IFIP Advances in Information and Communication Technology

468

Editor-in-Chief

Kai Rannenberg, Goethe University Frankfurt, Germany

Editorial Board

IFIP – The International Federation for Information Processing

IFIP was founded in 1960 under the auspices of UNESCO, following the First World Computer Congress held in Paris the previous year. An umbrella organization for societies working in information processing, IFIP's aim is two-fold: to support information processing within its member countries and to encourage technology transfer to developing nations. As its mission statement clearly states,

> *IFIP's mission is to be the leading, truly international, apolitical organization which encourages and assists in the development, exploitation and application of information technology for the benefit of all people.*

IFIP is a non-profitmaking organization, run almost solely by 2500 volunteers. It operates through a number of technical committees, which organize events and publications. IFIP's events range from an international congress to local seminars, but the most important are:

- The IFIP World Computer Congress, held every second year;
- Open conferences;
- Working conferences.

The flagship event is the IFIP World Computer Congress, at which both invited and contributed papers are presented. Contributed papers are rigorously refereed and the rejection rate is high.

As with the Congress, participation in the open conferences is open to all and papers may be invited or submitted. Again, submitted papers are stringently refereed.

The working conferences are structured differently. They are usually run by a working group and attendance is small and by invitation only. Their purpose is to create an atmosphere conducive to innovation and development. Refereeing is also rigorous and papers are subjected to extensive group discussion.

Publications arising from IFIP events vary. The papers presented at the IFIP World Computer Congress and at open conferences are published as conference proceedings, while the results of the working conferences are often published as collections of selected and edited papers.

Any national society whose primary activity is about information processing may apply to become a full member of IFIP, although full membership is restricted to one society per country. Full members are entitled to vote at the annual General Assembly, National societies preferring a less committed involvement may apply for associate or corresponding membership. Associate members enjoy the same benefits as full members, but without voting rights. Corresponding members are not represented in IFIP bodies. Affiliated membership is open to non-national societies, and individual and honorary membership schemes are also offered.

More information about this series at http://www.springer.com/series/6102

José Abdelnour Nocera · Barbara Rita Barricelli
Arminda Lopes · Pedro Campos
Torkil Clemmensen (Eds.)

Human Work Interaction Design

Work Analysis and Interaction Design Methods for Pervasive and Smart Workplaces

4th IFIP 13.6 Working Conference, HWID 2015
London, UK, June 25–26, 2015
Revised Selected Papers

 Springer

Editors
José Abdelnour Nocera
University of West London
London
UK

Barbara Rita Barricelli
Università degli Studi di Milano
Milan
Italy

Arminda Lopes
Madeira Interactive Technologies Institute
Funchal
Portugal

Pedro Campos
Madeira Interactive Technologies Institute
Funchal
Portugal

Torkil Clemmensen
Copenhagen Business School
Frederiksberg
Denmark

ISSN 1868-4238   ISSN 1868-422X (electronic)
IFIP Advances in Information and Communication Technology
ISBN 978-3-319-27047-0   ISBN 978-3-319-27048-7 (eBook)
DOI 10.1007/978-3-319-27048-7

Library of Congress Control Number: 2015955368

Springer Cham Heidelberg New York Dordrecht London

Printed on acid-free paper

Springer International Publishing AG Switzerland is part of Springer Science+Business Media
(www.springer.com)

Preface

Human Work Interaction Design (HWID) was established in September 2005 as the sixth working group (WG 13.6) of the IFIP Technical Committee 13 on Human–Computer Interaction (HCI). The scope of this group is the analysis and interaction design of a variety of complex work and life contexts found in different business and application domains. For this purpose, it is important to establish relationships between extensive empirical work domain studies and HCI design. WG 13.6 aims to provide the basis for an improved cross-disciplinary cooperation and mutual inspiration among researchers from the many disciplines that by nature are involved in deep analysis of a work domain. Complexity is hence a key notion in the activities of this working group, but it is not a priori defined or limited to any particular domains. WG 13.6 initiates and fosters new research initiatives and developments, as well as an increased awareness of HWID in the HCI curriculum.

This volume presents chapters developed from papers presented at the 4th HWID working conference held at the University of West London during June 25–26, 2015. The theme of this conference was on the integration of work analysis and interaction design methods for pervasive and smart workplaces.

Pervasive and smart technologies have pushed workplace configuration beyond linear logic and physical boundaries. As a result, workers' experience of and access to technology is increasingly pervasive, and their agency is constantly reconfigured. While in certain areas of work this is not new (e.g., technology mediation and decision support in air traffic control), more recent developments in other domains such as health care (e.g., augmented reality in computer-aided surgery) have raised challenging issues for HCI researchers and practitioners. The question now is how to improve the quality of workers' experience and outputs?

The chapters in this book focus on answering this question to support professionals, academia, national laboratories, and industry engaged in human work analysis and interaction design for the workplace. The first section provides an overview as well as instances of what could be classed as HWID methodologies. The second section offers different experiences on conceptualizing and researching the work environment in terms of how to sense and integrate its different dimensions into interaction design. The last section of the book presents chapters providing examples of HWID application in pervasive and smart workplaces across various domains such as aviation, education, product design, and archeology.

We hope this book becomes a resource for the type of discussion around HWID topics that took place at the working conference in London.

November 2015

José Abdelnour Nocera
Barbara Rita Barricelli
Arminda Lopes
Pedro Campos
Torkil Clemmensen

Organization

Organizing Committee

José Abdelnour Nocera   University of West London, UK
Pedro Campos   University of Madeira, Portugal
Torkil Clemmensen   Copenhagen Business School, Denmark
Dinesh Katre   Centre for Development of Advanced Computing (C-DAC), Pune, India
Arminda Lopes   Instituto Politécnico de Castelo Branco, Portugal
Effie Law   University of Leicester, UK
Barbara Rita Barricelli   Università degli Studi di Milano, Italy

Program Committee

Catherine Burns   University of Waterloo, Canada
Paola Amaldi   University of Hertfordshire, UK
Sergio España   Universidad Politécnica de Valencia, Spain
William Wong   Middlesex University, UK
Anirudha Joshi   Indian Institute of Technology, India
Anant Bhaskar Garg   HaritaDhara Research Development and Education Foundation, India
Ganesh D. Bhutkar   Vishwakarma Institute of Technology, India
Ebba Þóra Hvannberg   University of Iceland, Iceland
Ignacio Panach   Universidad de Valencia, Spain
Nathalie Aquino   Universidad Católica de Asunción, Paraguay
Frederica Gonçalves   University of Madeira, Portugal
Ali Gheitasi   University of West London, UK
Stefano Valtolina   Università degli Studi di Milano, Italy

Sponsors

IFIP International Federation for Information Processing
University of West London
M-ITI – Madeira Interactive Technologies Institute
Copenhagen Business School
SnitkerGroup

Sources of Support

Copenhagen Business School

Contents

Specific Contexts

Methodologies

Human Work Interaction Design: An Overview

Frederica Gonçalves[1(✉)], Pedro Campos[1], and Torkil Clemmensen[2]

[1] Madeira Interactive Technologies Institute, Funchal, Portugal
frederica.goncalves@m-iti.org, pcampos@uma.pt
[2] Department of Informatics, Copenhagen Business School, Frederiksberg, Denmark
tc.itm@cbs.dk

Abstract. In this paper, we review research in the emerging practice and research field of Human Work Interaction Design (HWID). We present a HWID framework, and a sample of 54 HWID related papers from workshops, conferences and journals from the period 2009–2014. We group the papers into six topical groups, and then attempt to map these groups to the framework to find research gaps for future research. We find that the groups of papers cover all areas of the framework well for a variety of work and leisure domains. The area in strongest need for more research papers is the development of the holistic framework itself. Furthermore, much focus has been on studying design sketching or implemented systems-in-use, while little attention has been paid to mature design (prototypes) or early implementation (content templates). In conclusion, we recommend an update to the framework so that it can be also useful for research in prototyping and early organizational implementation.

Keywords: Human work interaction design · User experience · Literature review

1 Introduction

The boundaries and work processes for how people work and interact are suffering changes due to the very fast emergence of new information technologies. To address this comprehensive problem, the Human Work Interaction Design Working Group (HWID) was established in September 2005 under the auspices of IFIP, the International Federation for Information Processing (Campos, Clemmensen, Abdelnour-Nocera, Katre, Lopes, Ørngreen, 2012). In this paper, we provide an overview of recent research related to HWID. Our focus is on identifying research gaps for future research.

Today, HWID is a comprehensive framework that aims at establishing relationships between extensive empirical work-domain studies and HCI design. It builds on the tradition of cognitive work analysis (Ørngreen, Mark-Pejtersen, Clemmensen 2008). In order to provide an easy understandable version of the framework that is applicable across domains, Clemmensen (2011) developed a revised HWID framework (Fig. 1). In recent workshops and scientific meetings, it has been discussed that the current mission should involve empowering users by designing smarter workplaces. HWID is currently positioned as a modern, lightweight version of Cognitive Work Analysis (CWA).

© IFIP International Federation for Information Processing 2015
J. Abdelnour-Nocera et al. (Eds.): HWID 2015, IFIP AICT 468, pp. 3–19, 2015.
DOI: 10.1007/978-3-319-27048-7_1

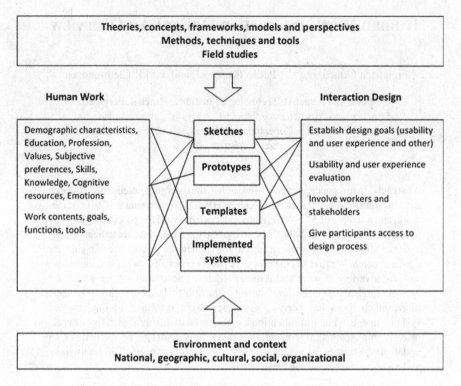

Fig. 1. Human Work Interaction Design framework (Clemmensen, 2011)

The characteristics of humans and work domain contents and the interaction during their tasks and decision activities, individually or in collaboration, are the base of this framework.

The top box illustrates the theories used, the left is the analysis of users' work and life, in the middle column the artefacts, and to the right the design of interactive information technologies. The box at the bottom indicates that environmental contexts, such as national, cultural, social and organizational factors, impact the way in which users interact with computers in their work and life. The lines connecting the left-right boxes illustrate the various relations between empirical work analysis and interaction design activities and products, which are the focus of HWID research.

For the early years of HWID research (2005–2008), Ørngreen et al. (2008) reviewed the theory and empirical evidence behind attempts to combine empirical work studies and interaction design. Since then, the research in this area has grown significantly, making the case for an updated survey and review. In this context, we reviewed and selected 54 research papers about HWID from workshops, conferences and journals from 2009 until 2014. This analysis has resulted in the identification of six groups of papers (see the Appendix for a list of the papers), which reflect diverse topics relating problems that the researchers perceive to be the major concerns and challenges in HWID. It is always a challenge to provide a sound overview of any research field. In this case, our literature review was quite broad and includes papers that do not cite or refer specifically to HWID, but are potentially important to HWID.

2 Exploring UX and Designs for Smart Places in Work Environments

The first group of research papers takes as the starting point the empirical analysis of human work and its relation to IT artefacts (the left side to center column of Fig. 1).

Understanding UX of Smart Workplaces. To design successful human-centered technologies for smart workplaces, Meerbeek et al. (2014) did a case study of automatic window blinds to acquire a better understanding of the current behavior of office occupants with respect to the control of daylight entrance. They used mixed methods to investigate the effect of user-controlled and system-controlled (automatic) changes of exterior venetian blinds on occupants' experience of the blinds' system and their satisfaction with the indoor climate, including lighting, noise, and temperature. They found that people's work habits tended to overrule artefact settings.

Smart and Pervasive Technologies. There are very few reports on how pervasive and smart characters of information and communication technologies shape the quality of the life, working and user experience of telecommuters. Law and Abdelnour-Nocera (2014) discussed, from different design and cultural perspectives, including emerging economies like India, the nature of sociotechnical gaps in telecommuting and the implications of these for the quality of work and quality of life teleworkers.

Identifying User Experience Goals. Clemmensen and Barlow (2013) used an interpretive phenomenological approach to find user experience goals in complex work systems such us an interactive climate management with growers and crop consultants. They presented a model of the essence of the emotional user experience with examples of how to capture the user experience in work contexts and with a qualitative methodology. In order to measure the identified emotions in other contexts than climate management or other climate management situation than greenhouses they suggested that futures research aim to develop work context sensitive user experience scales.

Ergonomic and Motivating Workplaces. Designing a platform for ergonomic and motivating workplaces, especially targeted at older employees, was the vision of Bobeth et al. (2014). The authors designed a smart and flexible work environment to support a prolonged, productive and satisfactory involvement of older employees in working life. Offering a range of assistive tools and services, both for the office and the home environment, was a goal driven by bottom-up insights into the work realities and contexts for this type of users.

Viz Reporter *in vivo*. Studying mobile journalism in the context of the professional news organization TV2 in Norway, Guribye et al. (2014) show in this paper through ethnographic inquires into the work practice of these journalists, how the adoption of a mobile application called Viz Reporter can be accomplished in practice. The authors identify design implications not only for the usability of the product but also for the ways in which journalists themselves can take part in configuring their digital habitats.

UX in a Work Context. To capture the user experience of the smart workplace, Yadav and Clemmensen (2014) present an approach discussing a pilot experiment where they integrate multiple data-streams of user experience, such us physiological, behavioral, and environmental and IT processes, in a work setting to give us a holistic view in user experiences due to Internet of Things. Their experiment provides one basic framework to new experiences in the future.

ICT Design and Evaluation for Trans-mediated Workplaces. Traditionally human work analysis is focused on user goals, user requirements, tasks and procedures, human factors, cognitive and physical processes and contexts. Abdelnour-Nocera et al. (2013) show a formal initiative at a European level to harmonize HWID as a substantive discipline supporting the interaction of workers through technology, at a time in which concepts of workers and workplace are changing significantly.

Evaluate the Work Environment of Future Work. Sandblad (2013) developed a checklist for analysis into aspects such us physical, psychosocial and cognitive work in order to prevent possible negative work environment consequences. It is not enough to simply introduce information technologies systems that support the organization's current work practice but also is important to use the full potential of the new technology to improve the organization, work practices and work environment. Developing this checklist based on the Demand-Control-Support model, Sandblad present a research approach with a focus on the work environment aspects.

Studying Contextual Interaction. In order to derive inspirations for designing future interactions Murer et al. (2014) provides an approach using industrial companies' habit to showcase their products as well as production facilities. Their strategy approaching extensive tours "behind the scenes" that are augmented with ad-hoc staging of contextual interactions, allows to study human work interaction in domains and facilities usually hard to access in research.

Workplaces for Creative Writers. Gonçalves and Campos (2014) describe an analysis based on HWID framework to make a simple analysis for a complex domain such as creative writing. The authors describe an analysis of connections between human work and interaction design from a creative writing support perspective.

Mind the Gap. Arguing there is a gap between the technological artifact produced and the social requirements that govern how well the system will fit in the organization, Lind et al. (2013) in this work in progress paper, present a framework – SOT (Social, Organizational and Technical) – to analyze the deployment of information systems (IT) from a sociotechnical perspective. The authors propose the concept of inertia to reflect the relative and varying ability of either of SOT aspects to adjust with respect to the other two. They believe that the sociotechnical gap is a result of the collective inability of these aspects to reach a middle ground within an organization.

Cognitive Work Analysis. Burns (2012) highlights the importance of cognitive work analysis (CWA) and their recent work focused on adapting CWA to face the new challenges and provides a solution that fits a truly social technical system in this paper.

Usage of Different Work Analysis Methods. Campos and Noronha (2012) describe and elaborate around the usage of different work analysis methods in a complex, real world work domain: collaborative review of large-scale 3D engineering models. They concluded that hierarchical task analysis was not effective in obtaining a clear, common vision about the work domain.

3 Improved Qualities in Health and Support in Work Design

The second group of papers are strong on work analysis in particular organizational contexts (right to bottom of Fig. 1).

How to Improve the Interaction Quality of Psychologists and Patients. Serra et al. (2014) look at the gap in the research about "computerized psychology". They present a work in progress project that consist on the development of an application that will support and facilitate the interaction among psychologists and patients. By interviewing several psychologists after and during the prototype evaluation phases, they showed that with the use of therapeutic writing could bring results for the clinical heath of patients.

Using Well-being Data. The advent of new technologies is changing the way people work. Valtonen et al. (2014), describe a new way to think about how we work. They propose the study of well-being from employees that are feeling overwhelmed and exhausted to design new ways of work and work environment to support productivity and well-being.

Designing a Health-care Worker-Centred System. Silvestre et al. (2013) report prototypes around personal schedules, games and personal digital artifact management that investigates different ways of looking at long-term health care based on multiple user-centred design iterations with the chronic mental care hospital staff. They established this approach as promising for improving overall care for the residents in long-term care.

Challenges in Applying a Participatory Approach. Scandurra et al. (2013) recommend increasing the use of "health informaticians" with usability and human work interaction design expertise within national and local eHealth development. In this paper, they present the experiences of applying a participatory approach in a nation-wide project. They considered that eHealth development is a challenging and complex activity, and best-practice methods from HCI related with HWID can support the business development within health and social care.

Usability Heuristics and Quality Indicators. Medical errors and cost the life of a patient can be caused by complexity in the user interface, features and functionalities of ventilator systems. Katre et al. (2009) presents a study about heuristic evaluation of three touch screen based ventilator systems manufactured by three different companies.

Evolving a specialized set of heuristics combined with objectively defined usability indicators for the usability evaluation of touch screen based ventilator systems was performed by four different usability evaluators to ensure the reliability of heuristics proposed. Findings on several observations in ventilators systems shows that the interface design of touch screen ventilator needs significant design enhancements.

The Influence of Mood Feedback. Sonderegger et al. (2013) offer experiences that examine the influence of mood feedback on different outcomes of teamwork in two different collaborative work environments. The authors present a new collaborative communication environment, using an avatar, which provides visual feedback of each team member's emotional state to support teamwork.

Do Usability Professionals Think about User Experience? Clemmensen et al. (2013) investigates how usability professional's thinking about system use is different from other stakeholder groups with different nationalities, in particular system developers and end users. The paper shows results that indicate usability professional focus on emotion-related aspects of system use, while users focus more on context in terms of utility and degree of usage.

Work and Speech Interactions Among Staff. Care services are often provided by the devoted efforts of care staff at long-term care facilities. Chino et al., (2012) observed bathing assistance, night shift operations, and handover tasks at a private elderly care home for eight days. The authors found that staff members are always speaking during the task, remote communication is rare, about 75 % of staff utterances are spoken residents, utterance targets are frequently switch, and about 17 % of utterances contain at least one personal name.

Usability Model for Medical User Interface. Bhutkar et al. (2012), in this paper used a usability model for medical user interfaces, especially for ventilator in Intensive Care Unit (ICU). They proposed this based on Norman's action-oriented seven-step model to capture a related medical context. This comprehensive model brings related medical context into human work analysis in terms of vital medical elements such us medical user, user interface, ICU environment and time required. The authors suggested that usability professionals for improved results could use this model as a template with medical user interfaces effectively.

4   Supporting Human Collaborative Work and Cognitive Strategies in a Global World

The third group of papers is strong on the environment and context, as they focus on the global world (bottom of Fig. 1).

Transnational Teams' Impacts. Global organizations can choose to configure and structure their teams in a wide variety of ways. Haines et al. (2013) found important to understand the implications of various transnational team configurations. The authors conducted a research in a large multinational technology company and they found that the development of social capital is impacted by whether a person is in their home context or transplanted and their expectations based on that context. They highlight factors in the creation of social capital as well as some mechanisms that may mitigate cultural difference.

Supporting Human Collaborative Works. Chino et al. (2013) proposed in their paper an application model to support human collaborative works. The model is designed based in a real field study at an elderly care facility in Japan and a virtual field experiment on the collaborative words utilizing a voice communication systems for human workers of what they called "action oriented intellectual services" that works in distributed work fields. To improve the interaction design among the system and the human workers, the authors suggest to use the data accumulated in the system itself to support the human work analysis.

Collegial Collaboration for Safety. Jansson et al. (2013) present a model for verbal probing procedures that is used to assess situation awareness in dynamic decision contexts – colleagues explore each other's cognitive strategies. In this paper the authors shows the results from a cognitive field studies using a method developed for knowledge elicitation in applied contexts and reviewed from previous studies – *collegial verbalization*. They purposed to evaluate whether the knowledge elicitation procedure can be used as a basis for exploring how colleagues can learn from each other, using studies that will take place at an intensive care unit.

Distributed Scientific Group Collaboration. Li et al. (2012) explored in this paper the collaborative practices, particularly information sharing, in scientific collaboration between different groups and over the distance of physical containment barriers in a biosecurity laboratory. Their findings contribute to the design of collaboration platform for this type of environment that can resolve common communications issues over distance.

An Integrated Communication and Collaboration Platform. In this paper, Müller-Tomfelde et al. (2011) present the design process, the technical solution and the early user experience of a collaboration platform, which integrates life-size video conferencing, and group interactions on a large shared workspace to support distributed scientific collaborations. This platform was developed to support the diagnostics and research scientists in an animal health laboratory to work collaboratively across a physical containment barrier.

Usability Testing in Three Countries. Triangulating how companies perform usability tests, Clemmensen (2009) in this paper reported and compared three ethnographic interviews studies in Mumbay, Beijing and Copenhagen. This study, using structural and contrast questions do a taxonomic and paradigm analysis, indicates that a typical or standard usability test across countries had some clear similarities.

5 HCI and Usability Research in Educational, Cultural and Public

The fourth group of papers focus on the global context's relation to usability and interaction design (bottom to right side of the Fig. 1).

Usability in a Cultural Context. The aspect of culture in design of user interfaces and interactive products is an issue important that Clemmensen et al. (2009) tries to underline in this paper. To understand the differences in how people with different backgrounds respond to directions and test methodologies, they focused on presenting and discussed the aim context, challenges, results, and impact of the Cultural usability named as CultUsab. This was a project with four-year international research effort from 2006 to 2009, supported by a grant from the Danish Research Councils for Independent Research in Culture and Communication.

Usability Research in Indian Educational Institutions. In this paper Yammiyavar (2009) traces briefly the evolution of human work interaction in educational institutions in India. The author highlights through samples of research work done the urgency for training more researchers in the field of emerging area such us HCI and the great potential in this country.

Usability Evaluation of State Government Portals. Katre and Gupta (2011) present in this paper a usability evaluation of 28 state government web portals of India. This evaluation was based on 79 parameters grouped under 7 broad categories such as accessibility, navigation, visual design, information content, interactivity, ownership and branding. The expert usability evaluation presented in this paper highlights the lack of human work analysis in the design of the state web portals.

A Rapid Ethnographical Study. Righi et al. (2011) conducted a rapid ethnographical study aimed at understanding attitudes of older people towards e-government related activities and Information and Communication Technologies. The authors presented initial results derived from their study and discussed a potential scenario for supporting information sharing and promoting a more active and dynamic participation of older people in their neighborhood. Their findings suggested that a variety of inclusive aspects, such as socialization, face-to-face contact, or mutual support impact the use and adoption of e-services by older people.

Narrative Interaction. Authors such as Schreder et al. (2011) suggested that narrative interaction could be used as a design possibility for human-machine interfaces in public information systems. They considered that using storytelling and narration for the graphical presentation of information in self-service technologies enables customers to draw on their everyday experiences. This paper presents a case study of a train ticket purchase process with a story structure that demonstrates the concept of narrative interaction.

Designing Accessible Public Information Systems. Campos (2011) presents in this paper a design approach towards the development of a fully interactive tourism information office. The author considered that public information was facing unique design challenges arising from the need to a diverse range of users, such as tourists, senior users, passers-by, children and teenagers. He concluded arguing that human work interaction design can be a solid, useful approach to better support the diversity of public information systems' users.

Success within User Centred Design. Hamilton et al. (2011) considered that E-Government websites and other online channels had the potential to empower citizens by making Government services more accessible and convenient to use. They examined three recurring challenges to applying User Centred Design (UCD) in the public sector and then described a successful service design project that overcame these challenges. Their experience in relation to UCD practitioners, was developed in the United Kingdom Government domain, and usability techniques were not being been sufficiently embedded in e-Government projects.

E-Government and Public Information Systems. Clemmensen (2011) outlines a revised version of the general HWID framework with a focus on what connects empirical work analysis and interaction design. Presenting a case study of the Danish government one-for-all authentication system NemID that has been briefly analyzed using ethno-methodology, work domain/task analysis, and the HWID approach for comparison. The author concluded that there were benefits in studying how human work analysis and interaction design in concrete cases are related and connected.

Cultural Elicitation in HCI. In Information and Communication Technologies (ICT) design many different approaches for techniques and frameworks are offered to eliciting culture and context in this field. Camara et al. (2009) in this paper argue that designers need to locally identify context and culture aspects and further explain their implications through the design process and at the global level.

Usability and Culture. Kurosu (2009) in this paper outlined the conceptual framework of the Artifact Development Analysis (ADA) and its relationship to the usability engineering. The author proposed to focus on the extent where the usability can provide the core satisfaction and also summarized the guideline on how the artifact should be designed.

Culture and Human-Computer Interaction. The interest in the correlation between culture aspects and Human-Computer-Interaction had grown significantly during the years. Clemmensen and Roese (2009), propose in this paper a review of current practice in how cultural HCI issues were studied, and analyzed problems with the measures and interpretation of their study. They found that Hofstede's cultural dimensions had been the dominating model of culture, participants had been picked because they could speak English, and most studies had been large scale quantitative studies.

'Adaptation' in Children. Deshpande et al. (2012) in this paper describe an exploration of how children adapt their interactions with different graphical user interfaces (GUIs) in carried task situations. They could observe that a GUI is rich in features facilities user adaptations in coping with differences in task complexities.

Library Usability in Higher Education. Based in UK university libraries, Wiles et al. (2012) in this study aims to find out how and to what extent user experience forms parts of university library policy, and how it can effectively be incorporated into it. The authors show that the creation of a library user experience policy begins with the identification of the social-technical gap between experiences and expectations.

6   Exploring Scenarios to Create Design Ideas

The fifth group of papers focus the relations between interaction design and artefacts (left side to center column of Fig. 1).

Using Storytelling to Create Design Ideas. Madsen and Nielsen (2009) in this paper explore the persona-scenarios method by investigating how the method can support project participants in generating shared understandings and design ideas. They contributed with guidelines that delineate (a) what a design-oriented persona-scenario should consist of product and (b) how to produce in order to generate and validate as many, new, and shared understandings and design ideas as possible.

Personas in Cross-Cultural Projects. To communicate data about users and to create a shared perception of them, Nielsen (2009) considered the method Personas in this experience using 16 participants in 9 different countries. The author asked participants to return a photo that resembled the persona and for them to explained their choice. Results in this analysis shows that there is a difference between the participants with professional experiences and those without.

A Game-Like Interactive Questionnaire. Dai and Paasch (2012) describe in this paper the use of a questionnaire to facilitate a photovoltaic (PV) application research, which led by University of Southern Denmark and with collaboration between local companies to popularize PV technology in both residential and the industrial markets.

Using Lego Mindstorms for Sensor-Intensive Prototype. In this paper, Pedersen and Clemmensen (2012) describe a design science framework for the use of interactive, sensor-intensive prototypes to develop interactive greenhouse climate management systems. This study provides a reference platform for combining micro information systems and human-computer interaction in design science research into environmental sustainability research.

UCD Guerrilla Tactics. Ericksson and Swartling (2012) in this paper present a case study within Sweden's military defense organizations, concerning the introduction of user-centred design (UCD). This paper describes the guerrilla tactics, how it was applied in this case study and factors that should be considered when using it.

Feedback in a Training Simulator. This paper aims to understand the importance of early work analysis in a real context during the design of such a simulator. Druzhinina and Hvannberg (2012) showed results that there were several significant differences.

7   Applications and Evaluations

The sixth group of papers focus on the IT artefacts as part of a holistic HWID context (center column and whole Fig. 1).

A Materiality-Centered Approach. To assess materiality from a user and artifact perspective, Fuchsberger et al. (2014) described an approach that puts the user and the artifact equally in the center of attention using a materiality-centered data analysis. Their approach allows identifying material attributes of actors that are less obvious.

Empirical Evaluation of Complex System Interfaces. Garg and Govil (2012) in this paper starts discussing two cognitive science paradigms and then present third approach related to interaction with the world as known as embodied cognition. They focused their analyze in work settings with the help of cognitive work analysis and human work interaction design approaches.

Natural Interactions. Proença and Guerra (2012) in this paper present a system for the development of new human-machine interfaces focused on static gestures recognition of human hands. Results shows that it is possible to interact with a machine naturally and intuitively through hand gestures without requiring support material such as gloves or markers.

Focus on Computing Practices. Franssila and Okkonen (2012) present a work in progress paper to considered the utility of current theoretical and methodological human computer interaction and work analysis in understating and supporting knowledge workers. They focused in the design efforts, instead of technical artifacts, into the observation, understanding and development of computing practices.

Mobile Probing and Probes. Duvaa et al. (2012) highlight in this paper the mobile probing as a method developed for learning about digital work situation and as an approach to discover new grounds.

Support of Multimodal. Velhinho and Lopes (2012) present a work in progress to evaluate frameworks used by business enterprises and to state the advantages and disadvantages in their use.

Safety Critical Social-technical System. This paper, authored by Amaldi and Smoker, (2012), used the UK service organization for Air Traffic Management Domain called NATS (National Air Traffic Service) as a case study to illustrate an example of an organization currently undertaking critical self-reflection about automation policy or lack of such.

8   Discussion and Conclusion

Figure 2 shows a mapping of the different groups of paper topics on top of the HWID framework: **(I)** Exploring UX and Designs for Smart Places in Work Environments; **(II)** Improved Qualities in Health and Support in Work Design; **(III)** Supporting Human Collaborative Work and Cognitive Strategies in a Global World; **(IV)** HCI and Usability Research in Educational, Cultural and Public; **(V)** Exploring Scenarios to Create Design Ideas; **(VI)** Applications and Evaluations. These are the groups that correspond to the previous sections. For instance, Group I (Exploring UX and Designs for Smart Places in Work Environments) is depicted on the middle left side of the Fig. 2 since this is where the HWID framework depicts the empirical analysis of human work and its relation to IT artifacts. The same applies to all of the other groups.

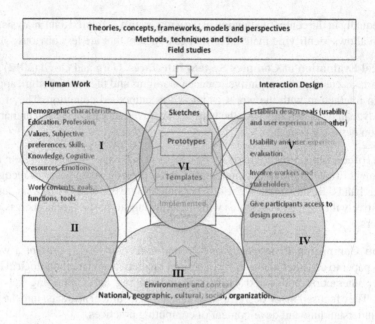

Fig. 2. Mapping groups of HWID papers to the HWID framework

It is obvious, from the analysis of missing bubble in the top of the framework's figure that one research gap is the need for better theories, concepts, frameworks, models and perspectives on HWID.

We do have theoretical work for different aspects of HWID, e.g. Burn's (2012) paper on social aspect of work analysis, but we need more papers that account for HWID as a holistic phenomenon that covers both work analysis and interaction design.

Second, we need more research on methods, techniques and tools, including field studies, for doing HWID research. Clemmensen (2011) suggested a specific way to use a combination of the HWID framework and grounded theory with digital qualitative analysis software (such as Atlas.ti), and we need more HWID-specific methods.

Third, Fig. 2 also indicates that we need more work explicitly dedicated to the relations (the lines in the framework figure), though we have the research papers represented by bobble I and V, and also earlier work on sketching for human work (Campos et al. 2006).

Fourth, when distributing the papers into the HWID framework, see Fig. 3, we can see that most of the papers are about human work and less about interaction design, and also, that there has been more studies of very early phases in system development (sketches) or, at the other end, late phases (studying implemented systems). There has been few studies of late prototypes or early stages of implementation (content templates for use).

Fifth, the work in this field has just started, and during the period that we analyzed, we had 38 empirical papers and 16 theoretical papers in order to explore concepts for the emerging area in HWID. Table 1 shows the number of papers per year we selected for the last six years, and the country of researchers. More

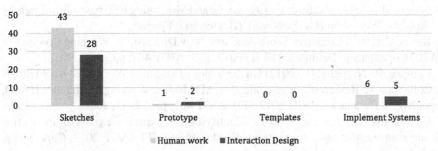

Fig. 3. Number of papers based on HWID Framework

researchers from more countries should be involved in this research, as human work and interaction designs may have many forms.

Table 1. Country of researchers and Number of papers per year

Year	Country of researchers	Number of papers
2009	*Denmark, India, Japan, UK.*	*9*
2011	*Australia, Austria, Denmark, India, Portugal, Spain, UK.*	*7*
2012	*Australia, Canada, Denmark, Finland, Iceland, India, Japan, Portugal, Sweden, UK.*	*17*
2013	*Brazil, Canada, China, Denmark, Germany, Japan, Sweden, Switzerland, USA, UK.*	*11*
2014	*Austria, Denmark, Finland, Germany, Greece, India, Netherlands, Norway, Portugal, UK.*	*10*

In summary, we believe that the papers presented in this review illustrates that researchers have developed the understanding of the HWID notion by experiencing and testing the contextualization of the concepts and framework, either empirical or theoretically. This is a good basis for future research in this area and focus on new challenging topics such a smart workplaces.

Appendix – the 54 Papers Included in the Review

1.1 Theme I: Exploring UX and Designs for Smart Places in Work Environments

Abdelnour-Nocera, J., Barricelli, B., Clemmensen, T., (2013) ICT Design and evaluation for trans-mediated workplaces: towards a common framework in human work interaction design. Workshop at INTERACT 2013, Cape Town, South Africa.

Bobeth, J., Gattol, V., Meyer, I., Müller, S., Soldatos, J., Egger, S., Busch, M., Tscheligli, M., (2014). Platform for Ergonomic and Motivating ICT-based Age-Friendly Workplaces. Workshop HWID, NordiCHI, Helsinki, Finland.

Burns, C. (2012) Cognitive Work Analysis: New Dimensions. Working Conference HWID, Copenhagen, Denmark. HWID 2012, IFIP AICT 407, pp. 1–11, 2013.

Campos, P., Noronha, H. (2012) On the Usage of Different Work Analysis Methods for Collaborative Review of Large Scale 3D CAD Models. Working Conference HWID, Copenhagen, Denmark. HWID 2012, IFIP AICT 407, pp. 12–21, 2013.

Clemmensen, T., Barlow, S. (2013) Identifying user experience goals for interactive climate management business systems. Workshop at INTERACT 2013, Cape Town, South Africa.

Gonçalves, F., Campos, P. (2014) Towards Pervasive and Inspiring Workplaces for Creative Writers: Simple Interactions for a Complex Domain. Workshop HWID, NordiCHI, Helsinki, Finland.

Guribye, F., Nyre, L., Torvund, E. (2014) Viz Reporter *in vivo – Design Implications for Mobile Journalism Beyond the Professional Newsroom.* Workshop HWID, NordiCHI, Helsinki, Finland.

Law, E., Abdelnour-Nocera, J., (2014) Towards a sociotechnical understanding of smart and pervasive technologies used by high-managed and low-managed teleworkers, NordiCHI, Helsinki, Finland.

Lind, T., Cajander, Å., (2013) Mind the Gap -Towards a Framework for Analysing the Deployment of IT Systems from a Sociotechnical Perspective. Workshop at INTERACT 2013, Cape Town, South Africa.

Meerbeek, B., Loenen, E. (2014). Understanding User Experience of Smart Workplaces: mixed methods. Workshop HWID, NordiCHI, Helsinki, Finland.

Murer, M., Tscheligi, M., Fuchsberger, V., (2014) Staged Inquiries: Studying Contextual Interaction through Industrial Showcasing. Workshop HWID, NordiCHI, Helsinki, Finland.

Sandblad, B., (2013) Using a vision seminar process to evaluate the work environment of future work. Workshop at INTERACT 2013, Cape Town, South Africa.

Yadav, M., Clemmensen, T., (2014) Multiple Data Stream measurement of UX in a work context. Workshop HWID NordiCHI, Helsinki, Finland.

1.2   Theme II: Improved Qualities in Health and Support in Work Design

Bhutkar, G., Katre, D., Ray, G., Deshmukh, S., (2012), Usability Model for Medical User Interface of Ventilator System in Intensive Care Unit. Working Conference HWID, Copenhagen, Denmark. HWID 2012, IFIP AICT 407, pp. 46–64, 2013.

Clemmensen, T., Hertzum, M., Yang, J., Chen, Y., (2013). Do Usability Professionals Think about User Experience in the Same Way as Users and Developers Do? Workshop at INTERACT 2013 Cape Town, South Africa.

Chino, T., Torri, K., Uchihira, N., Hirabayashi, Y. (2012) Work and Speech Interactions among Staff at an Elderly Care Facility. Third IFIP WG 13.6 Working Conference, HWID, Copenhagen, Denmark.

Katre, D., Bhutkar, G., Karmarkar, S., (2009) Usability Heuristics and Quality Indicators for the Usability Evaluation of Touch Screen Ventilator Systems. HWID 2009, IFIP AICT 316, pp. 83–97, 2010.

Scandurra, I., Åhlfeldt, R., Persson, A., Hägglund, M., (2013) Challenges in Applying a Participatory Approach in a Nation-wide Project-The Case of 'Usability of Swedish eHealth Systems 2013'. Workshop at INTERACT 2013, Cape Town, South Africa.

Serra, J., Leitão, J., Alves, P., Lopes, A., (2014) How to Improve the Interaction Quality of Psychologists and Patients: a Mediated Interface. NordiCHI, Helsinki, Finland.

Silvestre, R., Anacleto, J., Fels, S. (2013). Designing a Health-care Worker-Centred System for a Chronic Mental Care Hospital. Workshop at INTERACT 2013, Cape Town, South Africa.

Sonderegger, A., Lalanne, D., Bergholoz, L., Ringeval, F., Sauer, J. (2013) Computer-supported work in partially distributed and co-located teams: the influence of mood feedback, at the INTERACT Cape Town, South Africa.

Valtonen, T., Kalakoski, V., Paajanen, T., (2014). Using Well-being Data to Support Work Design, Workshop HWID NordiCHI, Helsinki, Finland.

1.3 Theme III: Supporting Human Collaborative Work and Cognitive Strategies in a Global World

Clemmensen, T. (2009) A Comparison of What is Part of Usability Testing in Three Countries. Working Paper NR. 04-2009, Copenhagen Business School, Handelshøjskolen.

Chino, T., Torri, K., Uchihira, N., Hirabayashi, Y. (2013). Supporting Human Collaborative Works by Monitoring Everyday Conversations. Workshop at INTERACT 2013, Cape Town, South Africa.

Haines, J., Olson, J., Olson, G. (2013) Here or There?: How Configuration of Transnational Teams Impacts Social Capital, at the INTERACT Cape Town, South Africa.

Jansson, A., Erlandsson, M., Fröjd, C., Arvidsson, M., (2013) Collegial Collaboration for Safety: Assessing Situation Awareness by Exploring Cognitive Strategies. Workshop at INTERACT 2013, Cape Town, South Africa.

Li, J., Robertson, T., Müller-Tomfelde, C., (2012). Distributed Scientific Group Collaboration across Biocontainment Barriers. CSCW'12, Seattle, Washington, USA.

Müller-Tomfelde, C., Li, J., Hyatt, A. (2011) An Integrated Communication and Collaboration Platform for distributed Scientific Workgroups. INTERACT 2011, Lisbon, Portugal.

1.4 Theme IV: HCI and Usability Research in Educational, Cultural and Public

Camara, S. Oyugi, C., Abdelnour-Nocera, J., Smith, A., (2009). Augmenting Usability: Cultural Elicitation in HCI. HWID 2009, IFIP AICT 316, pp. 46–56. 2010.

Campos, P. (2011) Designing Accessible Public Information Systems – An Interactive Tourism Office. International Journal of Public Information Systems, vol. 2011:3.

Clemmensen, T. (2011) A Human Work Interaction Design (HWID) Case Study in E-Government and Public Information Systems. IFIP INTERACT 2011 Workshop on Human Work Interaction Design for e-Government and Public Information Systems, Lisbon, Portugal.

Clemmensen, T., Yammiyavar, P., Orngreen, R., Katre, D. (2009). Usability in a Cultural Context: A report on the Scope, Process and Research Results of CultUsab – The Cultural Usability Project. HWID 2009, IFIP AICT 316, pp. 3–20, 2010.

Clemmensen, T., Roese, K., (2009) An Overview of a Decade of Journal Publications about Culture and Human-Computer Interaction (HCI). Working Paper NR. 03-2009, Copenhagen Business School, Handelshøjskolen.

Deshpande, Y., Yammiyavar, P., Bhattacharya, S., (2012) 'Adaptation' in Children – A GUI Interaction Based Task-Performance Study. Third IFIP WG 13.6 Working Conference, HWID, Copenhagen, Denmark.

Hamilton, F., Pavan, P., McHale, K., (2011) Designing usable E-Government services for the citizen – Success within user centred design. International Journal of Public Information Systems, vol. 2011:3.

Katre, D., Gupta, M., (2011) Usability Evaluation of 28 State Government Portals of India. IFIP INTERACT 2011 Workshop on Human Work Interaction Design for e-Government and Public Information Systems, Lisbon, Portugal.

Kurosu, M. (2009) Usability and Culture as Two of the Value Criteria for Evaluating the Artifact: A New Perspective from the Artifact Development Analysis (ADA). HWID 2009, IFIP AICT 316, pp. 67–75, 2010.

Righi, V., Sayago, S., Blat, J. (2011) Towards understanding E-Government with older people and designing an inclusive platform with them – A preliminary results of a rapid ethnographical study. International Journal of Public Information Systems, vol. 2011:3.

Schreder, G., Siebenhandl, K., Mayr, E., Smuc, M., Nagl, M., (2011) Narrative Interaction as Means for intuitive public information systems. International Journal of Public Information Systems, vol. 2011:3.

Wiles, A., Roberts, S., Abdelnour-Nocera, J. (2012) Library Usability in Higher Education: How User Experience can Form Library Policy. Third IFIP WG 13.6 Working Conference, HWID, Copenhagen, Denmark.

Yammiyavar, P. (2009) Status of HCI and Usability Research in Indian Educational Institutions. HWID 2009, IFIP AICT 316, pp. 21–27, 2010.

1.5   Theme V: Exploring Scenarios to Create Design Ideas

Dai, Z., Paasch, K. (2012) A Game-Like Interactive Questionnaire for PV Application Research by Participatory Design. HWID 2012, IFIP AICT 407, pp. 65–72, 2013.

Druzhinina, O., Hvannberg, E. (2012) Feedback in a Training Simulator for Crisis Management Compared to Feedback in a Real-Life Exercise. HWID 2012, IFIP AICT 407, pp. 124–138, 2013.

Ericksson, E., Swartling, A., (2012) UCD Guerrilla Tactics: A Strategy for Implementation of UCD in Sweden's Military Defense Organizations. HWID 2012, IFIP AICT 407, pp. 112–123, 2013.

Madsen, S., Nielsen, L., (2009) Exploring Persona-Scenarios – Using Storytelling to Create Design Ideas. HWID 2009, IFIP AICT 316, pp. 57–66, 2010.

Nielsen, L. (2009) Personas in Cross-Cultural Projects. HWID 2009, IFIP AICT 316, pp. 76–82, 2010.

Pedersen, R., Clemmensen, T. (2012) A Design Science Approach to Interactive Greenhouse Climate Control Using Lego Mindstorms for Sensor-Intensive Prototype. HWID 2012, IFIP AICT 407, pp. 73–89, 2013.

1.6 Theme VI: Applications and Evaluations

Amaldi, P., Smoker, A., (2012) An Organizational Study into the Concept of Automation in a Safety Critical Social-technical System. Working Conference HWID, Copenhagen, Denmark. HWID 2012, IFIP AICT 407, pp. 183–197, 2013.

Duvaa, U., Ørngreen, R., Mathiasen, A., Blomhoj, U., (2012) Mobile Probing and Probes. HWID 2012, IFIP AICT 407, pp. 161–174, 2013.

Franssila, H., Okkonen, J. (2012) Adjusting the Design Target of Life-Cycle Aware HCI in Knowledge Work: Focus on Computing Practices. HWID 2012, IFIP AICT 407, pp. 150–160, 2013.

Fuchsberger, V., Murer, M., Meneweger, T., Tscheligi, M., (2014) Capturing the In-Between of Interactive Artifacts and Users: A Materiality-Centered Approach. Workshop HWID, NordiCHI, Helsinki, Finland.

Garg, A., Govil, K. (2102) Empirical Evaluation of Complex System Interfaces for Power Plant Control Room Using Human Work Interaction Design Framework. HWID 2012, IFIP AICT 407, pp. 90–97, 2013.

Proença, R., Guerra, A. (2012) Natural Interactions: An Application for Gestural Hands Recognition. HWID 2012, IFIP AICT 407, pp. 98–111, 2013.

Velhinho, L., Lopes, A., (2012) A Framework in Support of Multimodal User Interface. HWID 2012, IFIP AICT 407, pp. 175–182, 2013.

References

Burns, C.: Cognitive work analysis: new dimensions. In: Campos, P., Clemmensen, T., Nocera, J.A., Katre, D., Lopes, A., Ørngreen, R. (eds.) Human Work Interaction Design: Work Analysis and HCI. IFIP AICT, vol. 407, pp. 1–11. Springer, Heidelberg (2013)

Campos, P., Nunes, N.: Principles and practices of work style modeling sketching design tools. In: Clemmensen, T., Campos, P., Ørngreen, R., Mark-Pejtersen, A., Wong, W. (eds.) Human Work Interaction Design: designing for human work. IFIP International Federation for Information Processing, vol. 221, pp. 203–220. Springer, New York (2006)

Campos, P., Clemmensen, T., Abdelnour-Nocera, J., Katre, D., Lopes, A., Ørngreen, R., (eds.) Human Work Interaction Design – Work Analysis in HCI. In: IFIP AICT, vol. 407, Springer, Heidelberg (2012)

Clemmensen, T.: A Human Work Interaction Design (HWID) Case Study in E-Government and Public Information Systems. In: IFIP INTERACT 2011 Workshop on Human Work Interaction Design for e-Government and Public Information Systems, Lisbon, Portugal (2011)

Ørngreen, R., Mark-Pejtersen, A., Clemmensen, T.: Themes in human work interaction design. In: Pejtersen, A.M., Paternò, F., Forbrig, P., (eds.) Human-Computer Interaction Symposium, International Federation for Information Processing (IFIP), vol. 272, pp. 33–46, Springer, New York (2008)

Reflections on Design-Based Research

In Online Educational and Competence Development Projects

Rikke Ørngreen[✉]

ResearchLAB: IT and Learning Design, Department of Learning and Philosophy,
Aalborg University, Copenhagen, Denmark
rior@learning.aau.dk

Abstract. Design-Based Research (DBR) is a relatively new intervention method investigating educational designs applied to real-life settings, and with a dual purpose to develop domain theories and to develop the design, iteratively. This paper is an integrative review, which draws on literature and empirical projects to identify and discuss critical elements in DBR, in particular when doing research in online educational projects, where the learning process expands from a traditional classroom to everyday work and life practices, as in competence development projects. Elements from two older, more mature, intervention approaches Interaction Design and Action Research, is included into the DBR discussion, and possible ways to work with the critical incidents are suggested. The paper argues that there is a risk of avoiding real-life factors by isolating the real-life intervention to the actors and actions in the classroom and thus mirroring some of the draw-backs in laboratory experimental research that DBR wanted to distance itself from. The discussion raises issues as users' needs, resistance, organizational relations, and alternative design solutions. Also, this type of online and competence development processes needs new empirical methods, and an argument for rigour in the DBR analysis and theory generation phases is presented.

Keywords: Design-Based research (DBR) · Educational research · Design science · Online and pervasive learning · Competence development

1 Background – Problem Space and Method

In recent years, the Design-Based Research (DBR) approach has increased in popularity within the field of education research. Though the root of this approach is mature, the actual term (i.e., DBR) only came into use in the year 2001. Between 2001 and 2010, a total of 1,940 papers using this term were published [2]. DBR is recognized as an intervention method that researches educational designs (products or processes) in real-life settings to generate theories in the domain and to further develop the specific design through iterative processes. DBR is useful to researchers investigating technological developments that support learning and learning processes.Researchers, as I, find it useful when investigating technological developments that support learning and learning processes. I research digital learning processes, and came app. 8 years ago from the

© IFIP International Federation for Information Processing 2015
J. Abdelnour-Nocera et al. (Eds.): HWID 2015, IFIP AICT 468, pp. 20–38, 2015.
DOI: 10.1007/978-3-319-27048-7_2

human computer interaction and information systems sciences, to the educational sciences. Though I had projects that were within the teaching and learning domain, they were often carried out as action research and interaction design studies, not as DBR projects. In my current research at faculties of education and humanities I find that there are elements from the interaction design and action science approaches that the educational design-based research approaches could benefit from (and probably vice versa, just not the scope of this paper). In this paper I give a brief (historical) introduction to Design-Based Research, where I among others utilize a couple of the good reviews that were written in the last 5 years. These reviews encapsulate some of the key characteristics, and I use them to reflect on the activities and actors involved in DBR research, and to derive the critical perspectives raised. I do this in relation to what I have experienced when discussing with peers and conducting DBR research projects. These projects use technological developments in educational settings, where the users are primarily online and distributed in space and time. Also, the learning process takes place during and transfers into a daily work practice, which means it is not possible to directly observe, as one can observe a classroom activity.

This paper is not a traditional literature review going through the full body of literature, though it does rely on a process of: identifying the key terms, locate literature, critically evaluate and select the literature and write a literature review [9]. However, this review consists also of experiences from existing empirical research, and combines this with the literature, similar to an integrative review [34], and combines it with inspiration from narrative ethnographic approach [9, 32]. Through this I aim to structure my reflections that are situated in cross-disciplinary experiences, and make the more subtle factors and findings explicit (even for myself).

An integrative review can contain theoretical papers, case studies etc. that apply different methodologies (quantitative and qualitative, experimental and non-experimental research) [35]. Whittemore and Knafl describes how this multifaceted approach provides a more rich picture of the topic being reviewed, but that this also raises the complexity and brings challenges: *"The integrative review method can summarize past empirical and theoretical literature on a topic of interest....Incorporate diverse methodologies in order to capture the context, processes and subjective elements of the topic. The integrative review method has been critiqued for its potential for bias and lack of rigour"* [35, p.552]. Whittemore and Knafl suggest bringing rigour into this process by among others applying Miles and Hubermans [24] processes of data reduction and data display in the qualitative analysis process. I take this a step further by applying an interpretative layer through personal experiences in own research projects, in a reflective narrative [24], thus making the personal elements explicit. This does not remove bias, but may provide insight and clarity to the interpretations made.

Thus this paper is primarily a discussion/reflection paper on a methodological level and it is not a rejection of DBR. The aim is to illustrate that DBR has a lot to offer, and I for one have research projects, where the methods makes great sense to apply and to continue applying. Empirical projects are in the paper included on a vignette and reference level representing the potentials and critical points raised. However, rather than seeing the critique as a rejection of an approach, it is an attempt to show where some of the critical incidents are hidden, leading to identification of possible elements for future action. The paper argues that there is a risk of avoiding real-life factors by isolating the real-life intervention to the actors and actions in the classroom and thus mirroring some of the draw-backs in laboratory experimental research that DBR wanted to distance itself from. The discussion raises issues as users' needs, resistance, organizational relations, and alternative design solutions. Also, this type of online and competence development processes needs new empirical methods, and an argument for rigour in the DBR analysis and theory generation phases is presented.

2   Design-Based Research

Though the design-based research as a term for an established approach in the educational sciences is new, and the first formal use was in 2001 (according to above), design science as such is of course far from new. Therefore, when I search: "design based research" OR "design-based research" in web of science, scopus and google scholar, the first appearances of one of these two terms is within Engineering, in a talk from 1973 on production technology [17]. Earlier appearances can exist as the databases may not contain a digital version of the papers, or the papers from before this period, are scanned versions, where the body text are not searchable.

No doubt the discussion on design science appears much earlier, which for example Cross provides an introduction to in Designerly Ways of Knowing: Design Discipline versus Design Science [8]. Cross also shows that within the technological domain, design science has primarily been about how to increase the knowledge pool on design methods, and less about how design processes used in research can improve theory generation in any domain [8].

Action research, is an intervention research approach, was primarily coined by Kurt Levin in the 1940-50, where Levin made his famous argument that in his objective one cannot understand something unless you change it. He formulated the unfreeze, change and freeze phases of action research, relying among others on group dynamics and democratic research process which today has evolved to more continues action research change models [18].

Design-Based Research in educational research primarily emerged as response to the need for more usable theories and models, similar to action research. Juuti and Lavonen [20] says that DBR bridges the gap between educational research and practice. The first two papers which have later been named the classical or first movers are Collins in 1990, who called for a design science of education [7] and Brown in 1992, who talks about design experiments [6]. One of the first papers to use the design-based research term is the design collective, with the *Design-based research: An emerging paradigm for educational inquiry* from 2003 [12]. Many of these people came from a psychological or teacher education research background, where experiments were applied in lab-like settings that tested hypothesis. To put it a bit squarely: real-life was for observations, and the laboratory was for experiments. The objective was to move to real contexts, to develop and work with practical usable methods and theories. [6, 7, 12, 14]. DBR are for some an hypothesis driven approach to theory development: *"Through a parallel and retrospective process of reflection upon the design and its outcomes, the design researchers elaborate upon their initial hypotheses and principles, refining, adding, and discarding - gradually knitting together a coherent theory that reflects their understanding of the design experien."* [14, p. 106].

According to Wang and Hannafin in 2005, DBR is *"a systematic but flexible methodology aimed to improve educational practices through iterative analysis, design, development, and implementation, based on collaboration among researchers and practitioners in real - world settings, and leading to contextually sensitive design principles and theories"* [33, p.6–7]. This is not much different from Anderson and Shattuck [2], who deducted the key characteristics through a review of the five most cited papers each year. Their paper is structured with a heading for each key characteristic, which is shown in the below list (and I will return to this list at the end of the paper). DBR are [2]:

- Being situated in a real educational context
- Focusing on the design and testing of a significant intervention
- Using mixed methods
- Involving multiple iterations
- Involving a collaborative partnership between researchers and practitioners
- Evolution of design principles
- Comparison to action research [which the authors describe as different from]
- Practical impact on practice

DBR in education primarily focus on an already designed product/process (perhaps a software prototype or an educational plan for use of a specific already developed technology) and its application into an everyday context, with all its messiness, chaotic and divergent nature. This design is then improved in iterative manners, through several interventions [e.g. 15, 22], which gives knowledge about how the design works, and informs the educational domain about how similar designs and situations would work. The design being used in the intervention can be a new technological product [22], or a technological enhanced learning process [34].

The DBR mind-set rest on an assumption that we as researchers can learn from the participants (teachers and learners) take on the design and the experienced learning process. Amiel and Reeves calls it a democratic research practice for researchers who believe in research as value-added, and that it is a possibility to use DBR to investigate in social responsible research [1]. Through this they distance themselves a little from the more researcher-defined hypothesis-driven approaches to DBR, and in the paper they illustrates the difference between a more typical/traditional predictive research approach and a more inclusive DBR approach were teachers are included in the formulation of the problems: *"In contrast, we suggest that design-based research begin with the negotiation of research goals between practitioners and researchers.... The practitioner is seen as a valuable partner in establishing research questions and identifying problems that merit investigation"* [1, p. 35].

Learning processes are complex in nature. The DBR researcher Sasha Barab argues from the perspective that cognition is not a disembodied activity of the mind, and that the whole person, the environment and the activity is part of a learning process [3]. However, this also makes it difficult to understand, measure, and differentiate between the dependent and independent variables, as many factors influence. Juuti and Lavonen mentions: classroom settings, social and psychological atmosphere, pupils' motivation, affection and conceptions toward a topic to be learned or toward schooling as such, and moreover, students' experiences outside the school [20, p.55].

DRB research results in understandings and knowledge which have the objective to be useful for and often change practice. This duality, and that both are equally important is seen in two sentences in the paper by Barab and Squire: (1) *Design-based research requires more than simply showing a particular design works but demands that the researcher (move beyond a particular design exemplar to) generate evidence-based claims about learning that address contemporary theoretical issues and further the theoretical knowledge of the field* [4, p.5–6] (2) *Design-based research that advances theory but does not demonstrate the value of the design in creating an impact on learning in the local context of study has not adequately justified the value of the theory.* [4, p.6] Pragmatism is by many authors seen at the underlying paradigm [2, 4, 20, 33]. This entails an ontological perspective of the world as complex and chaotic, where people with ideas and solutions through interaction change the context and the reality; and an epistemology that we need to try our ideas and solutions in real world settings in order to gain knowledge of the world; that the theories we generate need to be practical solutions to real world problems, and the methodological validation, that we can know something substantial about this world through repeated interventions. This is not similar to an understanding that a solution or a theory is final and will always work.

There are however inherent challenges on a methodological level, which has also been discussed and raised by several researchers. I have in particular learnt from the work of Yrje Engeström [16] and Chris Dede [10, 11]. Not everyone who criticizes DBR rejects DBR, but to do this to be aware and work with these factors as the DBR method matures. An often discussed issue is over-methodologized studies: Applying mixed methods strategies often means using many and varied methods in the same DBR study. The extremely large data-sets which these methods lead to, makes alignment and analysis difficult [10]. Another criticism is that it can be difficult for a researcher to stay trustworthy and unbiased, when he/she is involved with the design and the intervention (designing, planning, conducting and evaluating it) [4], and at the same time also is the one interpreting the quality and the lessons learned of the research practice [2], which btw. is comparable to the epistemology in a constructivist and interpretionist viewpoint. A third issue is that the design evolves over time, and with this the methods applied may shift as well [10]. As such, DBR lack rigor in the research process, which means we need robustness of evaluations, as well as ways to determine what a successful design is [10, 20].

Lyon and Moats point out in a paper on intervention research in general (i.e. on reading interventions not specifically DBR) that it may be difficult to replicate interventions because we do not have enough insight in a number of factors [21]. They mention: Sample heterogeneity and definition; Poorly defined interventions; Inadequate control groups; Inadequate intervention time and transfer effects; Effects of past and concurrent instruction; Method or teacher effects; consistency across teachers, and Generalization and maintenance issues [21, p.580]. Though some of these factors shows a desire to aim at a more positivistic paradigm of wanting to find the rules that govern the world (as the desire to replicate), they raise interesting issues relevant for research interventions. Issues that I find are seldom discussed explicitly in DBR (or in interaction design for that matter), as which effect does the teacher has on the intervention, and consistency across teachers. Another discussion is that there are many projects that have very well defined interventions, but because of the evolving nature of these, it is difficult in papers to disseminate knowledge about these precisely enough, to document what took place.

Engeström criticizes that design experiments have what he calls a linear view: "*In discourse on 'design experiments', it seems to be tacitly assumed that researchers make the grand design, teachers implement it (and contribute to its modification), and students learn better as a result. Scholars do not usually ask: Who does the design and why? This linear view is associated with notions of perfection, completeness and finality.*" [16, p3] A point Dede also raise when stating that: "*People fascinated by artifacts also are often tempted to start with a predetermined "solution" and seek educational problems to which it can be applied, a strategy that frequently leads to under-conceptualized research*"[10, p.107].

Engeström shows how DBR seldom discuss that the linear view makes some research studies blind for how interventions also brings about resistance to change from participant; how people reinvent a strategy and perhaps changes it, while it is being implemented. He sees resistance as natural force (as in action research) and discards design experiments and argues instead for formal interventions, where he among others presents a model to analyze and understand the interventions, namely his renowned model of activity theory [16]. He argues that all actors thereby get a language to talk about what is and has happened in the process. He also argues that the formal intervention unlike DBR has an open starting point, and that the intervention is subject for negotiation, with the aim to focus more on a localized solution than general applicable solutions, and thus a research role that have the aim to foster expansive transformation owned by the participants rather than a process where the researcher tries to control all variables [16].

Majgaard, Misfeldt and Nielsen [22] made use of inspiration between DBR, ID and AR in their case study, which focus on a specific design for children. It shows how even children can aid in the design process, though it does not raise the issues of how to align variables and findings, and to work with resistance or alternative designs as I do here, it does show an interesting example of how the children pointed to theory generation issues within the factor: motivation for learning, which the researchers had not found, if they had relied only on the teachers input [22], which I will return to later. The three approaches, DBR, ID and AR, all have an starting point in pragmatism, and it is possible to get inspiration from ID and AR perspective at the overall level, which I will do in the following sections. I look to interaction design (ID) and action research (AR) for inspiration to some of these issues of resistance, linearity and difficulties in alignment, as well as on working with alternative designs, users' involvement and methods for knowing about your online and time/space distributed users.

3 Online and Pervasive Settings

Where DBR projects were relatively small to begin with, many projects like the ones I work with today are large in scale, are longitudinal studies over several years, and involves many participants, and/or several research partners [e.g. 23, 25]. Barab writes in his introduction: *The goal of DBR is to use the close study of a single learning environment, usually as it passes through multiple iterations and as it occurs in naturalistic contexts, to develop new theories, artifacts, and practices that can be generalized to other schools and classrooms.* [3 p. 153]. There are a lot of technology enhanced education that involves designs which are in-class designs (using smartboards, mindstorms, programming computers, using iPads etc.), but what if the single learning environment is not confined to a single physical location?

The projects I work with have an extra dimension of participants working distributed in either time or place or both, and in settings, which physically or mentally are not strictly classroom-like [24, 34]. This means the use situation, the intervention, is not always easily identified, but permutate into other everyday situations and the question becomes: how do we as researchers' deal with a design and an intervention, which we cannot follow directly due to its pervasive nature?

Anderson and Shattuck [2] reviewed approximately 50 DBR studies, and none of these were explicitly in the competence development domain. They did categorise 5 studies to teacher training, but teacher training does not necessarily entail competence development, and the citations they use refer to results that are presented as useful in pre-service teacher training [2]. However, as the teachers often play a vital role in the studies, a competence development perspective as training experienced teachers could certainly be part of some of these studies, just not an explicit mentioned objective.

Even though many of my projects are situated in a formal educational system, they often have competence development for teachers as one of the objectives, and I have also worked with knowledge workers in consultancy firms, and health care professionals. All of these situations differ from the traditional classroom setting, not only because of the online time and space distribution, but also because the primary learning objective is different. Learning objectives in school contexts (regardless of this being primary school or higher education), are often related to learning outcomes and retention. Of course engagement and satisfaction are important factors, but in the end students are assessed on their knowledge and ability to utilise their domain knowledge, also in more constructivist approaches in for example project work with empirical data, problem-based learning approaches etc. Nearly everything is measured at an exam. However, in competence development, transfer from learning context to working contexts is the key factor. And if users are online, how can we gather information about both the users' interaction with the solution and the intervention, how do they communicate with and reflect with peers, and how do we know about the effects that intervention have afterwards on their everyday practice?

In the IFIP working group 13.6 on Human Work Interaction Design a number of tools and techniques for exploring the relationship between extensive empirical work-domain studies and interaction design has been presented. The workgroup encourage empirical studies and conceptualizations of the interaction among humans, their variegated social contexts and the technology they use both within and across these contexts (see the proceedings and activities at http://blog.cbs.dk/hwid_cbsdk/). The methods: sketching and mobile probing and probes are relevant in this context and methods that I have worked with in the HWID group. Sketching can work as a way of getting to user needs and requirements as well as unaffordable ways of trying out alternative designs [37]. Mobile Probes and probing is a method in between cultural probes and interviews, where the unknown are explored through questions and assignments send via SMS. Questions about what people are doing here and now, what they have done in a particular area that day, which challenges they met etc.; And assignments as encouraging to use a specific technique the following day, or to interview one of their students/colleagues etc. We find it a fruitful method, when the users are distributed in time and space from the research team and because we gain knowledge about this person while they are "doing" [13].

Methods as this, work with uncovering the unknown and serve as a catalyst for the daily practices. They open for areas that we as researchers did not know we could or should ask about, and that partcipants' had not verbalized as interesting issues [13, 37]. Other methods that can carry results in these pervasive settings are auto-ethnographic methods of digital nature - as in self-reporting on use via log-books, rich qualitative questionnaires, and digital storytelling/narratives. Interestingly this relates to the use of digital narratives in DBR. Here, digital narratives are reported to be used as reflective tool inbetween researchers, when analysing and discussing the project findings [see 20, which reference to Bell, Hoadley, and Linn (2004)]. Finally, of course many traditional mixed methods strategies are applicable in online environments, as online interviews and focus groups using video conferences, online surveys etc.

In conclusion, I argue that as DBR expand to educational settings that exceed the traditional formal educational classroom setting, so must the methods applied embrace this.

4   The Participants and the Organisation

DBR emphasize interventions in a representative real world setting understood as the classroom setting; investigating learning, learning strategies, perhaps teacher-student relations or even political agendas [2, 33]. Juuti and Lavonen [20] says that design research has three parties: (a) a designer (e.g. researcher), (b) a practitioner (e.g. teacher), and (c) an artefact (e.g. web-based learning environment for science education), but do not mention any other roles in the organization. However, there are many more roles, structures and activities which could be considered, than those present in the classroom. For example the team of teachers, which the teacher in the intervention collaborate with on a daily or almost daily basis, the it-people and administration, the management, or other intangible artefacts as the culture at the school, the voice of the municipality, perhaps even national or international strategies etc. The objective here is not to make educational research into grand scale organizational, social or financial studies, but to illustrate that if real world settings are important, then the organization as a whole is important, and we need to understand or at least reflect upon its role.

Action research has its roots in organisational studies and tends to be more sensitive to the systemic nature of organisations, where many aspects of the organisation and its network relations needs to be taken into account in change and intervention studies. There are many action research methods, but one of the common denominators is that researchers co-construct knowledge together with the practitioners (of course to various degrees in the various methods) [18]. Though there is here some similarity to AR and DBR, AR often provides the opportunity for participants to take ownership over the design and the interventions to a larger degree - sometimes even to a degree where the participants' finds that the process the organization has been through would have happened anyhow, i.e. without the researchers being present, which is in a way a positive thing. I have also seen, how too much ownership from management means that teachers then almost tacitly agrees to thinking less constructive and engage less in the DBR study. This is in line with the previous mentioned thinking of Engeström who works with resistance as a natural force [16], and in much organizational development literature resistance to change is seen as inherent human trace.

In learning processes that expand the classical classroom, I as researcher know less about how the users interact with the solution and about how it effect their everyday practice, only the users themselves can provide this input. If we at the same time believe in a contextual setting, where interaction among peers, in and around the organisation effect their learning and how their learning transfer to practice, then if we only investigate the three before mentioned parties (the designer, the teacher and the artefact) we may create yet another closed lab-like setting. It may happen in real-life, but it will be an artificial real-life research setting, where we omit too many factors of influence. The problematic about such a statement is of course, that we on the other hand open op for the vast myriad of variables to take into account, and to yet again over-methodologies our studies in order to "capture" these factors effects. But if we could early in the process make a real-life, in a true messy context, explorations of the different possibilities and factors influencing, perhaps this can aid in a better alignment. I will discuss one possible way of dealing with this issue in the following section.

There are certainly some DBR researchers who have become aware of this, and Barab and Squire mentions the naturalistic context boundaries, and provides a rare and much appreciated example of a design in a singular place, that did not scale well, because aspect from the surroundings regarding usability were not adjusted for [4]. So, we need to begin contemplating how to see and investigate such factors.

One challenge is, that the parties involved in an intervention may have different interests, not necessarily opposing interests, but with variation in what they priorities. One example is the difference in focusing on a micro or macro pedagogical level or on differences in time scale. The learners may be interested in learning and motivation with respect to their own learning process (here and now), where the organization is also interested in changes over time (next year students, other classes etc.), and the researchers may be interested in what can be learned from the intervention, which can inform theories and practices in general (meaning even bad examples can be learnt from). Also, who is concerned with the afterlife of the project in the organisation - after the researchers has left? Therefore it is pivotal to start from understanding and working with participants needs, and perhaps even clearly identify the success criteria's for all parties/ stakeholders.

5   Problems and Potentials, Solutions and Suggestions

"The idea that DBR is initiated to address problems that are both scientifically and practically significant has been repeatedly addressed in the literature" [23, p. 98], and this objective to make practical useful research results are also present in AR and ID. AR has a similar starting point of addressing problems, whereas in ID one can also work with potentials (as developing design innovations that there is no observed need for yet).

In both ID and AR the underlying belief is to work from a starting point that is explorative in nature, identifying needs and requirements of users in the context, before settling on the design specifications. This initial starting point is somewhat different in DBR, where some are hypothesis driven (in particular in the first papers of Collin [7] and Brown [6]), and often starts with a technological design, full functioning solution or a working prototype (as shown earlier). Ejersbo et al. presents two types of DBR studies, which had different starting points and different iterations. One where the design came first and another where a more ethnographic process of understanding the context was first applied [15]. They do not claim one is better than the other, but argue for what they call the "osmotic mode" of balancing the development of an artefact and the theory generation, and claim that as such DBR is not linear (which can be related to Engestöms [16] critique of DBR as linear discussed earlier).

In AR and ID a distinction is made between user centred design and participatory design. The first is an approach that values users, but where users are not directly involved in making the actual design or change process; whereas in participatory approaches, users are co-designers and not only co-creators of the knowledge, but make co-interpretations [18, 28]. Educational research could certainly work with both user-centred and participatory aspects, and just need to be explicit about the choices made. What is interesting is that the element of being 100 percent participatory may not always be an adequate solution in educational arenas, when for example the participants are on new grounds. This is perhaps best highlighted in the classic Spinuzzi paper [30], where the argument raised is, that users do not always know about thinking creatively about their own situation and henceforth cannot be as innovative as experts are. My experience is, that when participants are at the same time learning about an area, that they now little about, this may very much be the case. It is not only difficult to be creative, for some it is also difficult to leave the comfort zone of "what I usually do".

It is noteworthy that even though ID and AR researchers start with explorations of user needs and have them participate in the development of the change process, the design of a product/process; the researchers always comes with their expertise in a certain domain, and so the area of research is bound to be within this researchers practice. For example I seldom see empirical studies where the solution is abandoned (it happens, but is rare). In a worst case scenario, intervention research of any kind may end up investigating large scale technological eLearning solutions for problems and opportunities, where a simple paper poster could have done the work. My point is that this form of bias is seldom discussed in any of the three approaches – DBR, ID or AR.

6   Working with Alternative Designs

When working with people in educational research whether in small design experiments or larger DBR projects, I have often asked colleagues, professional it and learning designers, as well as students, if the project they are presenting is iterating on the best way or the first vision? This question deals with the notion that often we as DBR researchers have a vast knowledge of new technological innovations and their possible impact on learning. We are therefore often quite innovative and come up with interesting suggestions for new pedagogical designs. The field of online learning is for example in these days exploding due to the ease of making one's own digital production, whether as instructional material in a flipped classroom like setting; or as students' own video-production as a reflection on an interesting topic, to be shared with peers; or as synchronous video conferencing for teaching or informal talks. All of these enable online and distributed learning settings that flows in to our everyday practice. When we as researchers suggest learning designs that involves these, we change both the learning process, as well as the everyday work life. Sometimes these learning designs are great suggestions, which show that there is something important to be done in this area. However, the first vision about something often needs to be reworked into sustainable ways forward. But how do we know if we are working on a vision or one of the best ways forward, out of the many possible ways to reach that vision? i.e. the best way equals the currently best sustainable, scalable and usable design.

One of the suggested criteria for determining if a design is successful are when there are comparable experiences across participants' roles (as students and teachers, boys and girls etc.), across contexts and when an exhaustion level has been reached (e.g. [25]). This is however only possible with smaller incremental changes of the design, and if what we are comparing are if version 2 works better than version 1. So how do we define criteria's and find a process for when to abandoning designs that are different designs, rather than seeking to improve a design (a learning solution or process) which may be better off discarded?

Perhaps researchers are in fact already applying alternative designs, but are not doing so explicitly. It is unclear when reading the many studies (that the sheer volume of a reference list cannot cope with in this paper, but for lack of examples look to [2, 33]). If a design or intervention has changed significantly over time, well how many changes can one make, before it is no longer the same design? My point here is not that designs cannot change over time, they will, but rather that there seem to be no work on alternative designs early in the DBR process, that act out the first vision, and few studies that explicitly deals with the fluctuating designs trajectories.

Working incrementally with prototypes with real context serves great purposes - it was and still is a well-renowned ID and systems development approach. In 2005-8 Bill Buxton gave a series of talks with clear distinction between sketching and prototyping, where prototyping leads to refining the same idea, sketching was seen as a way of quickly and affordably trying out various ideas. (This discussion with reference to his talks and book is also shown in [37]). Trying out various ideas of the original vision, has shown me, how the vision in projects, may be fair and reasonable suggestions to an opportunity or problem, but that there are sometimes better ways of realizing that vision in concrete designs.

This and similar arguments has permutated into ID models. For example, in the period between two edition of the renowned interaction design book by Preece, Rogers and Sharp, the simple interaction design cycle change from having the second phase called: (Re) Design (in Fig. 6.7 in 2002 and in the 2007 editions), to its name being Designing Alternatives (in the 2011 and Fig. 9.3 in the 2015 editions) [28].

I believe working with alternative designs, and getting users view on these, is one of two suggested mechanisms for aiding us working in educational contexts and with DBR, that is to get pass the desire to or risk of confirming existing assumptions. The challenge is to implement this to larger DBR projects with external funding that demands relatively set project timelines and milestones. The other mechanism is about rigor in the analysis, which I will discuss in the next section.

7 Theory Generation and Rigor in the Analysis

Many DBR studies often gives rich conducts of the research methods and tools applied when creating and gathering empirical material (as observations, interviews, question-naires, log-files etc.). The process of analysis on the other hand seems less in focus. Publications include discussion of theories that talks about the same phenomenon as seen in the research results, with quotes from students or teachers, but no signs of how did the researchers choose these citations over others, how were the various data compared, worked-through etc. [15, 22]. Of course the journals have a maximum paper length, which means that all processes cannot be documented. Nevertheless DBR creates a huge number of data and as any qualitative study, the need to perform and document meaningful data reduction and data displays exist [24].

As Baskerville and Pries-Heje [5] I have found great use in grounded theory as a mean for bringing rigour into the analysis process of data in AR projects and as mech-anism for theory generation [36]. Though criticized for being a-theoretical this is far from the situation today (if ever depending on which strand one follows). In for example informed grounded theory, the literature and the knowledge we had prior to commencing the study does not leave us, but the approach do take a deliberate starting point in the data, from here open and axial coding begins [31].

While discussing an educational research study, DBR lifecycles and video analysis, Mike Rook wrote in his blog (quoting Doris Ash), that dialog progress discontinuously, and that we need tools to scientifically make sense over time and make connections [29]. Discontinued discussions and learning process are certainly part of online distributed educational and competence development projects, and digital analysis software have enabled me to analyse multimodal material that are dispersed and disjoint. The analytical software present today, as Atlas.ti and NVivo provides the possibility to make open and axial coding on the recordings, rather on transcriptions. This allows for mapping of concepts, working with displays, and applying theories, without loosing the link to the original empirical material. This supports the validity and verification process bringing visibility to myself and others, who can follow the arguments made in the studies.

Nortvig presents a project on video conferencing, where the DBR process did not evolve as planned, and she used grounded theory to align the varied input into categories of mutual and conflicting factors [27]. In this perspective it is the participants in the DBR study, who talks about the findings, and they point to theory-generating subjects via their utterances about what works, about experiences, what motivates and engage, and about what does not work, engage etc. i.e. the participants points to events of interest, and the researcher(s) have the right and responsibility to interpret how these utterances interrelate, and to relate them to which theories says something relevant about this phenomenon.

Another aspect which is seldom visible in the publications on larger DBR project is how research collaboration and findings in-between researchers take place. It is difficult to see how researchers agree on the aforementioned input from the participants. In ID the evaluator effect in usability studies has been discussed for the last almost 20 years. The evaluator is the person, who investigates a number of use situation, and who on the basis of that investigation determine, if there are critical issues in the design. Those issues which are very critical are called major incidents. The evaluator effect deals with the phenomenon, that if two or several evaluators investigate the same use situations (often via recorded sessions) they will not identify the same issues as critical or major incidents. i.e. even those that they do agree on may not be rated to the same severity-level. A new large and systematic study published in 2014, walked through previous studies, and conducted a major study confirming the evaluator effect [19]. Here, it was found that nearly 1/3 of the reported incidents by 19 experienced expert evaluators, which were found to be major incidents of high importance by one evaluator, were at the same time reported as a minor incident by another evaluator. The authors found that: it is important to have several evaluators on a design project; evaluators can benefit from consulting local or domain knowledge; evaluators can consolidate and gain further insights through group processes; unmoderated (and thus also remote evaluations) resulted in the same evaluator effect (and that it can be a cost-effective way of gaining insights); and that reliability as perfect reliable reported incidents are not the objective (but that the process converge through iteration and re-design) [19].

The big issue in this DBR context is not so much that experts within a design science, find and priorities differently. The issue is how we match these findings. Though a group process may be used in DBR, it is not clear how this matching occurs today, neither in the literature nor from the discussions that I have with my peers. This entails two perspectives. First having clear objectives and criteria's for what we are valuing in the specific DBR project is pivotal. (For example in a study of what authors deem as effective eLearning when doing empirical development studies (in general not just DBR), we found that 10 % did not say what effective learning meant for them [26]). Secondly, if we as researches want to make our arguments robust by combining and do collaborative analysis, how can we ensure that a group process are not enlarging rather than diminishing our blind spots? For example, if we in this process omit the less critical incidents or if we agree to focus on those that we agree is important – could it be that we are omitting those rare incidents that actually changes learning or are vital symptoms of something more crucial? I do not have a clear cut answer, but as being aware of the evaluator effect, and to discuss the incidents reported seem to be a way forward in itself [19], similarly being aware and explicit of DBR-researcher-effects can be important.

8 Unlearning, Capacity Building and Dealing with the Obvious

Part of a well-conducted research process is to make: *"assumptions and theoretical bases that underlie the work explicit. At times, this has meant defining assumptions and theory before the design work and other times these have evolved out of the work. However, as theoretical claims became apparent, we discussed them as a group and wrote them down on paper – even if they were only naïve conjectures."* [3, p.167] There could be a risk of that DBR with ID and AR perspectives result in solely localised knowledge that is tied to the intervention or the design. However results can also be general insights, and sometimes even these naïve conjectures, turn out to be important inherent naiveties, which need a push.

Majgaard et al. illustrates this in their ID and AR inspired intervention in the domain of mathematic, which led to insights about how children enjoyed and engaged more in the formal learning process, when they could experiment with huge numbers with many digits, than smaller and in the children's eyes uninteresting small numbers. [22] The paradox, in this specific case, was that teachers found that children should not "play around" with such large numbers, as they did not yet grasp their meaning. However, many of us can probably relate to this state when we were children, or if we have children now. I remember playing with my grandparent's calculators, making the most outrageous numbers, and trying to get my grandparents to pronounce them for me. And I saw how my children when they were smaller went through the same phase with much joy, fun and laughter, but also with good conversations about which number represented the hundreds, the thousands etc. This type of knowledge that Majgaard et al. extracted could therefore also be criticized of concluding the obvious common sense knowledge for people with educational experience, as Dede claims many DBR studies do [10]. Though I understand the reasoning, I also reason, that if no one makes these observations explicit, then common practical phenomenon may not be translated into what they mean for learning designs and learning materials in the future. In this case, teachers, developers and publishers of learning materials claim that children are not ready for large numbers and need to learn more about the smaller ones and their structures first, before large numbers can be used in school context. But in fact the opposite in this situation seemed the case. Perhaps the children need a dosage of both, and the teachers, developers and publishers need to change their practice. As often, I find that the research findings are of course linked to the possibilities that technologies bring to learning, but that it is also opens for blind spots or difficult issues, where we need to "unlearn".

In competence development projects, where the aim is changed practice in adults' work-life, unlearning and capacity building is very much at play. For example in one of our larger projects where science teachers are in focus, the first iterations shows that the facilitation or scaffolding of a learning process is vital. We find that some sort of "voluntarily but pushed" interaction with the teachers is usefull. It makes them explicitly reflect over their own teaching processes, which is necessary if the online learning is to transcend into changed behaviour/changed teaching habits. The online design consists of materials that illustrates and discuss an approach to science teaching, which is based on inquiry and problem-based learning, and the suggested learning model is to work in teams. The material is structured into modules, (but can be used in any sequence) and for each module a suggested route is laid out. This route is based on a mix of getting input from the material online, input from colleagues and from trying things out in one's own teaching and reflecting on the result. For example one route could be to: First discuss issue A with a colleague, using a pre-defined questions (as how do you normally deal with this issue in your classes); View the video B together with you colleague and discuss the video; Try this approach which video B presentd in your next session; Finally, reflect on the results and discuss this with your colleague. Now, even though the online design suggest that people "walk through this route", unless one of the researchers are sitting observing the teachers, the teachers would seldom work through the material as suggested. Only a few would remember to talk about what current practice they had, some would skip through large parts of video, text, etc. Even when the researcher was present, as in an early pilot, some teachers would in their discussions with colleagues come up with various strategies for why they should not adopt the material [see 26]. However, we also saw in this early pilot and in another iteration this spring 2015 that others because they used the time, they reflected on current practice and what could be changed, they clearly became inspired from the material online, and this was reflected in their teaching practice. For example in the spring 2015 iteration, mobile probes gave us insight into what the teachers were doing in their practice without us as researchers actually being there. A side effect of this became clear in the post-focus group interviews, where teachers said that getting a question or assignment, was like a gentle but also disciplinary reminder to act and reflect.

Now, stating that scaffolding and facilitating a learning process is vital to do in online distributed education may, as the previous example, state the obvious and naïve. The argument is, that the DBR process with an included explorative angle, has aided us in trying out various alternative design solutions to this vision and enabled our partners to see the necessity of providing a scaffold that provides a subtle "voluntarily but pushed" interaction to support the unlearning and capacity building process.

9   Framing Findings

This integrative review with a personal narrative element is an argument for an approach to DBR that stays true to the ontologies and epistemologies, which open for being explicit about the factors that influence research results in all its phases.

As a reflection on Anderson and Shattuck's headings [2] (shown earlier in this paper, and represented in *italic* below), the discussion in the above sections is about getting inspiration from ID and AR. I argue that we could perhaps mature the design-based research approach by reflecting on the consequences, barriers and potentials of working with alternative designs, focusing on the whole organization, on considering how to gain knowledge about the users and their work context, and to consider how to align our empirical data, and even when to reject designs or theories.

DBR [2]:

Evolution of design principles and
Practical impact on practice
Comparison to action research

DBR is different from AR (according to [2],

> **but could be inspired from AR and ID,**
> **particular in online educational and competence development projects, as follows:**

Being situated in a real educational context

> Broaden the concept of users to include the various roles in
> - the organisation
> - its stakeholders
> - the culture,
> - administration
> - etc.
>
> Understand users and the context first, and then begin designing. Working with
> - potentials as well as problems
> - with suggestions as well as solutions

Focusing on the design and testing of a significant intervention

> Work with alternative designs
> I.e. there can be several designs (rather than refining on the same first vision)

Using mixed methods

> Contemplate distributed online environments and with uncovering the unknown
> as getting inspiration from digital methods and tools, from sketching and mobile probes.

Involving multiple iterations

> of the chosen design
> Establishing requirements or setting criteria's for when to abandon designs

Involving a collaborative partnership between researchers and practitioners

> Consider how to align when several research partners analyse data
> and provide rigour in the analysis for example through grounded theory

---

10   Conclusions

This research discussion is situated in online educational projects, where participants are distributed in time and space, and where the learning process expands from a traditional classroom and the single physical context, to everyday work and life practices, as in competence development projects. The paper argues that there is a risk of avoiding real-life factors by isolating the real-life intervention to the classroom and thus mirroring some of the draw-backs in laboratory experimental research that DBR wanted to distance itself from. We may work with these issues by investigating factors as users' needs, resistance, organizational relations, and alternative design solutions. Another issue is that as the educational processes are distributed in space and time, and with many researchers, DBR needs new empirical methods, and rigour in the analysis and theory generation phases, and to consider how to leverage between several researchers evaluations. On the other hand by opening for these steps that I outline in this paper, there is a risk of adding to the volume of techniques, tools and factors involved, leaving the research vulnerable to even more over-methodologizing and making alignment difficult.

However, even with this risk of over-methodologising and adding to the number of factors involved, I argue that as DBR expand to educational settings that exceed the traditional formal educational classroom setting, so must the methods applied embrace this. I suggest methods as mobile probes. A method that mixes interviews/cultural probes over distance, using tasks and questions received during a full day with time intervals and via the mobile. This method and similar methods, as digital narratives and other auto-ethnographic productions made by the users' themselves, may represent a way to gain knowledge about what we as researchers do not know about the work-context. It also represents an opportunity for the users to reflect on their own learning process and its relation to their practice, and give insights about the organizational factors as a whole. These methods therefore also scaffold the participants learning process, which can of course be in one perspective a bias to the result, but on the other hand also be viewed as excellent tools for learning, not only as techniques for gathering empirical data.

I conclude that the objective is not to make educational research into grand scale organizational, social or financial studies, neither is it to make them into full blown grounded theory or usability studies, rather the objective is to illustrate that if real world settings are important, then the organization as a whole is important, and we need to understand or at least reflect upon its role. Such perspective is also important, if the DBR project is not only interested in the project results, but in how to anchor results and create sustainable theories and solutions. Therefore it is pivotal to start from understanding and working with participants needs, and perhaps clearly identify the success criteria's for all parties/stakeholders.

I have presented an argument for working with alternative designs as a way to get pass the desire to or risk of confirming existing assumptions. Another mechanism is about rigor in the analysis, and about how to leverage findings, also when many researchers are participating in these large DBR projects that are emerging today. Here I think an interesting point is to find ways of not omitting those rare incidents that actually changes learning or are symptoms of something more crucial.

References

1. Amiel, T., Reeves, T.C.: Design-based research and educational technology: rethinking technology and the research agenda. Educ. Technol. Soc. 11(4), 29–40 (2008)
2. Anderson, T., Shattuck, J.: Design-based research a decade of progress in education research? Educ. Researcher 41(1), 16–25 (2012)
3. Barab, S.: Design-based research: a methodological toolkit for the learning scientist. In: Sawyer, R.K. (ed.) The Cambridge Handbook of: the Learning Sciences, pp. 153–169. Cambridge University Press, New York (2006). pp. 627
4. Barab, S., Squire, K.: Design-based research: Putting a stake in the ground. J. Learn. Sci. 13(1), 1–14 (2004)
5. Baskerville, R., Pries-Heje, J.: Grounded action research: a method for understanding IT in practice. Account. Manag. Inform. Technol. 9(1), 1–23 (1999)

6. Brown, A.L.: Design experiments: Theoretical and methodological challenges in creating complex interventions in classroom settings. J. Learn. Sci. **2**(2), 141–178 (1992)
7. Collins, A.: Toward a Design Science of Education, pp. 15–22. Springer, Heidelberg (1990)
8. Cross, N.: Designerly ways of knowing: design discipline versus design science. Des. Issues **17**(3), 49–55 (2001)
9. Creswell, J.W.: Educational research: Planning, conducting and evaluating quantitative and qualitative research. Pearson, Boston (2008). 3rd edition
10. Dede, C.: If design-based research is the answer, what is the question? a commentary on Collins, Joseph, and Bielaczyc; diSessa and Cobb; and Fishman, Marx, Blumenthal, Krajcik, and Soloway in the JLS special issue on design-based research. J. Learn. Sci. **13**(1), 105–114 (2004)
11. Dede, C.: Why design-based research is both important and difficult. Educ. Technol. **45**(1), 5–8 (2005)
12. (The) Design-Based Research Collective: Design-based research: an emerging paradigm for educational inquiry. Educ. Researcher, 5–8(2003)
13. Duvaa, U., Ørngreen, R., Mathiasen, A.-G.W., Blomhøj, U.: Mobile Probing and Probes. In: Campos, P., Clemmensen, T., Nocera, J.A., Katre, D., Lopes, A., Ørngreen, R. (eds.) Human Work Interaction Design: Work Analysis and HCI. IFIP AICT, vol. 407, pp. 161–174. Springer, Heidelberg (2013)
14. Edelson, D.C.: Design research: what we learn when we engage in design. J. Learn. Sci. **11**(1), 105–121 (2002)
15. Ejersbo, L.R., Engelhardt, R., Frølunde, L., Hanghøj, T., Magnussen, R., Misfeldt, M.: Balancing Product Design and Theoretical Insights, The Handbook of Design Research Methods in Education: Innovations in Science, Technology, Engineering and Mathematics Learning And Teaching, pp. 149–164. Lawrence Erlbaum, New Jersey (2008)
16. Engeström, Y.: From design experiments to formative interventions. Theor. Psychol. **21**(5), 598–628 (2011)
17. Gejji, R.K.: Production technology today. Prod. Eng. **52**(10), 353–360 (1973)
18. Greenwood, D.J., Levin, M.: Introduction to action research: social research for social change. Sage publications, California (2007). 2nd edition
19. Hertzum, M., Molich, R., Jacobsen: What you get is what you see: revisiting the evaluator effect in usability tests. Behav. Inform. Technol. **33**(2), 144–162 (2014)
20. Juuti, K., Lavonen, J.: Design-based research in science education: one step towards methodology. Nord. Stud. Sci. Educ. **2**(2), 54–68 (2012)
21. Lyon, G.R., Moats, L.C.: Critical conceptual and methodological considerations in reading intervention research. J. Learn. Disabil. **30**(6), 578–588 (1997)
22. Majgaard, G., Misfeldt, M., Nielsen, J.: How design-based research, action research and interaction design contributes to the development of designs for learning. Des. Learn. **4**(2), 8–21 (2011)
23. McKenney, S., Reeves, T.C.: Systematic review of design-based research progress is a little knowledge a dangerous thing? Educ. Researcher **42**(2), 97–100 (2013)
24. Miles, M.B., Huberman, A.M.: Qualitative Data Analysis. Sage Publications, Thousand Oaks (1994)
25. Nelson, B., Ketelhut, D.J., Clarke, J., Bowman, C., Dede, C.: Design-based research strategies for developing a scientific inquiry curriculum in a multi-user virtual environment. Educ. Technol. **45**(1), 21–27 (2005)
26. Noesgaard, S.S., Ørngreen, R.: Understanding and utilizing the effectiveness of e-learning: a literature study on the definitions, methodologies, and promoting factors of e-learning effectiveness

27. Nortvig, A.-M.: Design Experiments and the Generation of Theory. In: Designs for learning, Extended Abstract, Stockholm, Sweden, 7 p. (2014)
28. Preece, J., Sharp, H., Rogers, Y.: Interaction Design: Beyond Human-Computer Interaction, 1–4 Edition. Wiley (2002, 2007, 2011, 2015). (author-order change in the editions)
29. Rook, M.: The Use of Video in DBR. In: The Design Stories blog, post from 9 November 2010 (visited January 2015). http://www.personal.psu.edu/mdm392/blogs/design/2010/11/the-use-of-video-in-dbr.html
30. Spinuzzi, C.: A Scandinavian challenge, a US response: methodological assumptions in Scandinavian and US prototyping approaches. In: Proceedings of the 20th Annual International Conference on Computer Documentation, pp. 208–215. ACM (2002)
31. Thornberg, R.: Informed grounded theory. Scandinavian J. Educ. Res. **56**(3), 243–259 (2012)
32. Van Maanen, J.: Tales of the field: On writing ethnography. University of Chicago Press, Chicago (2008). 2011
33. Wang, F., Hannafin, M.J.: Design-based research and technology-enhanced learning environments. Educ. Tech. Res. Dev. **53**(4), 5–23 (2005)
34. Weitze, C.L., Ørngreen, R.: The global classroom model simultaneous campus-and home-based education using video conferencing. Electron. J. e-Learning **12**(2), 215–226 (2014)
35. Whittemore, R., Knafl, K.: The integrative review: updated methodology. J. Adv. Nurs. **52**(5), 546–553 (2005)
36. Ørngreen, R.N.: Multimedia teaching cases. Forskerskolen i Informatik, Handelshøjskolen i København (2002)
37. Ørngreen, R.: The Design Sketching Process. In: Clemmensen, T., Campos, P., Orngreen, R., Pejtersen, A.M., Wong, W. (eds.) Human Work Interaction Design: Designing for Human Work. IFIP TC 13.6 WG Conference, vol. 221, pp. 185–202. Springer, Heidelberg (2006)

Insights from User Experience Research in the Factory: What to Consider in Interaction Design

Daniela Wurhofer$^{(\boxtimes)}$, Verena Fuchsberger, Thomas Meneweger,
Christiane Moser, and Manfred Tscheligi

Center for Human-Computer Interaction,
Christian Doppler Laboratory "Contextual Interfaces",
University of Salzburg, Salzburg, Austria
{daniela.wurhofer,verena.fuchsberger,thomas.meneweger,
christiane.moser,manfred.tscheligi}@sbg.ac.at

Abstract. During the past few years we investigated humans' work in a semiconductor factory, both in relation to digital and non-digital artifacts. With this paper, we provide an overview of aspects that are relevant in production environments. In particular, we present factors accounting for workers' experience as well as influences on their user experience (UX). Based on a meta-interpretation approach, we analyzed our previous studies on the basis of publications that presented our previous research results. In total, we annotated 21 publications, which reported results from qualitative (e.g., ethnographies, interviews) and quantitative approaches (e.g., questionnaires). Overall, this work contributes to an orientation for designers and researchers regarding the interplay between user, system and context in a factory environment by pointing out relevant aspects of and influences on workers' experiences.

Keywords: Factory · Production environment · User experience · Interaction · Design · Context · User · System · Work

1 Motivation

Research on user experience (UX) is often highlighting the relevance of the context, in which the interaction with an artifact takes place. Consequently, rich descriptions of contexts are needed, but according studies are still rare [3]. Many studies only focus on particular aspects of experiences, but widely ignore the multidimensionality of UX and the interrelationship of UX dimensions in specific contexts. Further, UX research has primarily been focusing on art and consumer products, while lacking devotion to work contexts [3]. This might be due to access restrictions, i.e., research faces a variety of limitations when trying to investigate competitive or safety-critical environments (e.g., [4,14]). Another reason could be that the potential of performing experience research is less obvious in a factory context [25].

© IFIP International Federation for Information Processing 2015
J. Abdelnour-Nocera et al. (Eds.): HWID 2015, IFIP AICT 468, pp. 39–56, 2015.
DOI: 10.1007/978-3-319-27048-7_3

This paper represents an attempt to summarize a series of different studies in the context of a semiconductor factory in order to identify relevant aspects with regard to UX (i.e., workers' experience). We aim to provide an orientation for researchers and designers by creating awareness that workers' experience is crucial for their well-being and performance. We present aspects that account for workers' experiences in a factory context which can be researched and designed for, reflecting that workers' experience is multifaceted. In order to better understand this context with regard to UX, we conducted a range of qualitative and quantitative studies. These provided us with a comprehensive understanding of workers' routines and experiences and helped us to identify aspects that are of particular relevance for UX in the factory (e.g., trust, stress)[1].

In this paper, we provide an overview of relevant factors, which we found in our previous work. These factors include aspects of the workers' experience when interacting with systems in such a context, as well as influences on workers' UX in form of system properties (e.g., efficiency), user characteristics (e.g., attitude), as well as characteristics of the social (e.g., hierarchy) and physical (e.g., space) context. Although these aspects are interrelated, they address specific notions of users' interactions that need to be taken into account in the design of interactive systems for the factory.

The paper is structured as follows. After motivating our work, we provide background information about research in the factory in general, as well as research on UX in the factory in particular. Then, we present our research approach by introducing the study context, method and procedure, as well as the materials used. Next, we present our findings according to identified UX factors as well as influences on UX. We then discuss our insights with regard to particularities of the factory context, design, methodology, UX factors, value of UX research, specifics of the use case, as well as opportunities and challenges. Finally, we conclude the paper and provide an outlook for future work.

2 Background

In this section, we point out related work in the area of UX and factory research. This provides a basis to better understand our research with regard to the specifics of the context (i.e., factory) and the theoretical grounding of our work (i.e., UX).

2.1 Research in the Factory

In general, industrial contexts pose a variety of challenges and restrictions, for instance, fieldwork must not impact work practices [4,37,40]. For decades, scientists have been occupied with investigating factory work from a point of view of classical or social psychology (e.g., [6]). A great number of research addresses health or safety aspects as well as ergonomics. Regarding humans' interaction

---

[1] in the following considered as "UX factors".

with systems, the factory context has been less prominent in HCI research and publications. Few material can be found that puts factory workers into the focal point of attention when designing interfaces. In the beginning of the 1990s, an IEEE Colloquium was held on "HCI: Issues for the Factory", dealing with the psychological basis for computer system design, operator support systems and industrial inspection [15]. This colloquium, however, remained a unique event and was not continued in the following years. One of the few pointing out the importance of investigating new technologies in the factory context is Fallman [10], considering the industrial use of information technology (IT) as "paradigm shift".

Our own research is primarily concerned with UX in challenging contexts, one of them being production environments (e.g., [25,37,41]). As part of a national large scale project - the Christian Doppler Laboratory "Contextual Interfaces" (CDL) [11] - we examine contextual interaction from qualitative, constructional, and methodological viewpoints in different application areas. Apart from basic research activities focusing on methods and tools for contextual research, the laboratory explores the contexts "car" and "factory" from these three perspectives. In the context "factory", we conduct research on UX in a semiconductor fabrication plant, where microchips are produced. There, we investigate, design, develop and prototype elements of novel human-centered, integrated, production interface systems. These systems are based on the intelligent cooperation between humans and (intelligent) computing systems, enabling enhanced user experience qualities. By this research, we advance the field of situated interface development (including "robotic interfaces") as well as the area of contextual user experience.

2.2 Research on (Workers') User Experience

Researchers still stress the need for a precise understanding of UX as well as a comprehensive formulation of the concept and its constituting factors (e.g., [12,19,24]), covering a range of contexts and situations. According to McCarthy and Wright [20], experience is constructed out of the interplay of the human and the technology in a situation. Thus, experiences are dynamic, situated, and never the same. McCarthy and Wright emphasize the situatedness and uniqueness of experience and object reductions of experience into separate areas of study (i.e., holistic approach on experience). In contrast, Hassenzahl and colleagues [13] suggest categorizing experiences on the basis of psychological needs and link them to affect and product perception. They highlight the need for some kind of generalization of experiences in order to be useful for HCI, and for designing interactive products (i.e., reductionistic approach on experience). In our research, we acknowledge the situatedness of interactions, which we take into account by investigating very specific, situated interactions. At the same time, we aim to generalize our findings in the sense that we summarize and cluster the observations to provide an overview of relevant aspects in order to open up the research and design space of production environments.

Especially in industrial domains and production environments, the value of UX research may not be obvious at a first glance. There are still many companies that do not focus on their workers' experience, or do not properly consider it [2]. Following Alben [1], we consider UX as being comprised of all the aspects of how people interact with an interactive artifact; e.g., how it feels in the hands, how well it is understood, how it is perceived during interaction, how well it serves their purposes, and how well it fits the context of use. With regard to the work domain and in particular factory work, with "people" we refer to factory workers. "Interactive artifacts" comprise all systems, devices, equipment and interfaces workers have to interact with regarding daily work. According to Kaasinen et al. [16], the key prerequisite for experience-driven design is to define what experience to design for. UX factors (e.g., from existing frameworks) can be employed as the basis for setting UX goals for design. The main challenges are to create a solid value argumentation for focusing on workers' experiences and showing the link between the monetary value it can create [38]. According to [38], positive experiences with the technology are for example related o the user's efficiency, work satisfaction, and professional pride. Similarly, on a customer level, there could be effects on productivity, competitiveness, or brand image. Better UX may lead to reduced learning time, reduced sick leaves, or more satisfied users in general. Satisfaction may reduce employee turnover and support the customers image as an attractive employer. Further, UX research in the industrial domain can act as a differentiating factor by offering competitive advantage.

UX research is closely linked to specific challenges. For example, measuring UX or investigating which characteristics contribute to a positive UX may be a difficult endeavor. In particular, this affects research on UX in production environments, as the context poses a variety of further constraints and challenges that increase the complexity of such investigations. Within the Christian Doppler Laboratory "Contextual Interfaces" (nationally funded for seven years), we address this issue [11]. There, we aim to research *contextual* interaction from different viewpoints, e.g., understanding users in contexts or designing interfaces and interactions for challenging environments. For example, we already stressed the importance of UX in the factory [25] and provide initial insights on workers' everyday experiences and contextual influences on it [44].

3   Approach

To provide comprehensibility and traceability of our research, the following section gives details about the context of our study, the methodological set up and procedure, as well as the materials used for the analysis.

3.1   Study Context: The Semiconductor Factory

In our work, we collaborate with a semiconductor fabrication plant, where microchips are produced. The overall goal of the semiconductor fabrication plant is a "zerodefect" production of microchips, i.e., ideally there are no defects during manufacturing, as they would be very costly. Consequently, the following aspects are crucial: continuous improvements of the work place, processes, and equipment, fast feedback loops, detection of weak spots, avoidance of redundant work, and ongoing enhancement of wafer quality. The production takes place in so called cleanrooms, which are categorized in different micro dust halls. The interaction in a factory is challenging, as the work has to be done quickly and exactly. Human errors can lead to high costs. Furthermore, operators often do have to work together and rely on each other and since a factory often is a closed and special environment, microcosms arise among operators within a factory.

The main challenge for semiconductor manufacturing plants is the coordination of many operators working on different machines to guarantee an efficient production process. As soon as we talk about factory ergonomics like safe, usable, and comfortable interfaces, we are also addressing aspects of UX (e.g., perceived safety). Despite the obvious relevance of UX in the factory, little research has dealt with this issue. This might be partly rooted in the difficulties and limitations of such a context, or due to the fact that the investigation of UX might lead to competitive advantage, and are thus not published for a greater audience. Further, the cleanroom poses several challenges for research, e.g., 24/7/365 production, high complexity of processes, interfaces and interactions, or the need for special equipment, like cleanroom suits.

3.2   Method and Procedure

In order to summarize and cluster UX factors based on our previous work, we drew on the approach of meta-interpretation [39]. Traditional literature reviews give an overview of the field, i.e., they are often descriptive and are rarely able to make sense of what the collection of studies reviewed has to say. In contrast, the meta-interpretation approach of Weed [39] maintains an interpretive epistemology by focusing on the interpretive synthesis of qualitative research (i.e., meaning in context). The meta-interpretation approach is based on the evaluation of eight research methods or approaches that include some form of synthesis (literature review, systematic review, meta-analysis, meta-ethnography, grounded theory, cross-case comparison, secondary analysis of primary data, and interpretive phenomenological analysis).

As suggested by Weed [39], our first step was to identify the overlying topic according to our research goal, namely to identify factors which account for operators' experience in the semiconductor factory. Afterwards, we established the "meaning in context", i.e., we collected an initial set of relevant publications and analyzed their content in terms of the goal of the literature synthesis. Based on this initial analysis, we included further studies and excluded those, which did not fit our objective (e.g., studies that did not address or detail their understanding of UX). The analysis was continued until theoretical saturation was reached, i.e., no further findings regarding UX were identified in the publications (see Table 1 for an overview of publications included in the analysis). Finally, we summarized the findings.

3.3   Overview on Materials Used

All publications that are mentioned in this subchapter were included into the analysis for this paper (see Table 1). In total, we analyzed 21 papers. Thereof, 14 were published as conference proceedings, 2 as book chapters, and 5 as workshop position papers. The work covered was published between 2010 and 2014, with most of the papers being published in 2012 (n=8) and 2013 (n=7). In order to provide an overview of how they relate, their origin, objective, or approach is described in the following.

Overall, our theoretical perspective on UX was both holistic and reductionistic. Initially, we followed a holistic perspective on UX in order to get an understanding of the heterogeneity of the contextual constraints and conditions in the cleanroom and the task diversity of different workers (e.g., operators, shift leads, maintainers) in this area. By applying qualitative methods like contextual inquiry, interviews, probing, or creative workshops (e.g., [17,18,25,27,41,44]), we gained a comprehensive picture of workers' routines and experiences.

In this early phase of our research, we focused on the uniqueness of experience, aiming to describe individuals' situated experiences in detail. Based on these findings we identified different factors, which play an especially important role in this context (e.g., trust, stress). In later stages of our research, we focused on these selected UX factors to explore them in detail, reflecting the adoption of a reductionistic perspective. In particular, the change of workers' specific experiences over time when introducing new interfaces turned out to be a promising field for future research [8]. For instance, we conducted a study on industrial robots in the cleanroom, where we accompanied the deployment of a new robotic arm over one and a half years [8], investigating changes of the workers' experience. Based on the findings from studies in the cleanroom (e.g., [8,40]), we also focused on specific UX factors relevant in the factory by conducting lab studies. In terms of human-robot interaction, we studied the role of feedback [30], anthropomorphism [31], training [32], social cues [42], or input modalities and task complexity [33–35]. Furthermore, the studies were the basis for designs and UX prototypes. In these designs, we focused on wearable devices [26,28], or ambient, persuasive displays in the factory [7,22,23,36].

The diversity of the above listed research activities and studies provided us with a comprehensive framing of UX in the factory and allowed us to identify factors which account for the workers' experience. The next section provides details about our insights regarding workers' experiences in the factory as well as influences on it.

4   Findings

In this section, we describe relevant aspects of the interplay between user, system and context regarding workers' experiences in a factory environment. With *user* we refer to the workers in the factory (e.g., operators, maintainers, shift leads). With *system* we mean interfaces, devices, or robots, the user has to work with in the factory. *Context* refers to the physical or social environment in which the

Table 1. Overview of analyzed papers and associated factors

	Paper Title	Author	Year	Publication Type	UX Factors Discussed
1	Assisting maintainers in the semiconductor factory: Iterative co-design of a mobile interface and a situated display	Buchner et al.	2013	Conference Proceedings	* Perceived Workload * Feeling of Control * Perceived Usefulness * Perceived Ease of Use * Trust
2	Robots in Time: How User Experience in Human-Robot Interaction Changes over Time	Buchner et al.	2013	Book Chapter	* Stress * Perceived Safety
3	Collaborative Reporting Tools: An analysis of maintainance activites in a semiconductor factory	Kluckner et al.	2013	Conference Proceedings	* Perceived Workload * Perceived Ease of Use * Satisfaction
4	Repair Now: Collaboration between Maintainers, Operators and Equipment in a Cleanroom	Kluckner et al.	2012	Conference Proceedings	* Perceived Ease of Use * Satisfaction * Trust
5	Ambient Persuasion in the Factory: The Case of the Operator Guide	Meschtscherjakov et al.	2011	Conference Proceedings	* Perceived Workload
6	The Operator Guide: An Ambient Persuasive Interface in the Factory	Meschtscherjakov et al.	2010	Conference Proceedings	* Stress * Perceived Usefulness * Perceived Ease of Use
7	User Experience Research in the Semiconductor Factory: A Contradiction?	Obrist et al.	2011	Conference Proceedings	* Stress * Emotions and Feelings
8	Using Participatory Design to Investigate Technology Usage in the Cleanroom of a Semiconductor Factory	Osswald	2012	Workshop Position Paper	* Stress * Perceived Usefulness
9	Designing Wearable Devices for the Factory Rapid Contextual Experience Prototyping	Osswald et al.	2013	Conference Proceedings	* Perceived Workload * Perceived Safety
10	Designing for the Factory: Wearable Experience Prototyping for Idea Communication	Osswald et al.	2012	Conference Proceedings	
11	I trained the robot: The impact of pre-experience and execution behavior on robot teachers	Stadler et al.	2014	Conference Proceedings	* Perceived Workload * Perceived Usefulness * Trust
12	Anthropomorphism in the Factory - A Paradigm Change?	Stadler et al.	2013	Conference Proceedings	* Stress * Feeling of Control * Performance Expectancy * Perceived Safety
13	Feedback is like Cinderella! The important role of feedback when humans and robots are working together in the factory	Stadler et al.	2012	Workshop Position Paper	* Feeling of Control * Perceived Safety * Trust
14	Input Modality and Task Complexity: Do they Relate?	Stollnberger et al.	2013	Conference Proceedings	* Performance Expectancy
15	"The Harder it Gets": Exploring the Interdependency of Input Modalities and Task Complexity in Human-Robot Collaboration	Stollnberger et al.	2013	Conference Proceedings	* Perceived Workload * Performance Expectancy * Satisfaction * Trust
16	The effect of input modalities and different levels of task complexity on feedback perception in a human-robot collaboration task	Stollnberger et al.	2012	Workshop Position Paper	* Satisfaction
17	Combining Implicit and Explicit Methods for the Evaluation of an Ambient Persuasive Factory Display	Strasser et al.	2013	Conference Proceedings	* Performance Expectancy
18	"Contextual Researches" - Challenges and Approaches in the Factory Context	Weiss et al.	2012	Workshop Position Paper	* Perceived Workload * Emotions and Feelings
19	Rethinking the Human-Agent Relationship: Which Social Cues do Interactive Agents Really Need to Have?	Weiss et al.	2012	Book Chapter	
20	Exploring Human-Robot Cooperation Possibilities for Semiconductor Manufacturing	Weiss et al.	2011	Workshop Position Paper	* Perceived Usefulness
21	Research in the Semiconductor Factory: Insights into Experiences and Contextual Influences	Wurhofer et al.	2014	Conference Proceedings	* Stress * Perceived Usefulness * Satisfaction * Trust * Emotions and Feelings

factory work is accomplished. Our findings are structured in form of *UX factors* (i.e., aspects of experience) as well as *influences on UX* stemming from the user, the system, or the context.

4.1 Identified UX Factors

Table 2 provides an overview of the identified UX factors. *UX factors* represent a component-oriented approach on UX, decomposing UX into specific aspects, which account for the users' experience when interacting with a system in a context. They represent measurable units of UX and thus support the operationalizability, measurability, and comparability of UX.

Taking a meta-perspective on our work, we found ten factors to be relevant for operators' experience in the semiconductor factory: perceived workload, stress, feeling of control, perceived usefulness, perceived ease of use, performance expectancy, satisfaction, perceived safety, trust, as well as emotions and feelings (see Table 2 for an overview). Thereof, perceived workload was described in most of the papers (7 out of 10). Stress, perceived usefulness, and trust were mentioned in 60 % of the papers (6 out of 10). Emotions and feelings were highlighted least often (3 out of 10). In the following, we outline those UX factors, which we have identified as relevant with regard to interactions in the semiconductor factory, in more detail.

One aspect regularly mentioned by workers when interacting with systems in the factory is **perceived workload** ([7,18,22,28,32,35,41]), meaning the cognitive effort required when interacting with a system in order to solve a task.

Table 2. Identified UX factors and their frequencies (N) with regard to publications

UX factor	Description	Source
Perceived workload	*Cognitive effort required when interacting with a system in order to solve a task*	[7,18,22,28,32,35,41]
Stress	*Workers' tension and perceived pressure induced by the interaction*	[8,23,25,27,31,44]
Feeling of control	*Workers perceived influence on the system's actions*	[7,30,31]
Perceived usefulness	*Utility attributed to interacting with the system*	[7,23,27,32,40,44]
Perceived ease of use	*How easy the interface is to handle in the interaction*	[7,17,18,23]
Performance expectancy	*Degree to which a worker believes that using the system will support his/her performance*	[31,34–36]
Satisfaction	*Workers' contentment with the interaction*	[17,18,33,35,44]
Perceived safety	*Workers' perception of the level of danger when interacting with a system*	[8,28,30,31]
Trust	*Extent to which the user feels confident that the system will behave as intended*	[7,17,30,32,35,44]
Emotions and feelings	*Affective states of positive or negative valence*	[25,41,44]

Attention and awareness are needed when interacting with a factory system; information overload increases the perceived workload.

Perceived workload is closely related to **stress** ([8,23,25,27,31,44]), which reflects the workers' tension and perceived pressure induced by the interaction. Time pressure, shift cycles, problems with equipment and priorization of interfaces were often mentioned in relation to stress when interacting with the system.

Feeling of control ([7,30,31]) is another relevant UX factor, meaning the workers' perceived influence on the system's actions. Particularly, this factor is crucial in human-robot interaction, e.g., that the human stays in control of the robot. Further, unnecessary information on interfaces promotes a feeling of losing control.

Another UX factor crucial in the factory is **perceived usefulness** ([7,23,27, 32,40,44]), which denotes the utility attributed to interacting with the system. In the factory, a system is perceived as useful and supportive if it improves, for example, the workers' efficiency or effectiveness. Otherwise, if a system works slow or even freezes sometimes, it is perceived as a hindrance regarding workers' performance.

Perceived ease of use ([7,17,18,23]), i.e., how easy the interface is to handle in the interaction, is closely related to learnability and intuitiveness/complexity of the system. Information overload and slow performance of interfaces in the factory are considered as the main problems when using them. Such problems are often mentioned as a source of stress for workers.

Performance Expectancy ([31,34–36]) means the degree to which a worker believes that using the system will support his/her performance. In the factory context, the expected performance is often decreased due to external factors like technical problems, bad work organization, or equipment related issues such as slow delivery of lots or too many equipment items in service.

We further identified **satisfaction** ([17,18,33,35,44]), i.e., the contentment with the interaction, as a UX factor. Workers are satisfied either when they consider their performance as being good, or when they get positive feedback regarding their performance from others (i.e., colleagues or superiors). The more difficult a task, the more satisfied they are.

Another UX factor is **perceived safety** ([8,28,30,31]), describing the workers' perception of the level of danger when interacting with a system. This aspect of UX is especially relevant when dealing with robots. For example, certain security mechanisms (e.g., emergency stop button) or displaying the robot's current and next state convey a feeling of safety in human-robot interaction.

Trust ([7,17,30,32,35,44]) is also an important issue regarding workers' experience at the factory. With trust we refer to the extent to which the user feels confident that the system will behave as intended. Trust is closely related to perceived safety and the feeling of control. Reliable and error-free system processes as well as feedback modalities that inform about the system's current state might help to improve trust towards the system.

Emotions and feelings, i.e., affective states of positive or negative valence, further shape the workers' daily experience in the factory. Negative emotional experiences we identified were **anger, fear**, and **frustration** ([25,41,44]). Regarding anger, workers often mention usability and work organization as a cause. For example, workers are bothered when the machines are difficult to handle, or when action space is limited. Similarly, frustration is, for example, related to slow response time of the interfaces or information overload and thus closely related to stress. Fear is often associated with human-robot interaction, as workers are afraid of being replaced by robots. Positive emotions mentioned with regard to factory work are **joy, fun**, and **pride** [44]. Overall, production tasks are rather linked to negative emotions, whereas administrative activities are experienced rather positive, fostering emotions like fun, joy or pride.

4.2   Influences on UX

Influences on UX can arise from characteristics of the user, the system, or the context (e.g., [13,20]). In our work, we differentiate influences on UX that origin from the user (individual influences), from the system (system influences), and from the context (contextual influences).

Individual Influences (e.g., [7,8,17,26,31,32,35,36,44]). **Motivation** can be considered as a characteristic of the worker influencing his or her experience. Sources for motivation are, for example, an increase of productivity despite having a lot of equipment down, working passionately for a common goal, or getting invited for a coffee to speak about the company. Further, the workers' **attitude** towards the system to interact with is crucial. Another influence on the experienced interaction is the workers' general **well-being**. **Pre-experience**, i.e., already gained know-how, was also found to influence the workers experience, similar to **reflexivity** (in the sense of conscious retrieval of knowledge and competences). Further, the workers' **flexibility** as well as their **routines** influence their UX.

System Influences (e.g., [7,17,26,28,30–36,44]). In the factory, the system's **appearance** in the sense of aesthetics and form as well as **visibility** of information and transparency of actions was found to influence the workers' experience. **Autonomy, adaptivity**, as well as **flexibility** of the system also shape UX. **Consistency** of the system's procedures, actions, or representations is important as well as the **persuasiveness** of the system in the sense of guiding the user in his/her actions or tasks. **Reliability** of the system in the sense of trustworthiness and functionality influences the workers' experience. Further, the **complexity** and **intuitiveness** of the system are crucial. This includes issues like training needed to interact with the system, understandability, or learnability. **Efficiency** (e.g., the system's performance) and **effectiveness** (e.g., error rate) are further properties of the system affecting UX.

Contextual Influences (e.g., [8,18,25–27,30,35,36,44]). With regard to the physical context, **noise** was found to be characteristic in the factory, representing a physical constraint and an influence on the workers' experience. **Light** as well as **temperature** (e.g., heat) represent further characteristics of the physical context of the factory. The special **clothing** required especially in the cleanroom is another constraint, needed to minimize **contamination** which has to be kept as low as possible (especially in the cleanroom). Additionally, the **action space** (i.e., amount of space to walk around) shapes the workers' experience.

Additionally, the workers? social context affects their experience, for instance, **interpersonal reliability**, i.e., the trustworthiness of colleagues. Further, **equal treatment** in the sense that everybody is treated in the same way by colleagues and superiors is another influence factor. **Appreciation**, e.g., positive feedback from colleagues or superiors, is also crucial for workers, shaping their experience. Finally, **hierarchy**, meaning the fulfilling of formal roles and associated expectations, affects UX.

5   Discussion

In the light of the factory being a challenging and hardly investigated context in HCI, the main intention of our work was to identify and collect UX factors as well as influences on UX in order to contribute a comprehensive picture of UX in the factory.

With the meta-analysis presented in this paper, we aim to create awareness that UX in factories is worthwhile to investigate and design for. Therefore, we illustrate differentiated needs and sources for the design of appropriate interactive systems. We provide reference points for designers which they can draw on when conceptualizing and developing systems for the factory context that support a positive experience at work. In the following, we discuss the main issues we were confronted with when researching UX in a factory context.

Restricted Accessibility and Complexity of the Factory Context. A factory presents a research context which is difficult to access in terms of sampling (i.e., access to the people who are in the focus of research) as well as physical presence of the researcher (i.e., access to specific areas in the factory). The first and foremost demand when doing research in this context is not to impact work practices [41]. This means that the factory's goals of error free production, efficiency of production processes, as well as cleanroom requirements (e.g., specific clothing) must not be impaired. Next to accessibility, the complexity of the factory environment (in terms of work practices, processes, and equipment) represents a hurdle for researchers. From our experience, basic knowledge regarding practices, processes, and equipment is necessary to conduct studies in this context (e.g., in order to have the "right" vocabulary in interviews).

The restricted accessibility and complexity of the factory context may be one of the reasons why UX research in this context is scarce [2]. Thus, with our contribution, i.e., factors accounting for workers' experience in the factory, we provide insights into a very restricted environment, allowing designers and researchers to better understand this context.

Designing for UX in the Factory. According to Kaasinen et al. [16], the core of experience design is the definition of UX goals, i.e., defining what experience to design for. With regard to industrial contexts, where various stakeholders are involved, concrete and shared UX goals are crucial to ensure a clear conception of the targeted experience and to support keeping UX in focus. We think that the UX factors we introduced in this work can be employed as a basis for setting UX goals for design in the factory context. This would be especially valuable with regard to factories of the future and future workplace designs.

We are aware that narrowing down the workers' experience to a list of UX factors is linked to specific drawbacks, rooted in the discussion of holistic versus reductive approaches on UX [5]. In particular, the uniqueness and situatedness of experience as stated by proponents of the holistic perspective (e.g., [20]) is lost. Following Redström [29], design should create and optimize a user's experience on the basis of predictions. Thus, such reductions seem to be necessary at this stage to break down empirical insights into concrete suggestions for the design. We consider our UX factors as such leverage points for interaction design. Nevertheless, we want to stress that designs should provide enough space for the user to act and improvise [29], ensuring that we do not lose the holistic viewpoint on experience.

UX Methodology. Throughout our work, we applied a range of methods, both qualitative and quantitative. In relation to this approach, we tried to consider UX from a holistic as well as reductionistic perspective. At specific stages of the research process (e.g., at the beginning of the project), it was meaningful to take a holistic perspective on UX, not narrowing it down to specific factors but trying to comprehend specific phenomena in as much detail as possible [20]. At other stages (e.g., after a basic understanding of the factory context was gathered), it was valuable to take on a reductionistic perspective in order to investigate very specific research questions or generalize findings [12].

Overall, our approach of taking different perspectives at different stages within a research process provided us with a comprehensive picture on workers' experiences in a factory. In our opinion, this approach supported us in uncovering otherwise (i.e., when just adopting one perspective) hidden factors. We think that such an approach has not been applied so far in this domain and therefore represents a methodological step forward towards studying UX in the factory.

UX Factors. Regarding the identified factors, some of them may be less surprising, given the context of a production environment, (e.g., perceived workload, stress, performance expectancy). Others, however, are more surprising (e.g., emotional experiences, such as fun, anger, or pride), pointing out possibilities for design that may not be initially thought of in this context. For example, we found that negative emotions like anger, fear or frustration are much more prominent regarding workers' experiences than positive emotions like joy or fun.

An implication of this finding may be to focus more specifically on positive experiences in future designs, wherefore we provided indications of what accounts for positive experiences in the factory in our work. Similarly, the results help us understand why designs may lead to different actions than imagined or intended (e.g., technology appropriation [9]). Thereby, the complexity is even increased through the interplay of the various factors and aspects. This poses serious challenges especially to the design of interactive systems, as it is difficult to decide what exactly to design for. Nevertheless, being aware of the situated nature of interactions and the range of experiences that may occur, as well as what may influence them, will help to explicitly decide for or against certain aspects, depending on their likelihood of appearance or relevance.

Valuing UX Research. An important aspect for our research was to show the relevance of UX research in the factory context. In particular, the stakeholders involved in our research (e.g., operators, maintainers, shift leads, management) learned about the value of UX and UX research. We think that is important to understand that positive experiences have a positive effect on workers (e.g., are for example related to efficiency, work satisfaction, or pride), which in turn provides competitive advantage in an industrial context [38].

In our experience, time was crucial for understanding the importance of UX. With progressing time, i.e., over the years, the stakeholders saw increasing value of our research. This could be due to the fact that at the beginning our scientific approach was not tangible for the stakeholders. As Ardito et al. [2] argue, scientific research and methods should be translated into something that makes sense for companies. In order to provide an understanding of what UX in a factory context is, we think that a list of dedicated factors accounting for the workers' experience in daily work is helpful. Such a list of factors represents something that is tangible and meaningful for companies, especially when illustrated by examples from daily worklife. Moreover, these UX factors provide a better contextual understanding of the factory.

Further, the active involvement of practitioners in the overall research process is also important [2]. Although not always possible in practice, we saw that presenting the results to the stakeholders and discussing them with them increased the acceptance and openness towards UX research in the factory.

According to Väätäjä et al. [38], showing the value of UX by measures is important. However, the question is what to measure, i.e., which factors account for UX in the context of production environments. We think that our paper represents a valuable contribution to this question, as it lists a range of factors which account for the workers' experience in a factory. By quantifying (i.e., measuring) specified factors, comparisons can be made and trends can be detected. Thus, UX factors provide an anchor for quantifying and improving workers' experience.

Specific Use Case. The described study environment represents a very specific use case. Thus, the factors presented above are subject to limitation, as they have been collected in a specific factory on basis of case studies, or within studies in a laboratory where the production context was simulated. Contextual conditions like light, temperature, noise, clothing might vary from factory to factory in their specific shape. Nevertheless, it is likely that the described influence factors are relevant in other factory environments as well, even if their manifestations differ.

With regard to UX factors, we assume a similar situation: differences to other production environments may primarily affect the degree of occurrence rather than the question whether the factors play a role at all.

An advantage due to the specific and single use case is the comparability of results. As all stakeholders involved in our studies work in the same factory, differences regarding their experience cannot be due to differences in the work environment (which could be the case if results from different factories are compared). Of course, the set of factors may be extended through further studies in other production environments.

Opportunities and Challenges. Critically reflecting on our work, it represents an exception as we had the opportunity to conduct studies for more than five years in a sensitive context which is challenging and hard to access. Thus, our research advanced from initial studies aiming to get to know the context to very specific studies investigating defined factors in detail.

A particular challenge we were confronted with was to gain the trust of the responsible stakeholders in the factory. This was especially hard at the beginning, when the stakeholders were skeptical about research in this challenging context. In particular, workers had concerns and doubts about anonymity of their statements and that superiors would be informed about their opinions. Therefore, it was especially important to emphasize anonymity and discretion whenever getting in contact with stakeholders. Further, we had the impression that the closer the contact was (e.g., individual interviews), the more open the stakeholders were towards the researchers. Next to closeness, time was a factor influencing openness of stakeholders. With progressing time, trust and openness towards the researchers increased and made it possible for researchers and stakeholders to work together closely.

Based on the insights gained within the last five years, we further developed and shaped our research. For example, we recognized that workers' experiences and attitudes are closely linked to specific incidents (e.g., the deployment of a robot), and that deeper investigation of such incidents provides knowledge about the dynamics and changes of workers' experiences. Therefore, we retrospectively investigated how workers experienced the deployment of a robot [21] and put a focus on the temporal transitions of workers' experiences in this context [43]. Such insights enrich the understanding of the UX factors in terms of comprehensively looking at experiential processes of workers in the factory.

6 Conclusion

This paper presents an analysis of UX in human-work interactions, which is based on several studies in the context of a semiconductor factory. Factors relevant in this context were identified and clustered to reveal the multiple facets of user experiences and influences on this experience. We presented UX factors occurring in the factory, ranging from stress, performance expectancy, trust, and satisfaction, to joy, pride, fear, and anger. Those factors are influenced by user characteristics, such as the user's attitude, well-being, flexibility, or routines. Furthermore, system aspects affect the users' experiences (e.g., complexity, appearance, visibility, accessibility, or persuasiveness). Contextual specifics may also influence human-work interactions, i.e., the physical context (e.g., noise, light, clothing, or action space) and the social context (e.g., interpersonal reliability, equality, or appreciation). Focusing on these factors also in the design of human-work interactions is a promising approach to improve users' experience at work, which eventually results in motivation and well-being at work.

For future work, we plan to extend our insights with studies from other factories. Similarities and differences should be explored across different factories in order to find out which factors are more or less stable when the specific environment changes. Further, we want to put a focus on the interrelations and dynamics of selected UX factors, which might be helpful for future factory and workplace designs. Finally, we aim to advance our research on temporal transitions of workers' experiences by studying newly deployed systems in the course of time.

Acknowledgments. The financial support by the Austrian Federal Ministry of Science, Research and Economy and the National Foundation for Research, Technology and Development is gratefully acknowledged (Christian Doppler Laboratory for "Contextual Interfaces"). Special thanks is dedicated to the researchers involved in the qualitative analysis: Axel Baumgartner, Elke Beck, Ulrike Bruckenberger, Roland Bucher, Alina Krischkowsky, Susanne Stadler, and Barbara Weichselbaumer.

References

1. Alben, L.: Quality of experience: defining the criteria for effective interaction design. Interactions **3**(3), 11–15 (1996)
2. Ardito, C., Buono, P., Caivano, D., Costabile, M.F., Lanzilotti, R.: Investigating and promoting UX practice in industry: an experimental study. Int. J. Hum.-Comput. Stud. **72**(6), 542–551 (2014). interplay between User Experience Evaluation and System Development
3. Bargas-Avila, J.A., Hornbaek, K.: Old wine in new bottles or novel challenges: a critical analysis of empirical studies of user experience. In: Proceedings of the 2011 Annual Conference on Human Factors in Computing Systems, pp. 2689–2698. CHI 2011, ACM, New York (2011)
4. Björndal, P.S., Ralph, M.B.: On the handling of impedance factors for establishing apprenticeship relations during field studies in industry domains. In: Proceedings of the 8th Nordic Conference on Human-Computer Interaction: Fun, Fast, Foundational, pp. 1107–1112. NordiCHI 2014, ACM, New York (2014)
5. Blythe, M., Hassenzahl, M., Law, E., Vermeeren, A.: An analysis framework for user experience (UX) studies: a green paper. In: Paper presented at the Proceedings of the 'Towards a UX Manifesto workshop' at HCI 2007, Lancaster, UK (2007)
6. Brown, J.A.: The social psychology of industry. Penguin Books (1954)
7. Buchner, R., Kluckner, P.M., Weiss, A., Tscheligi, M.: Assisting maintainers in the semiconductor factory: iterative co-design of a mobile interface and a situated display. In: Proceedings of the 12th International Conference on Mobile and Ubiquitous Multimedia, pp. 46:1–46:2. MUM 2013, ACM, New York (2013)
8. Buchner, R., Wurhofer, D., Weiss, A., Tscheligi, M.: Robots in time: how user experience in human-robot interaction changes over time. In: Herrmann, G., Pearson, M.J., Lenz, A., Bremner, P., Spiers, A., Leonards, U. (eds.) ICSR 2013. LNCS, vol. 8239, pp. 138–147. Springer, Heidelberg (2013)

9. Dix, A.: Designing for appropriation. In: Proceedings of the 21st British HCI Group Annual Conference on People and Computers: HCI... but not as we know it-vol. 2, pp. 27–30. British Computer Society (2007)

10. Fallman, D., Kruzeniski, M., Andersson, M.: Designing for a collaborative industrial environment: the case of the abb powerwall. In: Proceedings of the 2005 Conference on Designing for User eXperience. DUX 2005, AIGA: American Institute of Graphic Arts, New York (2005)

11. Grill, T., Reitberger, W., Obrist, M., Meschtscherjakov, A., Tscheligi, M.: The christian doppler laboratory on contextual interfaces. In: de Ruyter, B., Wichert, R., Keyson, D.V., Markopoulos, P., Streitz, N., Divitini, M., Georgantas, N., Mana Gomez, A. (eds.) AmI 2010. LNCS, vol. 6439, pp. 325–332. Springer, Heidelberg (2010)

12. Hassenzahl, M., Tractinsky, N.: User experience - a research agenda. Behav. Inf. Technol. 25(2), 91–97 (2006)

13. Hassenzahl, M., Diefenbach, S., Göritz, A.: Needs, affect, and interactive products - facets of user experience. Interact. Comput. 22(5), 353–362 (2010)

14. Heyer, C.: Investigations of ubicomp in the oil and gas industry. In: Proceedings of the 12th ACM International Conference on Ubiquitous Computing, pp. 61–64. UbiComp 2010, ACM, New York (2010)

15. IEE Colloquium: IEE Colloquium on HCI: Issues for the Factory (Digest No.047), IET February 1991

16. Kaasinen, E., Roto, V., Hakulinen, J., Heimonen, T., Jokinen, J.P., Karvonen, H., Keskinen, T., Koskinen, H., Lu, Y., Saariluoma, P., et al.: Defining user experience goals to guide the design of industrial systems. Behav. Inf. Technol. 34, 1–16 (2015). (ahead-of-print)

17. Kluckner, P.M., Buchner, R., Weiss, A., Tscheligi, M.: Repair now: Collaboration between maintainers, operators and equipment in a cleanroom. In: Proceedings of the ACM Conference on Computer Supported Cooperative Work, pp. 143–146. CSCW2012, ACM, New York (2012)

18. Kluckner, P.M., Buchner, R., Weiss, A., Tscheligi, M.: Collaborative reporting tools: an analysis of maintainance activites in a semiconductor factory. In: Collaboration Technologies and Systems (CTS), pp. 508–515 (2013)

19. Law, E.L.C., van Schaik, P.: Editorial: modelling user experience - an agenda for research and practice. Interact. Comput. 22(5), 313–322 (2010)

20. McCarthy, J., Wright, P.: Technology as experience. Interactions 11(5), 42–43 (2004)

21. Meneweger, T., Wurhofer, D., Fuchsberger, V., Tscheligi, M.: Working together with industrial robots: Experiencing robots in a production environment. In: Proceedings of the 24th IEEE International Symposium on Robot and Human Interactive Communication (RO-MAN) (2015)

22. Meschtscherjakov, A., Kluckner, P.M., Pöhr, F., Reitberger, W., Weiss, A., Tscheligi, M., Hohenwarther, K.H., Osswald, P.: Ambient persuasion in the factory: the case of the operator guide. In: ASCM2011 22nd annual IEEE/SEMI Advanced Semiconductor Manufactoring Conference, pp. 1–6. IEEE (2011)

23. Meschtscherjakov, A., Reitberger, W., Pöhr, F., Tscheligi, M.: The operator guide: an ambient persuasive interface in the factory. In: de Ruyter, B., Wichert, R., Keyson, D.V., Markopoulos, P., Streitz, N., Divitini, M., Georgantas, N., Mana Gomez, A. (eds.) AmI 2010. LNCS, vol. 6439, pp. 117–126. Springer, Heidelberg (2010)

24. Mirnig, A.G., Meschtscherjakov, A., Wurhofer, D., Meneweger, T., Tscheligi, M.: A formal analysis of the iso 9241-210 definition of user experience. In: Proceedings of the 33rd Annual ACM Conference Extended Abstracts on Human Factors in Computing Systems, pp. 437-450. CHI EA 2015, ACM, New York (2015)
25. Obrist, M., Reitberger, W., Wurhofer, D., Förster, F., Tscheligi, M.: User experience research in the semiconductor factory: a contradiction? In: Campos, P., Graham, N., Jorge, J., Nunes, N., Palanque, P., Winckler, M. (eds.) INTERACT 2011, Part IV. LNCS, vol. 6949, pp. 144-151. Springer, Heidelberg (2011)
26. Osswald, S., Buchner, R., Weiss, A., Tscheligi, M.: Designing for the factory: wearable experience prototyping for idea communication. In: Extended Abstracts of the ACM Conference on Designing Interactive Systems, DIS2012, Newcastle, UK (2012)
27. Osswald, S.: Using participatory design to investigate technology usage in the cleanroom of a semiconductor factory. In: Workshop The Message in the Bottle: Best Practices for Transferring the Knowledge from Qualitative User Studies at DIS'12 (2012)
28. Osswald, S., Weiss, A., Tscheligi, M.: Designing wearable devices for the factory: rapid contextual experience prototyping. In: 2013 International Conference on Collaboration Technologies and Systems (CTS), pp. 517-521. IEEE (2013)
29. Redström, J.: Towards user design? on the shift from object to user as the subject of design. Des. Stud. **27**(2), 123-139 (2006)
30. Stadler, S., Mirnig, N., Weiss, A., Tscheligi, M.: Feedback is like cinderella! the important role of feedback when humans and robots are working together in the factory. In: Workshop Feedback in HRI at RO-MAN 2012 (2012)
31. Stadler, S., Weiss, A., Mirnig, N., Tscheligi, M.: Anthropomorphism in the factory - a paradigm change? In: HRI 2013: Proceedings of the 8th ACM/IEEE International Conference on Human Robot Interaction, pp. 231-232 (2013)
32. Stadler, S., Weiss, A., Tscheligi, M.: I trained this robot: the impact of pre-experience and execution behavior on robot teachers. In: 23rd IEEE International Symposium on Robot and Human Interactive Communication (2014)
33. Stollnberger, G., Weiss, A., Tscheligi, M.: The effect of input modalities and different levels of task complexity on feedback perception in a human-robot collaboration task. In: Workshop Feedback in HRI at RO-MAN 2012, Paris, France (2012)
34. Stollnberger, G., Weiss, A., Tscheligi, M.: Input modality and task complexity: do they relate? In: HRI 2013: Proceedings of the 8th ACM/IEEE International Conference on Human Robot Interaction, pp. 233-234 (2013)
35. Stollnberger, G., Weiss, A., Tscheligi, M.: The harder it gets: exploring the interdependency of input modalities and task complexity in human-robot collaboration. In: Proceedings of the 22nd IEEE International Symposium on Robot and Human Interactive Communication (RO-MAN), pp. 264-269. IEEE (2013)
36. Strasser, E., Weiss, A., Grill, T., Osswald, S., Tscheligi, M.: Combining implicit and explicit methods for the evaluation of an ambient persuasive factory display. In: Paternò, F., de Ruyter, B., Markopoulos, P., Santoro, C., van Loenen, E., Luyten, K. (eds.) AmI 2012. LNCS, vol. 7683, pp. 113-128. Springer, Heidelberg (2012)
37. Tscheligi, M., Meschtscherjakov, A., Weiss, A., Wulf, V., Evers, V., Mutlu, B.: Exploring collaboration in challenging environments: from the car to the factory and beyond. In: Proceedings of the ACM 2012 Conference on Computer Supported Cooperative Work Companion, pp. 15-16. CSCW 2012, ACM, New York (2012)
38. Väätäjä, H., Seppänen, M., Paananen, A.: Creating value through user experience: a case study in the metals and engineering industry. Int. J. Technol. Mark. **9**(2), 163-186 (2014)

39. Weed, M.: Meta interpretation: a method for the interpretive synthesis of qualitative research. Forum Qualitative Sozialforschung/Forum: Qualitative Social Research, 6(1) (2005). http://www.qualitative-research.net/index.php/fqs/article/view/508

40. Weiss, A., Buchner, R., Fischer, H., Tscheligi, M.: Exploring human-robot cooperation possibilities for semiconductor manufacturing. In: International Workshop on Collaborative Robots and Human Robot Interaction, pp. 173–177 (2011)

41. Weiss, A., Kluckner, P.M., Buchner, R., Tscheligi, M.: Contextual researches - challenges and approaches in the factory context. In: Workshop at CSCW 2012 - Exploring Collaboration in Challenging Environments: From the Car to the Factory and Beyond (2012)

42. Weiss, A., Tscheligi, M.: Rethinking the human-agent relationship: which social cues do interactive agents really need to have? In: Hingston, P., (ed.) Believable Bots, pp. 1–28. Springer, Heidelberg (2012)

43. Wurhofer, D., Meneweger, T., Fuchsberger, V., Tscheligi, M.: Deploying robots in a production environment: a study on temporal transitions of workers experiences. In: Abascal, J., Barbosa, S., Fetter, M., Gross, T., Palanque, P., Winckler, M. (eds.) INTERACT 2015. LNCS, vol. 9298, pp. 203–220. Springer, Heidelberg (2015)

44. Wurhofer, D., Buchner, R., Tscheligi, M.: Research in the semiconductor factory: insights into experiences and contextual influences. In: Proceedings of 7th International Conference on Human System Interaction (HSI), pp. 129–134 (2014)

User-Created Personas – A Micro-cultural Lens into Informal Settlement's Youth Life

Daniel G. Cabrero[1,2(✉)], Heike Winschiers-Theophilus[2], and Hedvig Mendonca[2]

[1] School of Computing and Engineering, University of West London, St Mary's Road, Ealing, London W5 5RF, UK
Daniel@personas.technology
[2] School of Computing and Informatics, Polytechnic of Namibia, 5 Storch Street, Windhoek, Namibia
HeikeWinschiers@gmail.com,
Hmendonca@polytechnic.edu.na

Abstract. Participatory Design (PD) and service design have shown great potential in co-designing feasible solutions with marginalised societies. This study is part of a research project where dwellers in the informal settlement of Havana in Windhoek engage in context analysis for the establishment of a community centre offering technologies and services supporting the unemployed in finding work opportunities, self-employment and training. Participants first walked us through their neighbourhood pinpointing existing challenges they then communicated through persona sketches of local disadvantaged individuals like prostitutes and criminals. Societal issues, collective representations and sociotechnical gaps emerge, and participants reimagine these into work opportunities, enterprising, community cohesion, and overall alleviation and life improvement. The object of research is to align social realities, existing technologies, and design requirements to ensuring suitable usability, financial affordability, fulfilment of User Experience, and the ultimate self-sufficiency of community and overall project. This paper ultimately argues User-Created Persona (UCP) in PD as a fruitful inquisitive proceeding to explore and augment pervasive and smart work possibilities in locales with limited opportunity and resources.

Keywords: Participatory design · Service design · Work analysis · Personas · HCI4D · Micro-cultures · Walking-Method · User-created personas · UX

1 Introduction

Participatory approaches to development in the Global South have been established over the past decade. A number of participatory initiatives in Southern Africa have been launched with a primary focus on empowering and engaging marginalized youth currently excluded from the job market. While the youth unemployment rate is alarmingly high in Southern Africa, the potential in co-designing feasible solutions with marginalised youth has been demonstrated eclectically [25, 27, 32, 33] by deploying different methods of service design, PD and living lab approaches locally.

© IFIP International Federation for Information Processing 2015
J. Abdelnour-Nocera et al. (Eds.): HWID 2015, IFIP AICT 468, pp. 57–70, 2015.
DOI: 10.1007/978-3-319-27048-7_4

Much of the PD literature cautions researchers about fundamental differences of the conceptualization of participation in different contexts and the need for a situated adaptation of methods [37]. Personas have been a widely used technique in User-Centred Design (UCD), which, however, in a cross-cultural setting carries a high risk of misinterpretations [5]. Thus we propose the use of User-Created Personas (UCP) as one of the newly revised techniques in the form of a fruitful inquisitive, TV-based proceeding to explore and augment contextual understanding in a cross-cultural setting. Personas created by users hold the potential of empowering regular people to define who they are and what they need in their current lives, as well as in endearing regular users to the technological design process. This is possible because designing in their own footings regular people can naturally express their needs, requirements and aspirations.

Our current community outreach work, scientific research and aims concur with, and strive to align with some of the actual needs, requirements and aspirations of youth dwellers in the informal settlement of Havana in Katutura, Windhoek, Namibia. Scaffolding from the above, this study dissects and analyses a series of actions where youth living in Havana engaged in context analysis towards the establishment of a community centre that seeks to offer services and technologies to support the unemployed to finding work opportunities, self-employment and training.

In this paper we analyse and report how youth in Havana take-on, understand, and create persona artefacts as part of the context analysis and design of a better future. This specific study is part of the first author's research agenda on establishing how different ethnic groups in Namibia conceptualize and construct personas [13–15]. The objective of this intervention is, hence, to find out how user-created personas may assist to better understand the needs, requirements and aspirations of the youth in Havana, and how such personas may eventually benefit the development of the series of services and technologies proposed such as the job-search apparatus among others.

In the following section we briefly introduce the wider literature on personas in non-WEIRD (Western, Educated, Industrialised, Rich and Developed) countries [18]. We then introduce the project context, methods deployed, and a briefing on findings. Methods described and analysed in detail follow, while a discussion on them leads to conclude to have established the value of UCP as a participatory approach to appreciate the context and design services and technologies in collaboration with the youth.

2 Personas for Development

Human Work Interaction Design (HWID) endeavours to better understand relationships between concepts and methods in Human-Computer Interaction (HCI) and their meanings to local and indigenous groups [7]. A paucity of empirical HWID projects in developing venues, however, contrasts with ventures in HCI for development (HCI4D) that strive to enable and empower people in underserved or marginalized populations worldwide [1]. Some of these projects test, question and repurpose research and usability methods [2, 5, 6, 22], while others propose processes where engagement with locals is in their very own terms [9]. The array of perspectives, nevertheless, parallels present rates of unfruitful deployments [3], which some argue due to ideas in developing venues maturing slowly and over time [39].

Grounded on their work with unemployed youth in low-income settlements nearby Kampala, Uganda, [16] point out the significance of choosing the right methods to establish engaging research relations, as well as to gain a deeper contextual understanding. This, we argue, is because groups of humans coexisting in developing contexts do so under specific historical and geo-physical conditions that peculiarly characterise the dwellers and environments such as those in townships.

We postulate that such milieus function as micro-cultural contexts whereby to develop a small model of culture could either be gradually expanded into a larger model, or, to our current aims, it could evolve into a more manageable assembly of people's characterisation and placing regarding sociotechnical needs and aspirations [24].

Eyeing through such lens, we propose local youth in Havana to conform and design persona artefacts as characters for a TV-series based on the surroundings, as a possibility to mediate the improvement of their lives through the establishment of the community centre and technologies proposed. Such personas attempt to magnify the needs and requirements of locals to communicate them to the design process. Developing characters for the TV-series serves as training part of the overall engagement of the youth in activities proposed by this project to ameliorating lives in Havana [38].

In this vein, we propose the deployment of UCP as an means to (1) facilitating youth conveying their identities, surroundings and daily experiences; (2) continue exploring persona as a communicational tool in Namibian sites [13–15] by openly proposing it to final users through engagement, reciprocity and doing [4]; (3) keep investigating the debated and scarce pragmatism of persona in HCI [36]; and (4) to assist the overall 'discovery' of persona artefacts beyond Western settings [29].

Our argument on deploying persona scaffolds from the paucity of general empirical research [31] and the fact that the scarcity is even greater outside the West [30].

At the time of writing this manuscript, most research has positioned personas in contexts beyond WEIRD [17, 20, 23] by deploying template-styled outfits similar to the initially conceived by Cooper [8] in the US, namely a written narrative, a picture and a name [26] that strive to represent a group of users with common goals, attitudes and behaviours when interacting with a product or service [34]. Persona's core motivation, though, contrasts with recent ethnographic studies that reveal its dubious utilisation, and therefore effectiveness in UCD, WEIRD settings [11]. Lacking hence an ultimate consensus, many researchers and practitioners hold prejudices on the value of persona as a design communicational tool [36].

In India Katre [22] and Chavan and Prabhu [5] claim persona as it is commonly known is impeached with cross-cultural assumptions. Adapting persona a la Bollywood for usability testing, Chavan and Prabhu claim it facilitates a more effective user-designer communicational exchange in Indian settings [5].

Nielsen [29] hence ultimately problems whether the persona artefact, in taking the role of a translator of usability constructs and goals of User Experience (UX), may be taken-on, understood, created and transferred equally across cultures.

In this vein we first maintain the persona artefact has not yet been provided with ample enough occasions to be guided and fabricated by the consumers themselves. Based on previous [13–15] and ongoing experiences [12], then, we argue persona in Namibian sites holds potential in allowing people to genuinely depicting themselves for the usage of technologies.

3 "Live Design. Transform Life" Project

This project stems from an ongoing venture by the School of Computing and Informatics at the Polytechnic of Namibia (PoN) into co-designing new services and technologies with marginalized youth in urban and rural Namibia through service design. The overall project aims to explore how mobile applications and innovative service design balance formal education to develop youth, thereby opening new and viable career opportunities [32].

3.1 Research Site

Since October 2014, one of the pilot sites of this project has been the Kabila Community Centre in Havana, one of Katutura's informal settlements in Namibia's capital Windhoek. Katutura means *we do not have a permanent habitation*, as black communities were forcefully allocated, and tribally segregated here by apartheid during the 1950s and 60s [21]. This heritage makes Katutura to hold on to a historical susceptibility towards unemployment, lack of services and amenities [10]. This is despite more and more people move to Windhoek hoping to find employment and a better life. And yet approximately half of Windhoek's population lives in Katutura with a traditionally overwhelming majority of rural-urban migrants [28].

Havana is an informal settlement in Katutura that currently holds a scarcity of basic living facilities typical of slums [39], such as adequate housing, electrical reach, access to potable water, and hygiene resources like proper showers to serve sanitation. Wastelands surrounding inhabitants' shanties, drunkenness, and a lack of education are, instead, the daily encounters for the inhabitants in such site. In turn, this situation neither helps the intellectual and humanly growth, nor favours employment, a rather bleak issue in this particular locale, as well as in Namibia as a Nation [38].

3.2 Research Aim

The object of this particular research is to identify sociotechnical gaps, to communicate these to design through the UCP to eventually device optimal community interactions around physical spaces, available technologies and logistics anew. The pragmatic objective is to establish socio-technical requirements and align them both, with existing situations and to the technologies available. The final aim is to align social realities, existing technologies, and design requirements to ensuring suitable usability, financial affordability, fulfilment of UX, and the decisive self-sufficiency of the community and project.

3.3 Research Approach

This project is carried out within a PD framework encompassing service design as the pragmatic conceptualisation, and as the object of the technological design per-se. Theoretically, the focus of this research is grounded on previous UCP empirical experiences in Namibian ethnical contexts [13–15].

As per different phases and stakeholders involved in the process, an initial group of PoN and international students explored challenges and possible technical solutions in Havana and found out that there was a need for a job-search tool. Since then, a second generation of PoN students engaged in developing the job-matching-ranking system, as well as in promoting entrepreneurial activities through a challenge-based approach.

Participant youth in Havana, thus, engaged in work analysis in preparation to launch a community centre and a technological job-search tool initially identified as a need. Both items aim to alleviate local unemployment by providing training and work opportunities. The account narrated below consists of the phases and concurrent activities such as contextual mapping and need analysis that took place in the form of Walking Havana, User-Created Personas (UCP), Interviews and Enhanced UCP.

3.3.1   Walking Havana
Walking Havana aimed to inform researchers on local realities and socio-technical gaps by mapping-out the geography and physicality of the Havana area. Researchers proposed this as a 'location scouting' typically utilised in film and TV productions. The objective was to enable participants take-on the role of location scouts and spot and narrate genuine localities depicting realities in Havana for the TV-series.

3.3.2   User-Created Personas (UCP)
Participants then engaged in creating embodied sketches of regulars in Havana. The objective was to assist depicting characters for the TV-series that are distinctive of the settings shown through the Walking Havana method. In creating such characters, participants communicated explicit and implicit needs, requirements and aspirations towards the design of environments that hold the potential of facilitating a more humanly progress in life.

3.3.3   Interviews
Concurrently, semi-structured individual interviews attempted to find individuals' needs, requirements and aspirations. While these interviews support the findings of the larger project in regards, for instance, to technology ownership, it is in the informality of some of the conversations we found fruitful experiences in regards to the engagement and reciprocity between researchers and local participants in the process of doing [4]. This aids to better understand and therefore keep aligning the aims and objectives of the community and those of the researchers.

3.3.4   Enhanced Personas
In a later intervention participants further developed the above personas and reimagined these into enterprising and work opportunities, community cohesion, and overall alleviation and life improvement recounted as a series of challenges in [38]. In further proposing UCP, the aim was to build upon data previous participants had found relevant in representing some of the needs, requirements and aspirations towards promoting a grounding of the personas initially worked out to establishing sociotechnical gaps through the addition of scenarios.

Each of the sections introduced above and detailed below, presents now the method initially chosen and its intended in-depth utility, as well as the actual deployment and outcomes provided using each of them.

4 Walking Havana – Revealing Sociotechnical Gaps

Walking Havana assisted five female and male locals and five PoN researchers to initially identify local realities by mapping-out the area's physicality (Fig. 1).

The walk got proposed as "location scouting" for a pilot TV-series based on the joint-challenges and activities to be undertaken in Havana [38]. So, it got filmed and photographed for such purpose and for research analysis as well.

Participants pinpointed an overall paucity of electrical reach, grim access to potable water, wastelands around inhabitants' shanties, drunkenness, and scarcity of hygiene resources where public decaying open-showers serve locals for sanitation (Fig. 2).

Fig. 1. Participants walking Havana   **Fig. 2.** Hygiene, spirits, illegal wiring, water, wasteland.

They also indicated regular power cuts (as occurred in the persona session below), and pinpointed ongoing brick structures and cementations intermingled with shanties.

Mapping Havana revealed sociotechnical matters typically attributed to slums [39] for their basicness in needs and nature. For the purpose at hand, however, this seemed material enough to consecutively propose participants to create 'persona characters' inspired by Havana local inhabitants and their environments.

5 UCP - Embodied Underrepresented Sketches

Scaffolding from the walk, and continuing with the plans for the TV-series, participants plus two new late-arrivals developed some characters depicting Havana locals. Pens, markers, newspapers, magazines, and A4 and A1 paper were layout, and the youth split into Groups A and B. The aim was (1) to observe who in the community gets characterised; (2) to explore the reasoning behind such choice; (3) what information would emerge from characterising locals; (3) to what extend this facts resonate with issues encountered in the walking session, and (4) how the participants ultimately would build and depict characters on their own.

It is worthwhile noting participants have not yet been introduced to the persona tool. We postulate this legit to avoid rhetorical hurdles, jargon impediments, and the unnecessary inconvenience of some abstractions in technicality and HCI concepts [6]. Instead they were asked to create "actors" for a movie to be co-directed by them.

After 20 min Group A presented a written narrative entitled "Living like Slaves – Havana Location": 19 year-old Eddy came to live in Windhoek aged 16 and currently lives in a shanty; he cooks with firewood and has no direct access to electricity or water (Fig. 3).

Group B produced a collage entitled "Unemployed Youth" from press cut-outs and handwritten text (Fig. 4). The collage consisted of collective characters and several joint-background scenarios that explain why and how a local female and a male turn into prostitute and gang member respectively through time and unfavourable conditions in the vicinity.

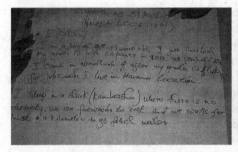 

Fig. 3. Description of "Eddy" character.   **Fig. 4.** Collective characters - holistic stories.

"Tselestina and her friend undergo hardship and decide to stand outside a club "for hunting" foreigners looking for escorting (Fig. 4, centred); Sequentially, Alom-gombe and Johanes got stopped and arrested to custody in a shopping mall (centre right). Meanwhile, 5 year-old Tselestina, Alomgombe and Johanes are "playing at their location" while dogs eat from a dumping site beside (top left corner). Top right corner, a press cut-out and written text tell on parents rallying against (1) high youth unemployment, (2) children standing by dumping sites, and (3) to achieve better housing. This is further supported by another cut-out (far right top) where there is a casserole with the words Education and Success embedded and steaming from the pot; and a burning fire underneath with the words Teachers, Parents, Pupils rooted in the logs. Bottom-left, the pictorial shows people rioting with burning tires, while the narrative describes shanties burnt because of paraffin stove and candles' indoor use.

While Group A portrayed a brief written description on Eddy's housing situation *living as a slave*, it delivered no further detail about situational causes on Eddy's life. Group B however provided relational causes and consequential effects through graphic and text association in the narratives of the two main characters of choice.

Relationally, Group B (1) interwoven Tselestina and Johanes' background stories from childhood, (2) implemented mothers as supporting characters, (3) rioters playing 'extras', (4) dogs, food leftovers, and car wheels as commonly encountered props, and (5) local sceneries as backdrops (Fig. 5 below). They also conveyed a particular pairing of pictures whereby people (i.e. personas) and settings (i.e. scenarios) were exposed side-by-side. Consequentially, individuals' personal issues came together depicting a strong sense of community support that illustrates the enrooted sense of holism in family union and public resilience prevailing in these settings through the years before apartheid [35]. This parallels previous political accounts of UCP research in other Namibian settings where alien invasion has also shown its signs of inheritance in the people's longing [14]. The accounts and major concerns perceived and expressed by the dwellers seem to furthermore resemble previous narratives collected with unemployed youth in the capital [32].

6 Individual Interviews and Informal Conversations

Along the above interventions, individual stories are continuously collected in the form of separate interviews. While this data will be used for different research purposes, the aim in relation to the present study is to compare "real stories" with those created in the actors' stories in order to evaluate the usefulness of UCP in this context. Moreover, this established a baseline data on the tenure of basic and smart cellphones.

Informal conversations with one participant, besides, revealed a genuine, quasi-adamant interest in acquiring a set of musical instruments for the community centre. As part of the overall community-centred system in Katutura, there are dated recounts of 'the tribal court' and the brass bands ethnic groups living in Katutura until

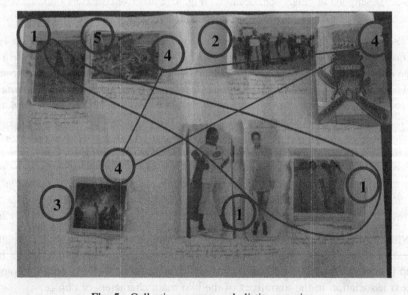

Fig. 5. Collective personas - holistic scenarios.

terminated by apartheid [35]. This may not seem part of work analysis to practitioners outside the Arts world or not acquainted to History. Yet, it provides with an array of implicit possibilities for the future of technological pervasiveness in these settings.

7 Reshaping UCP: Establishing Sociotechnical Gaps Through Sticky-Note™ Scenarios

From the persona-characters in the first UCP session, a further session attempted to reassess, align, and consolidate sociotechnical gaps through further developing the characters for the TV-series. Sixteen participants (eight new in this session) were orally and visually reminded of, or introduced to the previous persona outcomes. Then they split in 2 groups, i.e. Group C and Group D, and were provided of pens, markers, Sticky-Notes™ and both, blank A1 posters and the initial persona posters. Group C was compounded of children and teens, and facilitated by a PoN researcher. Group D were older participants, some with a genuine interest in entrepreneurship. No one facilitated the latter.

The facilitator to Group C opened the session emphasising the aim to further shaping the characters elicited by the previous group (i.e. Group A) towards the TV-series. The facilitator equally intertwined the words persona, person and character when inaugurating the session. This aimed to find out if one term may prevail over others.

Participants then scaffold from the initial characterisation of Tselestina, her friend, Alomgombe and Johanes (Fig. 5) and built further on them by first discussing existing findings, and subsequently proposing further themes, storylines, concepts and ideas summarised in the Sticky-Notes™ they tucked to the existing poster (Fig. 6).

Among the issues highlighted in this session, Group C reiterated matters pinpointed in the walking method (Sect. 4 above) such as poverty in the location, crime problems, hygiene, health, littering, and a lack of water and electricity. Further issues also emerged under the themes food, malnutrition, transport, money, care and parents.

Group C continued making relational pairings of some of the issues previously stated, in a similar way preceding participants had done in the initial UCP session. One Sticky-Note™, for instance, stated as follows in relation to parents and transport:

1. In our areas everyday parents walking a long way to fetch water and collect firewood. 2. Walking a long distance for Hospital and take child to school.

Participants implicitly related the above long distances walking and the physical effort this takes, and to the time, care and attention walking consumes from parents. Further issues such as the collection of firewood by having also to walk about, thus, added further socio-technical issues such as the one in further paired Sticky-Notes™:

Cooking everyday: By the use of firewood, gas and paraffin stoves can result in burning of shacks.

As for the electricity, participants opened a Sticky-Note™ where they stated: *Electricity for children/students to study properly at night for the tests and exams.*

Group C also concluded oral accounts of what a particular persona would sometimes say or think would be relevant. Such accounts were considered, though they were not materialised in the final personas.

 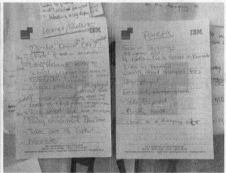

Fig. 6. Personas developed on Sticky -Notes™

Fig. 7. Two Persona profiles: student & parent

Eventually, Group C decided to summarise their findings into two character profiles typical of UCD personas proceedings: a learner/student and a parent (Fig. 7).

Meanwhile, Group D engaged in the local politics involved in the issues at hand, though they left aside the physicality of the initiating personas from groups A and B. Group D did not hence provide further insights to the existing personas as per needs, requirements and aspirations. Yet, by discussing political issues they implied further stakeholders and proposed ways to undertaking interactions with them (Fig. 8).

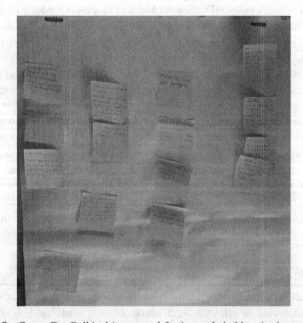

Fig. 8. Group D - Political issues and further stakeholders in the process.

One of the issues discussed'and summarised by Group D was on political leaders: *Our leaders they don't use to delivered information on time, they use to keep information; they don't use to come to people to look around to see the location.*

They went on stating a need for community togetherness to counteract positions: *People they must work together in the location to fight unemployment like to provide training to the people.*

A further Sticky-Note™ identified governmental programmes as present failures: *Decentralisation program for government services is far from people.*

Group D thus also expressed needs regarding Namibia's Police forces and crime: *Namibian Police should patrol at Havana location, and workers who use to work during the night should be dropped at their homes.*

The meeting ended with all participants thanking researchers for what they seemed to have learnt in the session and eagerly requested when the next session was to be.

In this session we found that when participants work in homogeneous group-ages, results evolved in two ways: groups of older participants with a flair for entrepreneurship conveyed more formal, bureaucratic, and implicit ways of embedding challenges in the community by extrapolating them to the involvement of other stakeholders such as councils, political representatives, police forces, etc. Yet, personas were not developed as such. Younger participants, though, stuck-in to the task at hand and implemented further user-data to the original personas. Besides, they explicitly and repeatedly referred to the characters dealt with as, we argue, these were youngsters like themselves. Thus, the personas were more relatable to youngsters, whereas experiences of older participants where to more mature community members and organisations.

8 Discussion

It is worth noting Havana participants have since the inception of this venture varied across the different activities, though most of the participants are youth, come on a voluntary basis, and most of them have attended more than one session. The number of participants per session also varies between four and fifteen, with often a great number of late comers in the middle of started sessions.

In testing methods, walking the neighbourhood provided researchers with an indication of the challenges faced as shown and explained by community members. Therefore, we corroborate walking as suitable in this setting to spot challenges and also in establishing those as part of work analysis. Further future walks may hence provide with on-site solutions to the challenges of unemployment. It can also create further awareness in possible actions to undertake by youth involved in the project.

The two UCP sessions have provided with both, an effective and engaging workability in using the TV-series proposal throughout and a provision of collective persona representations that acknowledged the main "actors" as local youth that could somewhat be anyone in the community due to the present challenges. Moreover, Group B in the first session showed a natural understanding in: (1) characterising main actors, (2) depicting and joining background stories, (3) supportive and engaging secondary characters, (4) extras, and (5) the props supporting and (6) enhancing scenarios. They have also shown a natural skill constructing narratives compounded of preparation (i.e. childhood), climax (i.e. characters' present situations) and resolution (i.e. mothers protest, others riot). This approach has hence enabled participants to elicit the risks undergone by youth in Havana, as well as sociotechnical gaps to be filled.

Group C were older participants who referred to issues beyond youth personas. While these concerns did not provide to the personas elicited, they enabled a further understanding of the pervasiveness of, and organisational and political issues in the community. Group D was formed by younger participants who readily related to the initial personas and provided with further relevant data both, orally and on paper. This all has shown UCP elicited in PD as a useful method to combining skill and experience, while forming complementary groups of in-situ stakeholders and those beyond.

9 Conclusions

This research attempted to elicit sociotechnical gaps in the informal settlement of Havana towards establishing a community centre and launching a job-search tool to alleviate youth unemployment in the community. We established that sketching personas in PD must be considered in developing pervasive systems for these settings, as this showed to provide towards community reliability, co-existence among stakeholders and activities carried out, as well as consistency, and mutual support as societal positives to nurture and maintain. The use of personas has also been fruitful as an inquisitive process to initially explore and augment pervasive and smart possibilities for work in locales with limited resources.

Finally, the TV lens provided of engagement and reciprocity in the doings in Havana. Adopting TV-related roles such as location scouters and proposing this exercise a potential TV-series, participants felt further motivated to get the venture going forth.

Acknowledgments. We wish to thank the Kabila Centre in Havana for hosting us and providing of electricity and shelter, as well as to the youth participants for engaging in the project in such a lively, genuine and thankful fashion. Special thanks go to "Eddie" from the Havana community for organizing the gatherings. We would like to acknowledge our co-researchers in the team. Furthermore, this work results from the financial support by the Namibian National Commission on Research, Science and Technology, for which we are grateful.

References

1. Al-Ani, B., Densmore, M., Cutrell, E., Dearden, A., Grinter, R.E., Thomas, J.C., Kam, M., Peters, A.N.: Featured community SIG: human-computer interaction for development. In: Proceedings of the CHI 2013, pp. 2473–2476. ACM Press, Paris (2013)
2. Anokwa, Y., Smyth, T.N., Ramachandran, D., Sherwani, J., Schwartzman, Y., Luk, R., Ho, M., Moraveji, N., DeRenzi, B.: Stories from the field: reflections on HCI4D experiences. ITID J. **5**, 101–115 (2009)
3. Blake, E., Glaser, M., Freudenthal, A.: Teaching design for development in computer science. Interactions **21**, 54–59 (2014)

4. Brereton, M., Roe, P., Schroeter, R., Lee Hong, A.: Beyond ethnography: engagement and reciprocity as foundations for design research out here. In: Proceedings of CHI 2014, pp. 1183–1186. ACM Press, Toronto (2014)
5. Chavan, A.L., Prabhu, G.V. (eds.): Innovative Solutions: What Designers Need to Know for Today's Emerging Markets. CRC Press, Boca Raton, London, New York (2011)
6. Chetty, M., Grinter, R.: HCI4D: how do we design for the global south? In: User Centered Design and International Development Workshop at CHI 2007. ACM Press (2007)
7. Clemmensen, T., Campos, P.F., Katre, D.S., Abdelnour-Nocera, J., Lopes, A., Orngreen, R., Minocha, S.: CHI 2013 human work interaction design (HWID) SIG: past history and future challenges. In: Proceedings of CHI 2013, pp. 2537–2540. ACM Press, Paris (2013)
8. Cooper, A.: The Inmates are Running the Asylum: Why High Tech Products Drive Us Crazy and How to Restore the Sanity. Sams Publishing, Indianapolis (1998)
9. Dourish, P., Mainwaring, S.D.: Ubicomp's colonial impulse. In: Proceedings of the UbiComp 2012, pp. 133–144. ACM Press, Pittsburgh (2012)
10. Friedman, F.: Deconstructing Windhoek: Urban Morphology of Post-Apartheid City (2000)
11. Friess, E.: Personas and decision making in the design process: an ethnographic case study. In: Proceedings of the CHI 2012, pp. 1209–1218. ACM Press, Austin (2012)
12. Cabrero, G., Winschiers-Theophilus, D., Ovahimba, H.: Knowledge through storytelling and personas: technologies, methods and challenges ahead. In: Workshop held at the C&T 2015, Limerick, Ireland (2015)
13. Cabrero, D.G., et al.: Reflecting user-created persona in Indigenous Namibia: what not to do when working in Foreign Land. In: Proceedings of C&T 2015. ACM Press, Limerick (2015a)
14. Cabrero, D.G., et al.: User-created persona: Namibian rural Otjiherero speakers. In: Proceedings of the SIGDOC 2015, Art. 28. ACM Press, Limerick (2015b)
15. Cabrero, D.G.: Participatory design of persona artefacts for user experience in non-WEIRD cultures. In: Proceedings of PDC 2013, pp. 247–250. ACM Press, Windhoek (2014)
16. Gough, K.V., Langevang, T., Namatovu, R.: Researching entrepreneurship in low-income settlements: the strengths and challenges of participatory methods. J. Environ. Urbanization 26(1), 297–311 (2013)
17. Guimarães, D.B., Carvalho, C.R., Furtado, E.S.: Panorama, Oportunidades e Recomendacões para o Contexto Brasileiro de Interação Humano-Computador e Design Centrado no Usuario a partir do uso de Personas. In: Proceedings of the IHC+CLIHC 2011, pp. 167–176. Brazilian Computer Society, Porto de Galinhas (2011)
18. Henrich, J., Heine, S.J., Norenzayan, A.: The Weirdest people in the world? J. Behav. Brain Sci. 33(2–3), 61–83 (2010)
19. Hisham, S.: Experimenting with the use of persona in a focus group discussion with older adults in Malaysia. In: Proceedings of OZCHI 2009, pp. 333–336, ACM Press, Melbourne (2009)
20. History of Old Location and Katutura. http://www.namibweb.com/hiskat.htm
21. Katre, D.S.: User persona: its application and the art of stereotyping. J. HCI 2 (2007). Article INS-17./Feb. 2007, http://www.hceye.org/HCInsight-KATRE15.htm
22. Lecomte, C., Blanco, E., Trompette, T., Cholez, C.: Towards a better frugal design using persona - issues and insights from an ethnography on prosthetics in Vietnam. In: Proceedings of the IICCI 2013, Paris, France (2013)
23. Löfstrom, A.: What is culture? Toward common understandings of culture in HCI. In: Forbrig, P., Paternó, F., Mark Pejtersen, A. (eds.) HCIS 2010. IFIP AICT, vol. 332, pp. 133–141. Springer, Heidelberg (2010)

24. Mendonca, H., van Zyl, I.: Youth empowerment: the role of service design and mobile technology in accessing reproductive health information. In: Proceedings of the PDC 2014, pp. 103–106. ACM Press, Windhoek (2014)

25. Miaskiewicz, T., Sumner, T., Kozar, K.A.: A latent semantic analysis methodology for the identification and creation of personas. In: Proceedings of the CHI 2008, pp. 1501–1510. ACM Press, Florence (2008)

26. Miettinen, S., Du Preez, V., Chivuno-Kuria, S., Mendonca, H.: My dream world 2: constructing the service prototype with Namibian youth. In: Proceedings of the PDC 2014, pp. 201–202. ACM Press, Windhoek (2014)

27. Nghiulikwa, R.V.: Re-situating and shifting cultural identity in contemporary Namibia: The experience of rural-urban migrants in Katutura, Windhoek, MA Thesis (2008)

28. Nielsen, L.: Personas in cross-cultural projects. In: Katre, D., Orngreen, R., Yammiyavar, P., Clemmensen, T. (eds.) HWID 2009. IFIP AICT, vol. 316, pp. 76–82. Springer, Heidelberg (2010)

29. Nielsen, L.: Acting as someone like me: personas in participatory innovation. In: Proceedings of the PIN-C 2012, Melbourne, Australia, pp. 1–7 (2012)

30. Nielsen, L., Hansen, K.S.: Persona is applicable: a study on the use of personas in Denmark. In: Proceedings of the CHI 2014, pp. 1665–1674. ACM Press, Toronto (2014)

31. Onwere, T., Lipito, H., Chivuno-Kuria, S., Winschiers-Theophilus, H.: Youth empowering the youth through participatory service design. In: Proceedings of DDR 2014, Cape Town (2014)

32. Parker, M., Wills, J., Wills, G.: RLabs: a South African perspective on a community-driven approach to community informatics. J. Commun. Inf. 9(3), 1–14 (2012)

33. Putnam, C., Kolko, B., Wood, S.: Communicating about users in ICTD. In: Proceedings of the ICTD 2012, pp. 338–349. ACM Press, Atlanta (2012)

34. Wagner, G.: Ethnographic survey of South West Africa, unpublished manuscript found in the Offices of the Department of Bantu Administration and Development, Ethnological Section, Windhoek. A copy of this manuscript has been placed in the National Archives by the author (1951)

35. Williams, I., Brereton, M.: A collaborative rapid persona-building workshop: creating design personas with health researchers. Int. J. Sociotechnol. Knowl. Dev. 6(2), 17–35 (2014)

36. Winschiers-Theophilus, H., Chivuno-Kuria, S., Kapuire, G.K., Bidwell, N.J., Blake, E.: Being participated: a community approach. In: Proceedings of the PDC 2010, pp. 1–10, ACM Press, Sydney (2010)

37. Winschiers-Theophilus, H., Cabrero, D.G., Angula, S., Chivuno-Kuria, S., Mendonca, H., Ngolo, R.: A challenge-based approach to promote entrepreneurship among youth in an informal settlement of Windhoek. In: Proceedings of the SATN 2015, Vanderbijlpark, South Africa (2015)

38. Wyche, S.: Exploring mobile phone and social media use in a Nairobi slum: a case for alternative approaches to design in ICTD. In: Proceedings of the ICTD 2015. ACM Press (2015)

Environment

Pervasive Technologies for Smart Workplaces: A Workplace Efficiency Solution for Office Design and Building Management from an Occupier's Perspective

Maria Ianeva[1]([✉]), Stéphanie Faure[1], Jennifer Theveniot[1], François Ribeyron[2], Cormac Crossan[2], Gilles Cordon[2], and Claude Gartiser[2]

[1] Colliers International France R&D, 41 rue Louise Michel, 92594 Levallois-Perret, France
{maria.ianeva,stephanie.faure,jennifer.theveniot}@colliers.com
[2] Le Hive, Schneider Electric, 35 rue Joseph Monier, 92500 Rueil Malmaison, France
{f.ribeyron,c.gartiser}@d5x.fr,
{cormac.crossan,gilles.cordon}@schneider-electric.com

Abstract. Corporate Real Estate (CRE) Management and office design are increasingly considered as a strategic resource for developing businesses and competitive advantage. Measuring the added value of CRE, as well as managing smart workplaces are an issue for academics and professionals. We consider that pervasive technologies offer potential for increasing workplace efficiency on a long-term basis. In order to gain insight of workplace and building management in practice from an occupier's perspective, Colliers International France designed its Paris office as a "living lab". We implemented a work environment based on desk-sharing and a set of activity-based workspaces. We also deployed Schneider Electric's WorkPlace Efficiency (WPE) solution aimed at monitoring the occupancy rate of our building as well as at supporting the effective use of shared office resources and employees' wellbeing. The paper presents our experience of this solution in the context of our Paris office and discusses its potential for building smart and sustainable workplaces.

Keywords: Office design · Real estate · Pervasive technologies · Smart building · Worlplace

1 Introduction

Corporate Real Estate (CRE) Management and office design are increasingly considered as a strategic resource for developing businesses and competitive advantage. Rather than a way of reducing costs, real estate decisions address challenges such as productivity, employees' wellbeing, innovation and flexibility. In this context, building and managing smart workplaces are an issue for both, academics and professionals. In order to meet these demands, an increasing number of companies choose to, fully or partially, implement "activity-based" workplace (ABW) environments. These office solutions are aimed at better supporting the "new ways of working", that is to say work practices as they actually take place in modern organizations. Indeed, in today's "knowledge-intensive firms", work

© IFIP International Federation for Information Processing 2015
J. Abdelnour-Nocera et al. (Eds.): HWID 2015, IFIP AICT 468, pp. 73–82, 2015.
DOI: 10.1007/978-3-319-27048-7_5

is "increasingly characterized by a temporary constellation of collaborators" [3] as people work in projects. It is also technology-dependent and thus distributed and distributable across time and space. Knowledge workers are likely to work anywhere, anytime and face growing requirements for cooperation and coordination of tasks and activities [6].

The concept of ABW appears complex and ambiguous [4]. ABW relies on the idea that space should fit the needs of employees' specific activities and the company's strategic goals in order to provide a basis for an effective CRE Management [1]. The activity-based office first emerged in the 1980's [13, 14]. The spread of Information and Communication Technologies (ICT) in the last two decades, as well as the low occupancy rate of offices [2] further supported this trend. As CRE managers are increasingly considering both financial and indirect benefits in real estate decisions (functional, strategic value), the focus in measuring CRE management effectiveness is moving towards a cost benefit ratio [1, 5]. Nonetheless, research on whether or not these office solutions truly increase productivity and employees' satisfaction show mixed results [12].

In the main, the idea of ABW is translated by architects, office planners and consultants into specific building and office layout (for instance activity-based workstations and workspaces such as "project rooms" for team work, non-reservable closed offices for individual concentration work or unplanned meetings) as well as into change management programs. The design and implementation of ABW involves a major transformation of work practices and habits [7], including behaviours and interactions with technology.

While ABW may be a good starting point for building smart workplaces, it raises questions related to the effective use of shared office resources such as space but also energy. In order to build flexible workplaces that truly fit organizations' needs and are able to adapt to corporate growth and restructuring, there is a need to both design and manage ABW. We think that pervasive technologies offer great potential in order to measure, manage and increase workplace efficiency on a long-term basis. In what follows, we present Colliers International France as well as our office in Paris. We use our building as a "living lab" in order to gain insight on flexible working and activity-based work environments. Then, we introduce a solution based on Radio Frequency Identification (RFID) technology, the WorkPlace Efficiency Solution (WPE), aimed at monitoring the occupancy rate of our building as well as at supporting the effective use of shared office resources. The solution was developed and implemented in partnership with Schneider Electric, a global specialist in energy management and energy efficiency. The post-occupancy evaluation of Colliers Paris office (Sect. 4) provided background and incentive for monitoring WPE performance and analysing the data over a ten-month period (January to October 2014). We conclude with a discussion on the implications of this solution for building and managing smart and sustainable workplaces and buildings.

2   Colliers International France

Colliers International France is a global independent Real Estate and Workplace Consulting and Project Management company. We help our clients to implement high performing flexible work environments, like ABW, and to reduce occupancy costs. In order to do so, we rely on a wide range of expertise (real estate and workplace consultants, architects, space planners, construction engineers) which allows us to address the different functional layers of buildings [9] in a coordinated manner. As Leamen [9] contends buildings are complex systems which are organized in functional layers, each setting constrains that influence characteristics on a smaller scale. Thus location, geographical characteristics, urban infrastructure may have an impact on size, shape, orientation, and accessibility of buildings, which in turn set the context for building services, like for instance heating, lighting, ventilation and for office design and layout (workstations, meeting rooms).

In our view, design and build processes (planning, architecture and build, interior design) require a systematic and an integrated approach to the building as a whole. This means considering and "aligning" a number of potentially conflicting perspectives on the system, those of the professionals or the stakeholders involved in the different stages of the project (architects, engineers, end-users, property developers, real estate and workplace consultants). The design of smart and sustainable workplaces is that of a building, but also that of the practical conditions of building management on a long-term basis from an occupier's perspective.

In order to gain a deeper understanding of workplace and building management in practice, our Paris office is organized as a "living lab". The design team was entirely composed of Colliers International France professionals and implemented a flexible work environment based on desk-sharing and a set of activity-based workspaces. Figure 1 provides a view of some of the workspaces available in our Paris office.

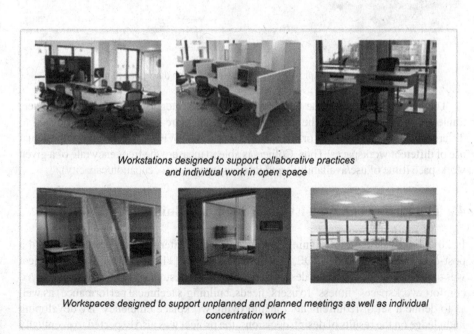

Workstations designed to support collaborative practices and individual work in open space

Workspaces designed to support unplanned and planned meetings as well as individual concentration work

Fig. 1. Different types of workstations and workspaces in Colliers International France.

In addition to office design and related issues ("ways of working", users' support in understanding and using space), we also implemented an indoor location-sensing system based on RFID technology. The system was designed by Schneider Electric and is aimed at providing us with data on the use of shared spatial resources such as meeting rooms, "bubbles" and the different kind of workstations.

The following section presents the system as well as its intended use and actual use.

3   The Workplace Efficiency Solution by Schneider Electric

Schneider Electric's WorkPlace Efficiency (WPE) is a solution designed to manage comfort and occupancy as well as to provide services to users in large office buildings. Colliers International France implemented the WPE occupancy monitoring system which connects a network of sensors with anonymous RFID tags inserted into employees badge holders. The tags transmit information to the sensors via radio which allows a real-time occupancy monitoring of the different spaces ("bubbles", meeting rooms, workspaces). Figure 2 shows the location of sensors on a standard floor of Colliers office as well as an employee badge holder.

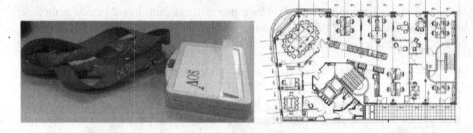

Fig. 2. An employee badge holder and a standard floor plan

The data transmitted by the tags includes the user category (for instance employee, trainee or visitor) as well as the detection zone (which are numbered and associated to different types of workstations or given workspaces). The WPE provides data on the actual use of different workspaces. Thus, Colliers is able to measure the frequency rate of a given workspace (time of use/availability) and its occupancy rate (occupation/capacity).

4   The Post-occupancy Evaluation of our Building

In 2013, two years after designing its office, Colliers International France launched a post-occupancy evaluation (POE) of its building-in-use [11, 15]. The aim of the project was to provide feedback on the designed environment (occupants satisfaction, perceived comfort, workspaces "fitness" to users' needs, building's technical performance) as well as to define a set of requirements for improving workplace efficiency. By developing knowledge on the results of design decisions, the project was also expected to eventually inform the practices of Colliers building-related professionals.

The initial phase of the project extended over a six-month period and included several field studies: (a) an online survey of employees' satisfaction of their office and perceived workplace efficiency was carried out by an independent provider; (b) focus groups with user representatives; (c) real-time observations of workspaces occupancy over a two-week period. The online survey questionnaire (a) included questions on employees' activities and satisfaction with physical features of their workplace (such as available workspaces and furniture, air quality, noise level, lighting) and facility services (mail, IT service, reception areas, access). The foçus groups (b) gathered user representatives and experts from various disciplines (architects, workplace and change management consultants etc.) and aimed to generate ideas on improving employees' comfort, as well as the workplace efficiency as a support for productivity and innovation. Finally, real-time observations of workspaces' occupancy (c) were carried out four times per day during two weeks. A group of surveyors walked through the building and recorded manually whether workstations and meeting areas were "used" (when a user is physically present), "in use" (when a user is not physically present but the workstation appears as occupied) or "unoccupied" (empty desk or space) by users. The survey provided data on peak, average and minimum occupancy rates as well as a map of most used areas in the building.

The results yielded by these studies suggested that concentration work as well as informal, un-planned meetings were insufficiently supported by the environment both in terms of workspaces availability and technical performance (noise level, air conditioning, air quality, etc.).

In this context, the WPE solution occupancy data highlighted workspaces occupancy trends over several months. The analysis sought to further develop post-occupancy evaluation (POE) diagnosis and to eventually provide a basis for recurring evaluation and continuous improvement of Colliers activity-based office. We analysed the data of the Schneider Electric WPE system over a ten-month period (January to October 2014). We specifically focused on the use of shared workspaces such as the non-reservable closed offices, called "bubbles", the meeting rooms and the cafeteria. The WPE solution reports the maximum number of users that occupied a given workspace ("room") per unit of time (1/4 of an hour, hour, day, week, and month). "Rooms" include workspaces with identified functional characteristics ("bubble", meeting rooms, and informal meeting areas, individual enclosed offices) as well as open spaces where different types of workstations ("benches", boxes) are available. The reports systematically feature rooms' capacity (number of seats) against the number of detected users.

The occupancy data reports were generated per hour, per day and per month. The analysis considered all user categories. In parallel, meetings rooms booking system provided additional information on the number of reservations of a given room per hour. Booking system data was compared to the frequency of occupation.

5 Implementation in an Activity Based Workplace

The ABW's underlying principles imply that employees choose their location according to their needs and preferences. While teams and services each have a dedicated area, people can potentially choose to work anywhere in the building. ABW is thus supposed to provide the means for an efficient management of peaks and troughs in user demand. Furthermore, functional characteristics of space are designed to match employees' needs (concentration, interaction, cooperation). For instance, open space meeting areas should support serendipitous interactions and trigger knowledge-sharing and workplace learning. In this context, the WPE system's data allows us to make hypothesis on the users' needs as well as on the current workspace "suitability" for employees' activities.

The Figs. 3 and 4 below display the occupancy of the cafeteria and one of the bubbles from January to October 2014. During observations and focus groups, the cafeteria was reported (b; c) to be regularly used outside lunch hour (Fig. 2) for planned and un-planned meetings. Analysis of WPE data on an hourly basis shows that cafeteria was occupied by a maximum of 45 users from 10:00 to 11:00 over a ten-month-period. Only 7 to 8 users were detected from 15:00 to 17:00.

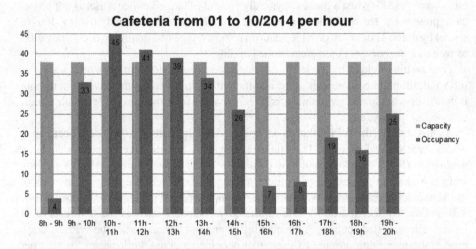

Fig. 3. Occupancy of the Cafeteria from June to October 2014

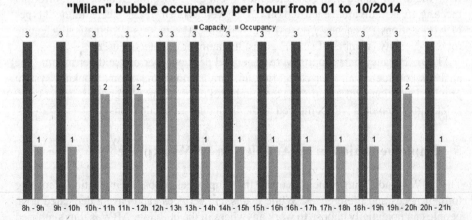

Fig. 4. Occupancy per hour of the "Milan" bubble from June to October 2014

Since occupancy refers to the maximum number of tags detected per hour of a working day over a five-month period, WPE reports highlight peaks values. From a design perspective, trough levels appear as important as peaks. Early afternoon occupancy of the cafeteria (from 15:00 to 17:00) was of a maximum eight users over several months. This neither confirm nor contradict the idea that cafeteria supports planned and unplanned meetings as reported by user representatives. Additional data is needed in order to draw meaningful conclusions on the average occupancy rate of a given space. In our case, observational study (d) tends to confirm cafeteria's "extended" use. This allows us to interpret the maximum observed as referring to a recurrent phenomenon, potentially related to a type of activity (planned or unplanned meetings of at least two people).

We also found that "bubbles" (Fig. 4) were frequently used by only one person over a day-long period, while their intended purpose is to support both concentration work and cooperation (2 to 3 users). Figure 4 shows the occupancy of the "Milan" bubble. The maximum of occupiers detected by the system nine hours per day, over the ten-month period considered, is of one user. Likewise, monthly reports over the same period highlight a maximum of one occupier six months out of ten. WPE data suggests that "bubbles" are under-occupied since peak occupancy levels detected rarely reach its maximum capacity.

Meeting rooms also appear as intensely used but under-occupied (1 to 4 users). The figures below display the frequency of occupancy of a meeting room compared with the number of reservations made by users via Outlook or directly on the reservation screen. Frequency of occupancy refers to the number of times the room was effectively occupied by one or several users. According to the number of occupiers considered (one, two or more) when defining "effective occupancy", there is a clear variation in results.

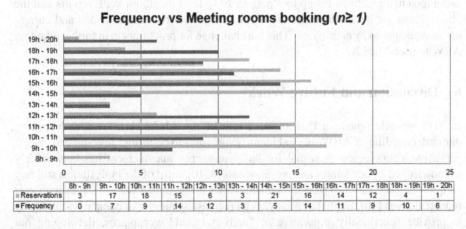

	8h - 9h	9h - 10h	10h - 11h	11h - 12h	12h - 13h	13h - 14h	14h - 15h	15h - 16h	16h - 17h	17h - 18h	18h - 19h	19h - 20h
Reservations	3	17	18	15	6	3	21	16	14	12	4	1
Frequency	0	7	9	14	12	3	5	14	11	9	10	6

Fig. 5. The frequency of occupancy of a meeting room versus the number of reservations n$\geq$1

For instance, if we assume a meeting room is regarded as occupied when at least one user is actually present, results (Fig. 5) highlight that occupancy exceeds reservations at noon (12:00 to 13:00) and at the end of the day (18:00 to 20:00). However, when occupancy involves at least two users, there is a considerable gap between the number of reservations and actual use (Fig. 6). This implies that a significant proportion of the reservations do not translate into actual use. This observation also suggests that meeting rooms are potentially "misused" since frequency of occupancy decreases when at least two occupiers are considered.

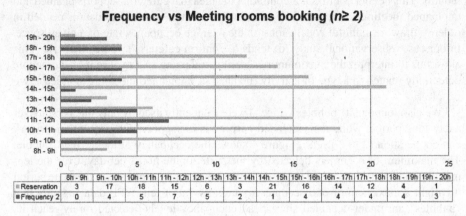

Frequency vs Meeting rooms booking (n≥ 2)

	8h - 9h	9h - 10h	10h - 11h	11h - 12h	12h - 13h	13h - 14h	14h - 15h	15h - 16h	16h - 17h	17h - 18h	18h - 19h	19h - 20h
Reservation	3	17	18	15	6	3	21	16	14	12	4	1
Frequency 2	0	4	5	7	5	2	1	4	4	4	4	3

Fig. 6. The frequency of occupancy of a meeting room versus the number of reservations n≥2

ABW is expected to provide an extensive supply of shared collaborative spaces such as meeting rooms or bubbles in order to increase employee comfort and effectively support collaboration. In the case of Colliers International France, bookable meeting rooms are intended for a group of at least three users since bubbles also support planned and unplanned meetings for up to 3 people. In spite of this, both WPE reports and the observations we have conducted highlight a difference between intended and current use of workspaces by employees. This is a challenge for practitioners in further adapting ABW to users' needs.

6 Discussion and Future Work

In 2015, we redesigned our Paris office. The WPE provided a basis for both deepening our understanding of ABW use and identifying issues to be further investigated. While pervasive technologies' potential for building energy management has been widely acknowledged by academics and professionals [8, 10], most of the POE studies still rely on questionnaire surveys, face-to-face interviews or facilitated work sessions with user representatives [10]. Be that as it may, as an increasing number of companies are trying to provide functionally supportive or "activity-based" workplaces, developing our knowledge of building-in-use is essential in ensuring the "adaptability" of workplaces to changing organizational needs.

So far, our results suggest that there is a gap between intended and actual use of shared workspaces and point at the need to better support concentration activities. The study also shows that successful implementation of a WPE solution is predicated upon a better understanding of the solution potential among the design and facility management professional communities.

A situated approach in understanding work practices, would greatly improve design process and could also contribute to develop the use of WPE. As a cafeteria is not intended for planned and unplanned meetings, just as informal meeting areas are not only for individual work, its "extended" use could be considered as "misuse" by designers and project managers. Yet in practice, having a meeting in the cafeteria, instead of in a meeting room, might be of value for users. It allows them to be seen and eventually heard by others. In other words, "misuse" could be considered as much as a resource for building mutual awareness as an inappropriate behaviour.

The use of WPE solution, in our experience, throws up several issues related to its acceptance by employees. While monitoring workspace utilization provides valuable input for design and has proven to be an effective "medium" for user involvement during workshops, further investigation is needed in order to assess and to deal with workplace "fitness" to employees' needs. Furthermore, the WPE system guarantees the anonymity of employees. Nevertheless, our experience shows that it can be perceived by users as a way of monitoring people rather than the use of space. In order to improve the acceptance of the system by employees, we recently introduced removable badge holders. Users are now able to separate their badges (by swiping it out) from the RFID badge holders and potentially swap with someone else's badge holder (within the same user category). A mobile application was also presented to employees. The application provides services such as a meeting room finder based on real-time occupancy data, a 3D building navigator designed to help users find their way in the building, as well as a comfort remote control. Additional third-party services are available, like transportation time estimation, carpark load information, restaurant information, company news etc. The recent developments of the WPE solution offer new opportunities for employees to actively engage with the system and thus develop their understanding of its possibilities and practical relevance. This is both an opportunity and a challenge for the design of pervasive technologies and smart workplaces. We are currently looking to develop the use of existing data pertaining to sustainability issues such as energy efficiency.

References

1. Appel-Meulenbroek, R.: How to measure added value of CRE and building design. Knowledge sharing in research buildings. Technische Universiteit Eindhoven (2014)
2. Appel-Meulenbroek, R., Groenen, P., Janssen, I.: An end-user's perspective on activity-based office concepts. J. Corp. Real Estate 13(2), 122–135 (2011)
3. Bjerrum, E., Bodker, S.: Learning and living in the 'New Office'. In: Kuutti, K., Karsten, E.H., Fitzpatrick, G., Dourish, P., Schmidt, K. (eds.) ECSCW 2003. Springer, Amsterdam (2003)
4. Cajander, A., Nauwerck, G., Lind, T., Larusdottir, M.: Challenges for action research on HWID in activity based workplaces. In: Proceedings of INTERACT 2015, Bamberg, 14–18 September (2015)
5. De Vries, J.C., De Jonge, H., Van der Voordt, T.J.: Impact of real estate interventions on organisational performance. J. Corp. Real Estate 10(3), 208–223 (2008)

6. Ianeva, M., Ciobanu, R.: Des compétences collectives en pratique. Le cas du travail d'articulation. Psihologia Resurselor Umane **12**, 34–47 (2014)
7. Ianeva, M., Chotel, P., Miriel, F.: Learnings from workplace user-centered design: the case of a media and communication company. In: Proceedings of ECCE 2015, Warsaw, Poland, 1–3 July (2015)
8. Labeodan, T., Zeiler, W., Boxem, G., Zhao, Y.: Occupancy measurement in commercial office buildings for demand-driven control applications – a survey and detection system evaluation. Energy Build. **93**, 303–314 (2015)
9. Leaman, A.: The logistical city. In: Worthington, J. (ed.) Reinventing the Workplace, 2nd edn, pp. 11–28. Architectural Press, Great Britain (2006)
10. Milenkovic, M., Amft, O.: Recognizing energy-related activities using sensors commonly installed in office buildings. Procedia Comput. Sci. **19**, 669–677 (2013). SEIT 2013
11. Vischer, J.: Post-occupancy evaluation: a multifaced tool for building improvement. In: Learning from our Buildings: A State-of-the-Practice Summary of Post-occupancy Evaluation. Federal Facilities Council Technical Report, No. 145. National Academy Press, Washington, D.C. (2001)
12. Vos, P., Van der Voordt, T.: Tomorrow's offices through today's eyes: effects of innovation in the working environment. J. Corp. Real Estate **4**(1), 48–65 (2002)
13. Worthington, J.: Reinventing the Workplace. University of York, Oxford (1997)
14. Worthington, J., Duffy, F., Greenberg, S., Myerson, J., Powell, K., Thompson, T.: The Architecture of DEGW. Birkhaüser Verlag, Boston (1998)
15. Zimmerman, A., Martin, M.: Post-occupancy evaluation: benefits and barriers. Build. Res. Inf. **29**(2), 168–174 (2001)

From Bottom-up Insights to Feature Ideas: A Case Study into the Office Environments of Older Knowledge Workers

Valentin Gattol$^{(\boxtimes)}$, Jan Bobeth, Kathrin Röderer, Sebastian Egger,
Georg Regal, Ulrich Lehner, and Manfred Tscheligi

Innovation Systems Department, Technology Experience, AIT Austrian Institute
of Technology GmbH, Giefinggasse 2, 1210 Vienna, Austria
{valentin.gattol, jan.bobeth, kathrin.roederer,
sebastian.egger, georg.regal, ulrich.lehner,
manfred.tscheligi}@ait.ac.at

Abstract. Given recent demographic changes, adapting the office environments of older knowledge workers to their needs has become increasingly important in supporting an extension of working life. In this paper, we present a case study research of older knowledge workers in Romania, with the goal of gaining bottom-up insights that support the ideation, design, and development of features for a smart work environment. Utilizing a multi-method approach, we combine (1) contextual interviews and observations, (2) an analysis of needs and frictions for deriving insights, (3) an ideation workshop for eliciting potential features, (4) an online survey among experts for evaluating the final feature ideas, and (5) early stage prototyping of selected feature ideas. Following this comprehensive yet efficient approach, we were able to gain a rich understanding of the work realities and contexts of older knowledge workers and to transform that understanding into a concrete set of prioritized feature ideas.

Keywords: Knowledge workers · Older adults · Requirements analysis · Multiple methods · Contextual inquiries · Needs-frictions analysis · NUF prioritization

1 Introduction

Within the European Union labor market participation rates currently reduce sharply along with age: while participation is high for the age group of 50–54 years (75.5 %), it drops noticeably for the age groups of 55–59 years (61.5 %) and 60–64 years (30.5 %) [1]. The OECD predicts that by the year 2050 the number of retired persons aged 50 and above will surpass the number of active persons in the workforce in Europe [2]. Given these demographic changes, policies geared towards motivating older persons to work longer have become more and more important. From a company perspective, older employees hold important knowledge and know-how, have high quality standards in their work, and are typically very loyal and dedicated to their organizations [3]. Moreover, positive effects on productivity have been reported for age-diverse teams, with performances of both younger and older team members being significantly higher

© IFIP International Federation for Information Processing 2015
J. Abdelnour-Nocera et al. (Eds.): HWID 2015, IFIP AICT 468, pp. 83–96, 2015.
DOI: 10.1007/978-3-319-27048-7_6

compared to less age-diverse teams [4]. Thus, the challenge is how we can support an extension in working life. On the one hand new policies are needed that strike the right balance between older employees' rights and interests and in increasing their employability [5]; on the other hand, efforts are needed that put a clear focus on innovation in the immediate environment of older workers.

In the present research we focus on the latter by means of a case study into the work environments of older knowledge workers in Romania. Older adults are a heterogeneous group with very different needs depending on physical, cognitive, and social constitution [6]. Also, experience with computers may vary greatly within this group and influence both the effectiveness and efficiency of using computers [7]. For this reason, it is crucial to provide tailored technology support that addresses the real needs of older knowledge workers. The case study presented in this chapter was part of a larger project, following the vision of developing a smart work environment that supports "a prolonged, productive and satisfactory involvement of older employees in working life" [8]. The aim of the case study was to provide feature ideas as input for the technical specification of a smart work environment. We followed a multi-method approach, combining (1) contextual interviews and observations for mapping the workplace environment, (2) an analysis of needs and frictions for deriving insights, (3) an ideation workshop for generating feature ideas, (4) an online survey among experts for prioritizing the feature ideas, and (5) early stage prototyping of selected feature ideas. As a result of this multi-method approach, we were able to gain a rich understanding of the work realities of older knowledge workers and to transform that understanding into a set of prioritized feature ideas. Such a list of feature ideas can serve as a valuable reference in the development of smart workplace solutions and offer crucial guidance on which features to select for further development and prototyping.

Our main contribution is an elaborate description of our comprehensive and efficient multi-method approach along with the results we obtained with this approach. We are confident that this approach will serve as a helpful tool for designers of smart workplace solutions.

The remainder of this chapter is structured as follows: in Sect. 2, background and related work, we discuss current workplace trends in today's knowledge-based economies and different approaches in the goal-oriented design of smart work technologies; in Sect. 3 we give a detailed account of the different phases in the multi-method approach; in Sect. 4 we present the results of the case study that were obtained with this approach; and finally, in Sect. 5, discussion and conclusion, we reflect on our experiences with the approach as a tool for informing the development of smart work place solutions.

2 Background and Related Work

In recent years, daily work in our increasingly knowledge-based economy is demanding a high degree of flexibility and adaptability [9] in order to perform tasks anytime and anywhere [10]. Within this context, smart work approaches as alternative ways of organizing work supported by technology have emerged. One indication for this trend is the already widespread use of mobile devices in business contexts, which blurs the boundary between work and personal life by enabling people to complete work tasks when at home or on the go [11]. Many of today's knowledge workers embrace this trend, as it allows them to more flexibly allocate their time between work and personal life; yet, others are skeptical of the new technological possibilities, fearing that it may lead to an expectation of round-the-clock availability, as expressed in today's knowledge workers increasingly felt obligation to answer phone calls or check emails outside of regular office hours. Especially for the latter group, this can lead to increased stress levels and an off-kilter work–life balance [9]. Smart work technology has the potential to alleviate some of these negative impacts on work–life balance by supporting employees with tailored solutions that are better aligned with their particular goals and working style. Greene [12], for example, distinguishes four knowledge worker types with different goals and working styles: the *anchor*, who represents the traditional sedentary office worker at the desk; the *connector*, who spends most of his/her time in meetings away from the desk; the *gatherer*, who mainly operates outside the office, for example, networking with clients and customers; and the *navigator*, who is rarely present at the office, working more independently and globally. The goal-oriented development of smart technologies thus requires a deeper understanding of workers' tasks and needs, in particular the special needs of older employees who cannot as easily adapt to new technologies as younger employees. Without such considerations, the adoption of smart work technologies remains rather low [10].

There are different approaches towards the goal-oriented design of supportive smart work technology. One approach is *Human Work Interaction Design* (HWID), a multidisciplinary framework combining work analysis (e.g., cognitive work analysis [9]) and interaction design, to promote a better understanding of the relationships between humans and work domain contents and the interaction during their tasks [13]. Another promising approach is *Contextual Design* [14]. According to this approach, great feature ideas evolve from the synthesis of a designer's detailed understanding of the users' needs (through direct involvement in data collection and interpretation) and his or her own in-depth understanding of the technological possibilities. This approach requires designers to visit the companies, in order to understand the workers' tasks and overall organizational processes, before technologies are customized for the company [15]. Visiting, in this case, means to apply some form of ethnographic research method, such as observations [16], contextual inquiries [14], design ethnography [17], or co-realization [18].

The many benefits of ethnographic research in the domain of computer supported collaborative work are reflected in the work by Blomberg and Karasti [19]. Design ethnography, for example, is based on the idea that observing and designing should not be strictly separated. In other words, the design process should not be limited to working in the reclusive environment of a design studio but experiment with design interventions on site and on the spot [20]. Similarly, co-realization emphasizes the need for a long-term engagement between designers and users, as the full implications of new technology for work practices can only be revealed in and through the system's subsequent use [18].

Given that many ethnographic approaches require considerable efforts in time and resources, we position our multi-method approach as a comprehensive yet efficient alternative to study the work realities and contexts of older knowledge workers. A key benefit of our approach is that it leads to a concrete set of prioritized feature ideas based on the involvement of relevant stakeholders. Designers and developers may consult such a list in selecting the most promising features for further development and prototyping.

3   Multi-method Approach

In line with the overall goal of providing feature ideas as input for the technical specification of a smart work environment for older people, we followed a multi-method approach as depicted in Fig. 1.

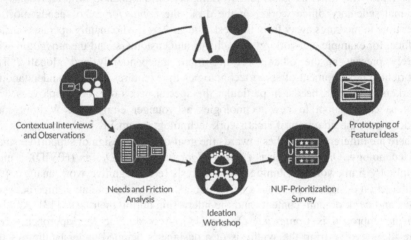

Fig. 1. Overview of the phases in the multi-method approach

Within the first phase (see Sect. 3.1), we aimed at gaining bottom-up insights into the work environments of older knowledge workers. Inspired by ethnographic approaches (see Sect. 2), we analyzed the work environment as a whole, utilizing a combination of semi-structured interviews and observations at the workplace. The goal of the second phase (see Sect. 3.2), was to identify needs and frictions from the interview transcripts and observation reports, which were then combined to insights. The goal of the third phase (see Sect. 3.3), was to derive feature ideas based on these insights by conducting an ideation workshop. The goal of the fourth phase (see Sect. 3.4), was to prioritize these feature ideas in an online survey among experts. Finally, the goal of the fifth phase (see Sect. 3.5), was to develop selected feature ideas into prototypes to communicate the overall concept and to gather feedback at an early stage.

3.1   Contextual Interviews and Observations

Participants and Setting. Older knowledge workers (aged 50 years and above) are a heterogeneous group, characterized by different needs depending on physical, cognitive, and social constitution [6]. For the present study we focused on a subset of that group: knowledge workers who use computers on a daily basis and spend most of their time in the office (cf. with the Anchor and Connector working types described by Greene [12]). A convenience sample of eight older knowledge workers (two women) was drawn to take part in the contextual interviews and observations. The mean age was 55 years ($SD = 3.93$). The participants were recruited from two small IT companies in Bucharest that worked in hardware and software engineering in the domain of fiscal accounting. All participants were frequent users of smartphones, tablets, and laptops. The interviews and observations took place directly at the participants' workplace (see Fig. 2 below) and lasted for 60–90 min.

Fig. 2. Study settings (clockwise from top left): (a) table for briefing participants, (b) open plan office area, (c) researcher and interpreter on site, (d) participant at her desk.

Procedure. Each session started with an informal conversation and the participant signing an informed consent document (see the setting in Fig. 2a). Afterwards, we started recording with a Blackberry Z10 smartphone and proceeded with the contextual interviews and observations. The choice for using an unobtrusive smartphone camera rather than a professional camera was made deliberately, so that participants would not feel intimated. We followed the participants through the office to their workplaces (see Fig. 2b) and encouraged them to present their work environment and typical tasks (see Fig. 2d).

In line with the open character of our approach, we relied on a loose structure ensuring that participants still had enough leeway to act and speak spontaneously. Behavioral prompts (e.g., "Can you show us around your desk?") and follow-up questions (e.g., "Why do you prefer to take down appointments in a physical calendar?") were used to direct the attention to specific aspects. The contextual interviews and observations were conducted by two researchers with backgrounds in design and psychology. They were supported by a local interpreter who was crucial in overcoming cultural barriers, building rapport, and generally ensuring proper translation (see Fig. 2c on the right). The researchers spoke English, the participants answered either in English or Romanian.

3.2   From Needs and Frictions to Insights

Data Preparation. More than 10 h of video material was transcribed using the open source software *easy transcript*[1]. For those participants that answered in Romanian, only the English translations were transcribed. All names were anonymized.

Data Analysis. The goal of the analysis was to identify needs and frictions from the interview transcripts and observation reports, which were then combined to insights. For our purposes, we defined needs as something required in the execution of work, frictions as a certain issue that stands in the way of satisfying a need, and insights as an intuitive grasp of a need–friction situation (e.g., 'I need to meet objectives but sometimes I forget them.'). The analysis of the data involved two steps:

Step 1: Reading the transcripts, highlighting relevant utterances and observations, and categorizing them to themes (i.e., certain recurring patterns). For example, "staying in touch with distant colleagues" and "being stressed by the daily email load", would both be coded to belong to the theme *Communication*. The themes (see Tab. 1) structured the process of identifying the needs and frictions.

Step 2: After categorizing the relevant utterances and observations to themes, we identified underlying needs and frictions. Insights were formed by combining a specific need with a specific friction and formulated from the user's perspective (e.g., 'I need to communicate via email but I cannot handle the high email load'). In some cases, more than one insight could be identified for a specific need due to several frictions for the same need.

3.3   Deriving Feature Ideas in an Ideation Workshop

Participants of the Ideation Workshop. In order to generate a wide range of ideas we involved 15 professionals with backgrounds in software engineering, wireless communications, user experience design, marketing, psychological evaluation, sociological research, serious gaming, eLearning and telemedicine.

Procedure. For having a structured yet flexible way of brainstorming, we slightly adapted the World Café method [21] by using insights of the needs–frictions analysis as input for deriving feature ideas. Thus, we formulated the overall question as:

---

[1] http://www.e-werkzeug.eu/index.php/en/.

considering these insights, which concrete feature would be helpful for users belonging to the target group of older knowledge workers?

We prepared four tables, each equipped with post-its, markers, and 9–10 insights. Each table was moderated by a host who stayed at the same table and took notes of the discussion. The other participants switched tables after each round (4 rounds in total). One round lasted for 20 min and always followed the same procedure: (1) *Introduction:* the host read out the insights and summarized the ideas discussed in the previous round; (2) *Brain writing:* each participant was given five minutes to write down as many ideas as possible; (3) *Discussion:* at each table participants discussed and developed feature ideas. At the end of the fourth round, the hosts consolidated the features ideas.

3.4 Prioritizing Feature Ideas in an Online Survey

Respondents. The goal of the fourth phase was to prioritize the feature ideas that resulted from the ideation workshop. For this purpose, the participants of the ideation workshop were asked to fill in an online survey. The prioritization was not part of the ideation workshop, as we wanted each expert to evaluate the ideas individually with no time pressure and unaffected by groupthink. We received 10 completed surveys.

Survey Design and Procedure. The survey relied on a simple design introducing each feature idea by its name and a short description, along with the insights from the needs–frictions analysis. The respondents' task was to score each feature on the three dimensions *newness*, *usefulness*, and *feasibility* (following the NUF approach, [22]). For each of the dimensions, respondents assigned any number of points ranging from 1 ('not new/useful/feasible at all') to 10 ('very new/useful/feasible'). Moreover, respondents were given the opportunity to leave comments in a text box for each feature. The survey was designed to take about 30–60 min to complete.

Data Analysis. The goal of the NUF is to arrive at an overall index score per feature. First, a total score per feature was calculated across the dimensions of newness, use-fulness, and feasibility. Second, means and standard deviations were calculated across respondents in order to generate a rank-ordered list of the feature ideas (see Table 2 for the 10 highest ranked feature ideas).

3.5 Prototyping of Feature Ideas

Scenarios. The goal of the fifth phase of the multi-method approach was to develop selected feature ideas into early stage prototypes. The first step in this process involved developing (use) scenarios. Scenarios describe a person, the person's goals and the steps the person takes to achieve these goals with the proposed system (cf. [23]). Using scenarios in an early stage of the design and development process provides a basic and shared understanding of the overall concept for the different stakeholders (cf. [24]).

Mockups. The second step in the prototyping process involved developing mockups based on the scenarios. For this we combined two of the highest-ranked feature ideas— the Private Digital Noteboard and the Digital Paper Calendar (see Table 2)—and developed them into a mockup utilizing off-the-shelf hardware (i.e., in our case a tablet, a smartphone and a paper calendar). Generally, mockups differ in fidelity along three dimensions: role, look and feel, and implementation (cf. [25]). We developed our mockup to the level of a medium-fidelity prototype covering the first two dimensions: role (i.e., functionality) and look and feel (i.e., size, form factor, overall design).

4 Results

Our comprehensive multi-method approach (see Fig. 1) allowed for gaining bottom-up insights into the work realities of our target group, which were then used to generate feature ideas for a smart work environment, and to develop an example scenario and a mockup based on a combination of two highly-ranked feature ideas. In this section, we present the results we obtained from our approach.

Themes and Insights. In Table 1 we provide two examples of insights for each theme that resulted from a needs–frictions analysis of the contextual interview and observation transcripts. While some insights left room for creative ideas, other insights were so straightforward to suggest an easy solution (e.g., 'I need to write proper Romanian but the default English keyboards come without diacritics.') or so general that smart workplace solutions cannot help (e.g., 'I don't want to work at home but sometimes I have to.').

Table 1. Themes and Insights

Themes	#	Insights (examples)
Task management	i1	I need to keep track of open tasks but carrying them over (e.g., from my agenda to Outlook) takes effort
	i2	I need to meet objectives but sometimes I forget them ("Out of sight, out of mind")
Communication	i3	I want to be able to send instant messages to both private and business contacts but without mixing contacts
	i4	I need to communicate via email but I cannot handle the high email load
Collaboration	i5	I need to solve bigger and complex problems but effective collaboration is difficult when people have different backgrounds/expertise
	i6	I need to share information digitally but there is no efficient way of digitizing hand-written information
Mind & body	i7	I want to train my mind but I don't know how to do it effectively ("To train my mind I'm reading, solving crosswords, and checking Facebook")
	i8	I need to take breaks but since I stopped smoking I remain mostly at my desk

(Continued)

Table 1. (*Continued*)

Themes	#	Insights (examples)
Work conditions	i9	I want to be flexible in the choice of my work environment but accordant company policies are required for that
	i10	I need to write in proper Romanian but the default English keyboards come without diacritics
Personal development	i11	I would like to train general skills but the company does not foster it
	i12	I would like to learn on my own but there is no dedicated eLearning content (e.g., video tutorials, interactive materials)
Personalization	i13	I want an always visible external memory resource for frequently needed information (e.g., important deadlines), but my current solution (i.e., post-its) is not reliable and cannot hold a lot of information
	i14	I want to work on my tasks in different contexts/environments but there is no seamless way of doing so
Tools	i15	I need to compile lists and make calculations but do it by hand because I lack the necessary computer skills (Excel)
	i16	I plan my day on paper because I don't see the benefit of digital solutions

Note. The insights were synthesized from the needs and frictions analysis and formulated from the perspective of a user. Quotation marks are used to indicate utterances that originated directly from participants.

Ranking of Feature Ideas. In Table 2 we present the top 10 feature ideas that resulted from the ideation workshop and the online prioritization survey. As can be seen from the list, some of the features obviously are more innovative than others. For example, the feature 'Private Digital Noteboard' (#1) is certainly more new to the world than the feature 'Walking Break Scheduler' (#9). By contrast, the 'Walking Break Scheduler' is certainly more feasible—that is, less complex and therefore easier to develop—than the 'Private Digital Noteboard'. Yet, both of these features are useful in the sense that they address a real need—supporting a healthy lifestyle and staying on top of things, respectively.

Table 2. The 10 highest ranked Feature Ideas

#	Feature name (ref. to insights)	Feature description	NUF score	
			M	D
1	Private Digital Noteboard (i1, i2, i13)	Always visible second screen at personal desk: •Urgent tasks are highlighted •Tasks are clustered according to projects/teams •Finished tasks can be crossed out •To-Do's/notes can be sent to public noteboard	23.90	3.78

(*Continued*)

Table 2. (*Continued*)

#	Feature name (ref. to insights)	Feature description	NUF score M	D
2	Cognitive training games (i7, i11)	A selection of serious games to train cognitive skills to prevent mental decline with personalized training • sessions	23.20	4.34
3	Exercise Prompter and Demonstrator (i7, i11)	A friendly exercise reminder: •Prompting physical/mental exercises through pop-ups •Avatar might demonstrate exercises •Connected to calendar to know about ongoing meetings/deadlines	22.70	3.71
4	Flexible Self-Learning Mini-Modules (i3, i12, i15)	Tutorials on how to use new software/tools: •Ca. 15 min per session •To be completed until a fixed date	22.10	4.12
5	Public Digital Noteboard (i1, i2, i13)	Always visible second screen at a wall: •see #1 Private Digital Noteboard •To-Do's/Notes can be sent to private noteboard	21.50	4.12
6	Knowledge base (i5)	Central internal knowledge base within organization: •"in case of problem X, contact Mrs. Miller..." •Wiki on frequent problems to post questions	21.40	5.83
7	Healthy Email Mgmt (i4)	Organized as e-learning content (e.g., Guidelines/tips on how to better cope with the email load)	21.30	6.04
8	Digital Paper Calendar (i6, i16)	Paper calendar capable of automatically digitizing hand-written notes: •Digital paper or digital pen as input device •Tagging system (e.g., offline with different stickers or directly on the tablet/PC)	21.00	4.90
9	Walking Break Scheduler (i8)	Walking time in nature as part of the daily schedule and encouraged by various means (e.g., calendar reminders, pop-ups...)	20.91	4.66
10	Remote Access (i9, i14)	A cross-platform tool to support task portability via secure remote access to company resources (i.e., files, software...)	20.40	5.06

Example Scenario and Mockup. We selected the Private Digital Noteboard (#1) and the Digital Paper Calendar (#8) for prototyping (see Table 2 above), resulting in the following scenario and mockup that combined both of these feature ideas (see below and Fig. 3).

> *Paul, a 55 + office worker, and his younger colleague Rachel work in the same building but on different floors. Paul needs to schedule a meeting with Rachel. Thus, he opens his Digital Paper Calendar to display her shared calendar. He sees an empty slot and writes down the following note with a smart pen on the 10 a.m. line: "Update on concept draft for BigHealth Inc. with Rachel". The Digital Paper Calendar interprets his hand-writing and suggests sending an invitation to Rachel. Paul confirms and a message is sent. Rachel responds via her Outlook calendar and suggests to meet an hour later at 11 a.m. Paul sees her request as a notification on his Private Digital Noteboard that he uses for displaying tasks and to-do's. He confirms the new time by touching the "accept" button on the display. He then also changes the time in the Digital Paper Calendar by simply drawing an arrow with his smart pen from the 10 a.m. to the 11 a.m. line.*

Fig. 3. A mockup representing the Digital Paper Calendar and the Private Digital Noteboard.

We developed our mockup to fit into typical workplace settings and to take advantage of people's existing and well-established mental models about paper and touch-screen based interactions. It can be used for organizing meetings, managing a list of to-do's, or simply for taking notes. The proposed concept, as illustrated in Fig. 3, consists of a paper calendar with a touch display along with a tablet used as noteboard.

By using page tracking mechanisms, the Digital Paper Calendar is aware of the analogue page that is seen by the user and provides digital information accordingly. The proposed combination of page tracking, pen and paper input, a digital display, and an additional private screen seamlessly integrates common behaviors and habits that are highly familiar to the target group of older knowledge workers. To simulate the page flipping mechanism in future user studies, we developed an application that allows for remotely switching screens in a Wizard of Oz setup [26], on both the Digital Paper Calendar and the Private Digital Noteboard.

5   Discussion and Conclusion

A primary goal of this case study was to map the contexts and environments of older knowledge workers in order to gain bottom-up insights that can support the ideation, design, and development of features for a smart work environment. In line with this goal, we followed a comprehensive multi-method approach, combining contextual interviews and observations, an analysis of needs and frictions for deriving insights, an ideation workshop for eliciting potential features, and an online survey among experts for evaluating the feature ideas on the dimensions of newness, usefulness, and feasibility. We want to emphasize that this list is not intended to be prescriptive or followed blindly but to serve as a basis for further specifications in the design and development of a smart work environment that caters specifically to the needs of older workers. Thus, its main value lies in providing food for thought to all project stakeholders and to inform rather than to enforce the decision on which features to select for further development. In our case, we used the list to select two feature ideas that we developed into a scenario and a mockup. This helped us to communicate the overall concept to future users and to gather feedback at an early stage.

The main contribution of this case study is the successful application of the compiled multi-method approach. Following this comprehensive approach, we were able not only to gain a rich understanding of the work realities and contexts of older computer workers, as is typical of ethnographically-inspired approaches in general (cf., [16]), but to transform that understanding into a concrete set of prioritized feature ideas that can form the basis for prototyping selected features. In the following, we briefly reflect on our experiences for each of the phases:

1. *Contextual interviews and observations:* using a smartphone camera rather than a dedicated camera to record turned out to be the right choice. Participants quickly forgot about the presence of the camera, which in our view helped to create a more natural setting. As a limitation we think it would have been useful to visit each participant not just once but more frequently, to align it more with the tradition in Co-realization that emphasizes the importance of a long-term engagement between developers and users [18].
2. *From needs and frictions to insights:* we followed a practical approach in transcribing the contextual interviews and observations, which put emphasis chiefly on what was said rather than how it was said (as might be of interest from a more

sociological perspective). This turned out to be sufficient for the purposes of our analysis that was focused on identifying needs and frictions.

3. *Deriving feature ideas in an ideation workshop:* a positive element of the workshop was the small number of people that sat at each table (three to four) that allowed for an active involvement of each participant. As a negative element, we noticed that having nine or ten insights per table was a bit overwhelming. We think that the number of insights discussed at each table can be reduced to around five.

4. *Prioritizing feature ideas in an online survey:* from our experience, it was a good choice to separate the prioritization of the feature ideas from the ideation workshop to prevent groupthink effects. However, if a 'safe environment' can be created during the workshop, then this phase might be merged with the previous one.

5. *Prototyping of feature ideas*: based on the prioritized feature ideas, we developed a scenario and a mockup. Such early prototypes are a fruitful way to communicate design decisions to the development team and to potential users. In addition to discussing the basic concept, they also provide input for discussions on details (e.g., particular functionalities, form factor, etc.).

To conclude, other than many ethnographic approaches that require considerable efforts in time and resources, our multi-method approach serves as a comprehensive, fairly easy to implement and efficient means of informing the design and development process, based on continuous direct involvement of users and other stakeholders in the design process. A key benefit of the approach is that the different phases efficiently combine to arrive at a concrete outcome, a set of prioritized feature ideas. Such an empirically well-founded prioritization can support designers and developers in selecting the most promising ideas for further development and prototyping. Future research may investigate how this holistic approach can be further streamlined to reduce costs and maximize the benefits for designers and developers of smart work place technology.

Acknowledgments. This work has been partly funded by the European Ambient Assisted Living Joint Programme and the National Funding Agencies from Austria, Denmark, Germany, Netherlands, Romania, and Switzerland: PEARL (AAL-2013-6-091).

References

1. Eurofound: Sustainable Work and the Ageing Workforce. Publications Office of the European Union, Luxembourg (2012)
2. OECD: Live Longer, Work Longer. OECD Publishing, Paris (2006)
3. Roundtree, L.: The Aging Workforce: Exploring the Impact on Business Strategy. Executive Briefing Series. Boston College Center for Work & Family (2004)
4. Gobel, C., Zwick, T.: Are personnel measures effective in increasing productivity of old workers? Labour Econ. **22**, 80–93 (2013)
5. van Dalen, H.P., Henkens, K., Schippers, J.: How do employers cope with an ageing workforce? views from employers and employees. Demogr. Res. **22**, 1015–1036 (2010)
6. Bobeth, J., Deutsch, S., Schmehl, S., Tscheligi, M.: Facing the user heterogeneity when designing touch interfaces for older adults: a representative personas approach. In: NordiCHI 2012, Copenhagen, Denmark (2012)

7. Wood, E.: Use of computer input devices by older adults. J. Appl. Gerontol. **24**, 419–438 (2005)

8. Bobeth, J., Gattol, V., Meyer, I., Müller, S., Soldatos, J., Egger, S., Busch, M., Tscheligi, M.: Platform for ergonomic and motivating ICT-based age-friendly workplaces. In: Workshop on Human Work Interaction Design for Pervasive and Smart Workplaces, NordiCHI 2014, Helsinki, Finland (2014)

9. Vicente, K.J.: HCI in the global knowledge-based economy: designing to support worker adaptation. ACM Trans. Comput.-Hum Interact. **7**, 263–280 (2000)

10. Eom, S.-J., Choi, N.-B., Sung, W.: The use of smart work in Korea: who and for what? In: Proceedings of the 15th Annual International Conference on Digital Government Research, pp. 253–262. ACM, Aguascalientes (2014)

11. Stawarz, K., Cox, A.L., Bird, J., Benedyk, R.: "I'd sit at home and do work emails": how tablets affect the work-life balance of office workers. In: CHI 2013 Extended Abstracts on Human Factors in Computing Systems, pp. 1383–1388. ACM, Paris (2013)

12. Greene, C., Myerson, J.: Space for thought: designing for knowledge workers. Facilities **29**, 19–30 (2011)

13. Clemmensen, T.: A Human Work Interaction Design (HWID) case study in e-government and public information systems. Int. J. Public Inf. Syst. **3**, 105–113 (2011)

14. Beyer, H., Holtzblatt, K.: Contextual Design: Defining Customer-centered Systems. Morgan Kaufmann, San Francisco (1998)

15. Cau-Bareille, D., Gaudart, C., Delgoulet, C.: Training, age and technological change: difficulties associated with age, the design of tools, and the organization of work. Work **41**, 127–141 (2012)

16. Leonard, D., Rayport, J.F.: Spark innovation through empathic design. Harv. Bus. Rev. **75**, 102–113 (1997)

17. Crabtree, A., Rouncefield, M., Tolmie, P.: Doing Design Ethnography. Springer, London (2012)

18. Hartswood, M., Procter, R., Slack, R., Voß, A., Büscher, M., Rouncefield, M., Rouchy, P.: Co-realization: toward a principled synthesis of ethnomethodology and participatory design. In: Ackerman, M.S., Halverson, C.A., Erickson, T., Kellogg, W.A. (eds.) Resources, Co-evolution and Artifacts, pp. 59–94. Springer, London (2008)

19. Blomberg, J., Karasti, H.: Reflections on 25 Years of Ethnography in CSCW. Comput. Support. Coop. **22**, 373–423 (2013)

20. Halse, J., Brandt, E., Clark, B., Binder, T. (eds.): Rehearsing the Future. The Danish Design School Press, København (2010)

21. Brown, J., Isaacs, D.: The World Café: Shaping Our Futures Through Conversations That Matter. Berrett-Koehler Publishers, San Francisco (2005)

22. Gray, D., Brown, S., Macanufo, J.: Gamestorming: A Playbook for Innovators, Rulebreakers, and Changemakers. O'Reilly Media, Inc., Sebastopol (2010)

23. Carroll, J.M.: Five reasons for scenario-based design. Interact. Comput. **13**, 43–60 (2000)

24. Alexander, I.F., Maiden, N.: Scenarios, Stories, Use Cases: Through the Systems Development Life-Cycle. Wiley, New York (2005)

25. Houde, S., Hill, C.: What do prototypes prototype? In: Helander, M., Landauer, T., Prabhu, P. (eds.) Handbook of Human-Computer Interaction. Elsevier Science B.V., Amsterdam (1997)

26. Kelley, J.F.: An empirical methodology for writing user-friendly natural language computer applications. In: Proceedings of the SIGCHI Conference on Human Factors in Computing Systems, pp. 193–196. ACM, Boston (1983)

Characterizing the Context
of Use in Mobile Work

Heli Väätäjä[(✉)]

Tampere University of Technology, Tampere, Finland
heli.vaataja@tut.fi

Abstract. The context of use has been widely acknowledged as important
when designing and evaluating systems for work related activities. This paper
describes in case of mobile news making the synthesized findings on the context
of use. Findings are categorized to five components and nineteen subcomponents and characterized with examples from our studies. The presented findings
validate a previously presented model for context of use in mobile HCI, extend
it, and elaborate the definitions for the components. The presented elaborated
model can be applied by academics and practitioners in development, research
and evaluation activities from identifying requirements to evaluating systems for
mobile work. Findings support understanding what circumstances and how they
can contribute to user experience and acceptance of designed systems.

Keywords: Context of use · Mobile · User experience · Model · Component ·
Work

1 Introduction

The importance of understanding and characterizing the context of use when designing
and evaluating systems for work activities and their user experience has been widely
acknowledged. In this research we approach context of use as the *circumstances under
which the activity [of mobile work] takes place* (adapted from [1]). Mobile work is
characterized by flexible use of time and place [2], that is, a person is able to move and
carry out tasks "anytime and anywhere" [2, 3, p. 14] with the help of wired or wireless
technology [3, p. 14]. However, relatively little research exists that explicitly con-
centrates on the characteristics of context of use in mobile work.

This paper addresses mobile news making as an example of mobile work. Mobile
news making activity takes place in a mobile context of use by using mobile handheld
technology, in this research smartphones, in one or several subactivities in the news
making process. News making consists of four main activities: (1) *discovering* the
potential news item [4], (2) *gathering* the news material [4, 5], (3) news *production* [5],
and (4) *distribution* [5]. These activities can be sequential or simultaneous [5]. They
can be carried out at the spot of the event with mobile handheld devices by a mobile
reporter, or specific activities, such as discovering and gathering can be done at the spot
while others can be carried out in a café or by editors in the news room.

Mobile workers are *"employees that work at and move between different places"*
[6, p. 6]. In mobile news making mobile workers refer to (1) employees of the news

© IFIP International Federation for Information Processing 2015
J. Abdelnour-Nocera et al. (Eds.): HWID 2015, IFIP AICT 468, pp. 97–113, 2015.
DOI: 10.1007/978-3-319-27048-7_7

organization [7], (2) other professionals in the news industry, such as freelancers that work, for example, for the news organization on event based contracts [7] or independently or with crowdfunding, or (3) mobile crowdworkers [8] or reader reporters, who carry out news reporting related tasks based on the news organization's initiative with open, coordinated, or focused calls for content, expertise, or reports [9], or (4) citizen journalists working alone or in small groups outside of news organizations.

This paper synthesizes findings reported in twelve publications based on twelve case studies carried out in the context of mobile news making, characterizing the components and subcomponents of context of use. The findings validate the model of context of use for mobile HCI, CoU-MHCI model [10], extend it, and elaborate the definitions for the components. The presented elaborated model can be applied by academics and practitioners when designing and evaluating systems for mobile work that utilize location technologies or context-awareness, such as for identifying typical combinations of context characteristics. Findings also support understanding how circumstances can contribute to user experience and acceptance of the systems when planning system uptake and selecting solutions for use.

The paper is organized as follows. First, related work on characteristics of mobile context of use is summarized and user experience is discussed. Then, the methods and results are presented. The paper ends with conclusions and proposes future work.

2   Related Work

The model for the context of use for mobile HCI, CoU-MHCI model [10], synthesizes findings from on an extensive literature review of components and characteristics of context of use. It describes five context components with their subcomponents and properties for the mobile context of use: (1) physical, (2) temporal, (3) task, (4) social, and (5) technology and information. As this model is one of the most comprehensive models for the context of use presented in the field of mobile HCI and it specifically addresses the mobile context of use, it is used as the framework for categorizing the related work, as well as the findings from our research discussing them in this paper.

The results of the summarization of related work is presented in Table 1 and briefly exemplified in the following.

Usage of mobile handheld devices in a mobile context of use is characterized by distractions, interruptions, and fragmented attention [13, 20, 24, 27]. Distracting characteristics of the mobile context of use, such as reflections on the screen and parallel tasks can influence user experience [28]. The split visual resources when interacting with the mobile devices (tapping with a stylus on a PDA) and walking, simultaneously trying to maintain an awareness of the environment, increases the task completion times, error rates, and work load, as well as reduces walking speed [29].

In relation to task context, the task hierarchy and task characteristics are important. The primary task, such as observing animals [24] or focusing attention on other tasks external to the mobile device: to avoid danger, to monitor progress, or to handle other objects [13], may call for a high level of attention and limit the use of hands for interaction with the mobile device. Multi-tasking, such as communicating on the phone while pursuing a target in police work, splits the attention of the user [14]. The

Table 1. Characteristics of the mobile context of use for mobile work from prior literature.

Component	Characteristic	Reference(s)
Task	Parallel primary task	[12, 13]
	Multi-tasking	[14]
	Handling of other physical objects simultaneously	[13]
	Evolving tasks based on locality and situation	[15]
	Task complexity, irregularity	[16–18]
	Task interdependence	[16]
	Work in dead time, in transit, in waiting	[19]
Temporal	Available time span	[19, 20]
	Time-criticality, time-pressure, deadlines, urgency	[11, 12, 14–16, 18, 21, 22, 25]
	Time of day	[14]
	Hours of work – extended & unpredictable	[23]
Physical	Environmental conditions	[14]
	Location	[23]
	Dynamic environment	[24]
	Interruptions	[20, 23]
	Location dependence of the task	[16, 25]
	Frequency of mobility	[16]
Social	Bystanders	[12, 14]
Technology and information	Available technology and access to information	[19, 23, 26]

fragmented attention caused by context characteristics, including interruptions (physical context), parallel tasks, multi-tasking, and the handling of other objects related to the task at hand, needs to be considered when designing for the mobile context of use.

The characteristics of temporal context, including, time-criticality of action, urgency, deadlines, and time-pressure, is emphasized in mobile work. In the case of freelance work, the hours of work are described as unpredictable and extended [23]. The physical context characteristics include environmental conditions, location, and dynamism of the environment, as well as interruptions, e.g., caused by traffic lights in police work. In relation to the technology and information context, availability and access to technology and information, and their uncertainty in a mobile context of work, or alternatively the opportunities offered by technology and available information has been emphasized. Finally, in relation to social context, bystanders affect the comfort of using mobile systems, as users consider whether bystanders experiencing the use of the system find it appropriate to the situation such as in case of firefighting [12]. Also, in the case of police work, unobtrusiveness and discreteness of using mobile systems can contribute to experience of users [14]. From the five components of context of use, social context has received relatively little attention in literature of mobile work.

3 User Experience and News Making

User experience is described as subjective, situated, complex and dynamic [30]. According to Hassenzahl et al. [30] context within which the interaction occurs is one of factors that contribute to user experience. In our research we found that the mobile context of use and its characteristics are one of the four components contributing to user experience [31]. The three other components contributing to user experience include the characteristics of the user, system and the outcome of using the mobile system as illustrated in Fig. 1 (see also [31, p. 94]). The fifth component in the model of user experience in mobile news making presented in Fig. 1 are the user's verbally expressible descriptive attributes related to his/her experience in terms of system and outcome quality and the perceived impacts. They can contribute to overall evaluative judgments. The impressions and perceptions of system and outcome quality, the perceived impacts, and the overall evaluative judgments can lead to consequences that can be moderated by the characteristics of the user, system, the context of use and the outcome.

To understand user experience in mobile news making, it is essential to understand the activity of news making and the context of the activity. The goal of news making is to publish news, share information, and tell a story. These stories are told to an audience. News are a selective version of world events with a focus on what is new or unusual.

Two types of news are often described. Hard news is new, timely information about significant events, describing factual details of what has happened or what has been said [32, p. 12, 33, p. 24]. Examples of this type of news are natural catastrophes, major accidents, or important political events. Soft news can be characterized as lighter, more colorful and entertaining (ibid.). They may neither be immediately important nor informative (ibid). Reporting a local community event could be an example of this type of news.

Journalists measure the news worthiness of potential news items against criteria that are known as news values, such as relevance for the audience, timeliness, and novelty. Technology that is used in news making needs to support its goals and the criteria that are used in assessing the news worthiness and journalistic quality. On the other hand, the selection of news is constrained and influenced by a number of structural factors, such as legal constraints, the system of media ownership, organizational routines, a shortage of time and market forces [34, pp. 17–34]. All of these factors exemplify what influences news making and are related to the concept of context.

How does the context of use contribute to user experience in mobile news making? Let's consider an example. The goal of news reporting is informing the public about current issues. Examples of requirements and values in news journalism are timely and truthful reporting. Constraints set by the organization are deadlines, or required immediacy of reporting directly from the spot of the event. The available technology and information available for a mobile reporter to carry out news making creates possibilities and at the same time may set constraints to the activity and quality of outcome. The ideals, needs and goals of a mobile reporter may have different importance for the mobile reporter depending on the situation. Situation, defined as the

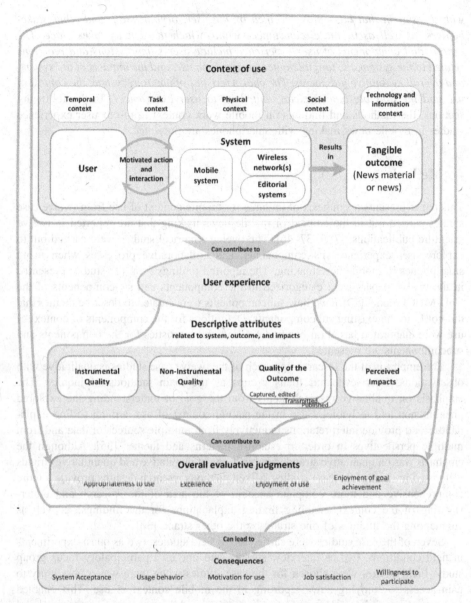

Fig. 1. The model of user experience in mobile news making (modified from [31, p. 94])

"relative position or combination of circumstances at a certain moment" (Merriam-Webster, retrieved 5.8.2013) as a combinations of previous examples when using the smartphone-based system in news making activity is one factor that can contribute to user experience in this domain.

We have defined user experience in mobile news making as follows (see Fig. 1 and [31, p. 91]): *"User experience is the consequence of motivated action and interaction with the system that has goals specified by the user, organization, and other stake-holders, as well as by the circumstances within which the activity takes place. The experiential components of user experience include user's impressions and reactions related to the system, the tangible outcome of system use, and the impacts of the system, and overall evaluative judgments. The characteristics of the user, system, the context of use and the tangible outcome can contribute to user experience.*" In the following sections, the methods and findings on mobile work context from our user experience studies in mobile news making with smartphones are presented.

4 Methods

This paper presents a synthesis of findings for mobile context of use from twelve case studies carried out in the context of mobile news making that are reported in twelve scientific publications: [7, 9, 37–46]. The twelve empirical studies were carried out to explore user experience, its components, and collaborative processes when using smartphones in mobile newsmaking. The reported findings from the studies presented in the twelve papers were categorized to the components and subcomponents of the CoU-MHCI model [10]. Two new subcomponents were created to describe themes that did not fit to the existing subcomponents. Definitions for the components of context of use were elaborated based on our findings and characteristics for the components and subcomponents are presented.

The emphasis of the research approach of the twelve case studies is qualitative with observations, interviews and focus groups as the main methods of inquiry. The emphasis on qualitative research stems from the goal of understanding the explored phenomenon and technology use in the natural context of use, aiming to find explanations and provide interpretations inductively from multiple sources of data and from multiple perspectives in order to establish patterns and themes [35]. Although the emphasis was on qualitative strand, combinations of qualitative and quantitative strands were used in most of the case studies. Mixed methods research designs provide a more comprehensive and more complete account of the area of the research and understanding of the context, enabling finding explanations for the findings, as well as augmenting the findings of one strand by the other strand [36].

Seven of the case studies were carried out as field studies, two as quasi-experiments in field conditions, two as interview studies, and one as a participatory focus group study. Field studies were chosen for the case studies when there was a possibility to gain access to studying news reporting in the mobile context of use. This enabled understanding of news making practice in context in addition to usage, experiences and requirements for mobile systems. Quasi-experiments enabled the study of user experience with news reporting tasks carried out with smartphones in the natural context of use, but using predefined reporting assignments created by the researchers, which was not possible in other studies conducted in field settings.

Seven of the twelve case studies include the usage of a mobile service client for news making in the mobile context of use. In six of the seven case studies the used client was a partly or fully functional prototype. Two of the twelve studies concentrate on reader participation in news making as a form of mobile crowdsourcing. The rest of the studies focused on professional use. Over one hundred participants participated in the studies. Majority of the participants were students of visual journalism with prior work experience in journalism to ensure experience as close to professional users as possible. On the other hand, it was not possible to use prototypes in professional's daily use with deadlines due to the possible unreliability of the prototypes. Within their journalism studies the students were reporting news in as close to authentic context of use as possible enabling us to study real news reporting situations.

A more detailed description of the methods of the twelve case studies can be found in the publications and in [31, pp. 46–59].

5 Findings on Context of Use in Mobile News Making

We categorized the findings on the factors of context of use that influence user experience in mobile news making to the five context components (temporal, task, physical, social, and technology and information context) and their subcomponents according to the CoU-MHCI model [10]. Our findings validate the model, and elaborate the definitions for its components in the case of mobile news making. In addition, our findings extend the model by two subcomponents. First, task context is extended with mobile assignment characteristics. Second, social context is extended by stakeholders, such as colleagues, editors, readers, or customers, who are not physically or virtually present when interacting with the device, but who assess the quality of the news material and reporting.

5.1 Temporal Context

Temporal context refers to the interaction and carrying out the activity with the mobile system in relation to time and it captures the nature of the activity in terms of time (adapted from [10]).

Temporal context is characterized by (1) duration - the time spent on the interaction, activity, subactivity, or task, (2) time of day, week, or year of the interaction, activity or task, (3) actions prior, simultaneously, or after the interaction with the mobile system or activity carried out with it, (4) the action's relation to time, and (5) synchronicity or asynchronicity of communication (Table 2). Time is one of the key characteristics related to news making. The work is time critical and calls for immediate publishing of breaking news or often directly from the spot of the event in mobile context of use to be competitive and relevant to the audience. This applies to professionals, reader reporters and citizen journalists alike. On the other hand, reporting in organizational context or by pro-amateurs is also carefully planned, scheduled and organized days, weeks or months ahead of known events, such as elections etc. When a surprising event occurs, it can change the plans and calls for immediate action and attention interrupting the current activity. Temporal context is therefore related to the news qualities in terms of immediacy, unexpectedness, and timeliness of news. According to described experiences by participants in our studies, the capability of the

Table 2. Summarized findings on the temporal context.

Findings related to the subcomponents	Publication(s)
Duration – the length of interaction, activity, or the event in which interaction takes place	
Time (delay, response time) to start up photo and video recording	[7, 41, 44]
Time spent on the activity, task or carrying out a sub-activity, such as recording, editing,submitting	[7, 9, 37, 38, 41–45]
Time of day, week, and year	
Deadline, schedule, or continuous deadline	[7, 37, 38, 42]
When the mobile reporter is available for locating and receiving mobile assignments	[42, 43]
Before, during and after	
Preparations for capturing, editing, and submitting	[7, 41, 44, 46]
Following up on submission, calling up the newsroom after submission to check on the success of mobile delivery	[42, 45]
The action's relation to time	
Hurried, waiting, speed, urgency, time pressure	[7, 37, 38, 41, 42, 44, 45]
The unexpectedness of events that call for action	[37, 38]
Synchronism (synchronous–asynchronous)	
Communication by phone calls, SMS, MMS, email, chat, mobile assignments	[42]

system to support the time-related needs and constraints, and the aimed news qualities related to time can have a major influence on user experience.

5.2   Task Context

Task context refers to the user's tasks and activities surrounding the interaction with a mobile system or when carrying out the activity with the system (adapted from [10]). Synthesized findings on subcomponents (multi-tasking, interruptions, task domain, and assignment characteristics) are presented in Table 3.

In our studies, multi-tasking included parallel tasks and activities, such as instances of interviewing while audio or video recording, or taking notes, for example. Mobile reporters also kept track of typed characters while writing if a specific length has been assigned for the story, as well as time, and possible deadline. When capturing photos and video footage, surrounding physical circumstances needed to be taken into account to ensure the sufficient technical quality of the footage. This may call for action from the users, such as turning on lights indoors, choosing an appropriate direction for shooting footage based on direction of natural light or taking into account the ambient noise conditions. Parallel other ongoing tasks and activities also contribute to the willingness to receive mobile assignments for reporting.

Table 3. Summarized findings on the task context.

Findings related to the subcomponents	Publication(s)
Multi-tasking – multiple parallel tasks alongside human mobile computer interaction that compete for cognitive resources	
Primary task interviewing, secondary task recording audio, photo, and video footage, or writing notes with the smartphone	[41, 44, 45]
Keeping track of the number of characters in the story while writing	[44, 45]
Keeping track of time and the deadline	[44]
Awareness of the surrounding physical conditions or constraints of the used smartphone that need to be taken into account when shooting footage (photo, video) or recording audio	[7, 39, 41, 44, 45]
Parallel tasks while receiving mobile assignments (no parallel task, during free time, when working or studying)	[42, 43]
Interruptions – events that break the user's attention from the current task to focus on the interruption temporarily	
Passers-by	[38
Interruptions by bystanders who make contact while the reporter is editing at a public location	38, 46]
The primary task is interrupted by a mobile assignment	[43]
Task domain – macro level of task context by dividing the situation of an interaction into two groups – goal-oriented (work) and action-oriented (entertainment) tasks	
Primarily goal-oriented for professionals, but can include action-oriented characteristics	[7, 37, 38, 41, 42]
Primarily action-oriented for readers, but can include goal-oriented characteristics	[9]
Assignment characteristics (added sub-component)	
The type of assignment or reporting to be carried out or the content asked for and attributes of content (no. of characters in text, length of audio and video footage, count of photos, requested quality, special requests like camera angles)	[42, 43]
Monetary incentive, incentive mechanism	[7, 9, 43]
Voluntariness of carrying out the task	[9]
Autonomy in reporting	[42]
No. of receivers	[42]
The creativity needed or allowed	[42]
The needed skills and equipment	[42]

Interruptions are one of the important subcomponents of the task context as they influence the activity carried out. As the mobile reporters typically work in public spaces, there may be interruptions due to passers-by, or bystanders may take contact and talk to the mobile reporter and interrupt the task being carried out.

On macro-level the task context is suggested to be divided to goal-oriented tasks in work related use and action-oriented tasks for entertainment [10]. In mobile news making, for professionals the tasks are primarily set by the organization or customer, but secondarily, the tasks may include action-oriented elements that could be related to concepts such as flow and enjoyment of the activity as such. For reader reporters participating to news making the enjoyment of the activity may be the primary motivation to participate. Participation of readers may, however, also include elements related to goal-oriented activity and motivations that professionals have or combinations of motivations as our later studies in using crowdsourcing in mobile news making indicate. The goal-oriented task setting may also apply to crowdsourcing, if the participation is primarily motivated by monetary benefit and has no hobbyist or enjoyment, or other motivational element.

The assignment characteristics, whether delivered as mobile assignments to the smartphone, e.g., via specific applications, email, or SMS messages, or received more traditionally, were added as a new subcomponent. Assignment characteristics frame the properties of the task context, and was addressed in our studies especially when studying use of mobile assignment delivery, carrying them out, and responding to them, but also in our other studies. Identified assignment characteristics include the types of assignment, reporting, and content or its attributes, the perceived voluntariness of undertaking and carrying out the assignment, the perceived and expressed extent of autonomy and creativity, needed skills or equipment as well as the incentives. Assignment characteristics can also contribute to user experience by moderating the willingness to undertake tasks and be motivated by the goal and activity.

5.3 Physical Context

Physical context refers to apparent features or physically sensed circumstances while interacting with the system or carrying out the activity with it (adapted from [10]). Its components include (1) spatial location, functional place and space, (2) sensed environmental attributes, (3) movements or mobility, and (4) artefacts (Table 4).

Mobile reporters work in multiple workplaces and dynamic locations. The work is often carried out in public spaces, either outside or inside. Stationary workplaces, which can be called third workplaces [3], include cafés, or waiting rooms, for example. Typical mobile workplaces are also trains, cars or airplanes, where planning the upcoming reporting or editing the materials can be carried out. The proximity of the reporting spot to the reporter's current location as well as the precision of locating mobile reporters can contribute to participation preferences in case of assignment-based processes. The sensed environmental attributes such as lighting, temperature and ambient noise can contribute to carrying out the activity and influence the capturing of photos and video footage. The quality of the outcome can then be influenced by the combination of the system characteristics and environmental attributes contributing to user experience, for example. Furthermore, the perceived characteristics and verbal descriptions of the area, location, or country (such as totalitarian, safe, shady) were found to be related to perceived privacy and safety issues and willingness to share location information, when studying locating reporters and location-based assignments.

Physical context is also characterized by movement of the user's body while interacting with the system. User may be sitting or standing while writing, capturing

Table 4. Summarized findings on the physical context.

Findings related to sub-components	Publication (s)
Spatial location, functional place and space – the aspects of location and material characteristics of location, functional space and in distance participation	
Geographical location (vicinity or distance)	[38, 42–45]
Third workplaces – cafés, hallways, canteens, waiting halls etc.	[37, 38, 44, 45]
The precision of locating mobile reporters	[42, 43]
Attributes related to the area, location or country such as shady, totalitarian, unacceptable place, safe, dangerous	[42, 43]
Sensed environmental attributes	
Light, lighting	[38, 41, 44, 45]
Temperature	[38]
Ambient noise, sounds	[38, 44, 45]
Movements and mobility – the position and motion of the user's body, the mobility of the user and the motion of the user's physical and functional environment	
Sitting while editing, reaching out to record footage	[38, 41]
Placement of artefacts in relation to the user's body (e.g. on the knee, on a table, on a sofa)	[38, 44]
Working while commuting	[7]
Artefacts – physical objects that surround a human-mobile computer interaction	
Proximity of artefacts (e.g. a notebook)	[44]
Chairs, sofas, tables	[38, 44]

photos or video footage, or kneeling or reaching out while using the system for capturing photo or video footage. The tools may be placed on the user's body such as on the lap or attached to arm, or placed on surrounding objects, such as on a table or sofa. Furthermore, smartphones were in some instances attached to surrounding other objects, such as a book, a bike or a window for photo or video capture enabling new ways of content capture and reporting.

5.4   Social Context

Social context refers to other persons present physically or virtually while interacting with the system or using it for the activity, or to other stakeholders of the activity who perceive and assess its outcome (adapted from [10]). Subcomponents include (1) persons present in the situation, (2) stakeholders not physically or virtually present, and (3) culture (Table 5).

Persons physically present while interacting can include interviewees, bystanders, and own colleagues or peers of the mobile reporter. Newsroom staff or a colleague

Table 5. Summarized findings on the social context.

Findings related to subcomponents	Publication (s)
The persons present in the situation classified to self, group, organization or public, physically or virtually present.	
Interviewees, bystanders, peers (colleagues) present while interacting with the smartphone-based system	[37, 38, 39]
Stakeholders not physically or virtually present while user interacts with the device or carries out the activity to produce an outcome (**added sub-component**)	
Editors, colleagues in the newsroom or from another newsroom, customers, audience/readers who asses the quality of the produced material or news (stories)	[7, 37, 46]
Culture – The macro level of social context including the values, norms, and attitudes of a certain culture, such as the work and organizational culture	
Journalistic and news values, norms etc.	[7, 37, 45]
Profession related values, identity, ideal, norms etc.	[7, 37]

working elsewhere in the field can be virtually present using synchronous (e.g. video or online calls) or asynchronous means of communication (instant messaging or social media services). Other stakeholders may also not be physically present, such as free-lancer's customers or the audience that consumes the news. The opinions and anticipated impressions and expectations of persons present or of other stakeholders on the used mobile system and the outcome of its usage can influence the user experience of a mobile reporter. The social acceptance of the used tool is important for users and it may differ based on the user group. Social acceptance may also change over time. What is considered a low-quality system, odd, and even shameful at first, may become part of everyday work practice within a few years as technology matures and is adopted to use providing new opportunities and value for the users as well as audience in case of news reporting. Furthermore, culture and practice of journalism and participatory journalism or the culture of the organization in question incorporate values, norms and ideals, that can as a subcomponent contribute to user experience.

5.5   Technology and Information Context

Technology and information context refers to the relation of other relevant systems and services to the user's interaction or activity with the mobile system. It includes as subcomponents (1) other systems and services, (2) interoperability between and across devices, and (3) informational artefacts (Table 6).

In case of journalism, other systems or services can include external components to the core mobile system, such as microphones, keyboards, and displays, or alternatively, mobile applications or services that can be used for mobile journalism. It also includes the wireless network with its attributes as well as the interoperativity of systems in transferring data or material from one device to another or to the editorial system. Paper notebooks with hand-written information on preparations, interview questions, and

Table 6. Summarized findings on the technology and information context.

Findings related to subcomponents	Publication (s)
Other systems and services – the device, applications and the network related to the user's system or service (note: in this study components external to the smartphone or installed after purchase on the smartphone)	
External components of a smartphone-based system, such as microphones and keyboards.	[38, 41, 44, 46]
Mobile journalism related applications	[7, 9, 37, 41, 42]
The wireless network and related attributes (availability, reliability, speed, interference)	[7, 37, 38, 41]
Interoperability between and across devices	
Transferring data from one device to another or material delivered from the mobile system to the editorial system	[44, 45, 46]
Informational artefacts and access to other artefacts that contain relevant information	
Notebooks	[7, 9, 37, 38]
Access to information via the Internet	[7]

interviewee's quotes as well as plans for editing video footage can still be important informational artefacts for mobile reporters. In addition, smartphones enable, with the available connectivity to the Internet, access to open information or organization's archives, for example. The multipart and complex systems form ecosystems of devices and services that can contribute to user experience when used in mobile newsmaking.

5.6 Properties of the Mobile Context Components in Mobile News Making

The model for context of use for mobile HCI, the CoU-MHCI model [10], describes four properties for context components. These properties are (1) the level of magnitude varying from micro to macro, (2) the level of dynamism varying from static to dynamic, (3) the patterns varying from rythmic to random, and (4) typical combinations of context components [10]. These are exemplified next in case of mobile news making.

The findings on the **level of magnitude** for the five context components in mobile news making can be mapped to three levels: macro-, meso-, and micro-level (see for levels of analysis [47]). Macro-level exemplified for social context refers to the context of news journalism with its journalistic standards, values, practices, ethical codes and goals as well as its role in the society and the community it is reporting to. Meso-level refers in case of social context to the organization, community of practice or peer group. Micro-level context of use is the individual level, referring to the situation and its characteristics when a mobile reporter is interacting with the system and using it while carrying out the activity of news making. All levels can contribute to user experience of a mobile reporter, by framing goals, requirements, possibilities, or constraints for mobile news making.

The **level of dynamism varies from static to dynamic** in the components of context of use in mobile news making. Activity within which the interaction with the mobile system occurs may be hurried or waiting. Breaking news bring urgency to news making, calling for reporting and publishing immediately from the spot of the event and changing the rhythm on the go. To be able to "capture the moment" needs fast action and undelayed recording of photo and video footage. Fast movement, changes in the environmental conditions, such as lighting and ambient noise, may need attention and adjustment when shooting of photo and video footage. The network availability and speed of connection may vary depending on the crowdedness of the area or movement of the mobile reporter. Dynamism in the context of use needs to be supported by the mobile system and its features and functionalities.

The **patterns in mobile news making can have a regular rhythm, or occur randomly**. A regular workday with a priori set plan and deadlines brings regularity to the workdays of professionals. As random events and happenings worthy of news reporting, such as breaking news about a big natural catastrophe or accident, unfold, the regular schedule breaks. In our studies we also noticed, that there are certain types of news stories, that are dependent on the time of year or have some other rhythm based on the public holidays, or national or local elections, for example. The locations of mobile news making and types of stories can also have patterns, like focusing on local issues from a certain area at a certain time of the week or month. Randomly happening unexpected events, and on the spot reporting seem to fit the capabilities and strengths of smartphone-based systems in news making.

Finally, **typical combinations of context components** with properties can be identified for mobile news making. Based on our observations, the combinations typically include all five context components, but their importance and emphasis can vary depending on the situation. The situation described by the combination of circumstances can influence the requirements and needs of a mobile user and therefore contribute to user experience in a particular situation.

6 Conclusions

Findings related to five components of context of use (temporal, task, physical, social and technology and information context) with a total of nineteen subcomponents were reported in case of mobile news making. Two subcomponents were added to the original CoU-MHCI model [10]. Task context was extended with assignment characteristics, and social context by stakeholders who are not physically or virtually present when interacting with the device, but who assess the quality of the news material and reporting. Situation as circumstances described by a combination of components, subcomponents and properties of context of use, can have significance for the users that influences their evaluation of the system quality and its appropriateness to use. The findings illustrate context of use related components and characteristics that can influence user experience in the field of mobile news making. Further studies could address the context related characteristics in other work domains to test and extend the model. The context model and presented findings can also be used as a framework in planning of studies, data collection, and measurement of context related aspects.

References

1. Roto, V.: Web browsing on mobile phones.– Characteristics of user experience. Doctoral dissertation. TKK Dissertations 49, Helsinki University of Technology (2006)
2. Vartiainen, M., Hyrkkänen, U.: Changing requirements and mental workload factors in mobile multi-locational work. New Technol. Work Employ. 25(2), 117–235 (2010)
3. Vartiainen, M.: Mobile virtual work – concepts, outcomes and challenges. In: Andriessen, J. H.E., Vartiainen, M.'(eds.) Mobile Virtual Work: A New Paradigm?, pp. 267–288. Springer, Heidelberg (2006)
4. Reich, Z.: The process model of news initiative. Journalism Stud. 7(4), 497–514 (2006)
5. Bradshaw, P.: Model for a 21st century newsroom – redux. How digitization has changed news organisations in a multiplatform world. Leanpub. (2012). https://leanpub.com/s/0JmP8wqPD40vEznX1aNa5r.pdf
6. Andriessen, E., Vartiainen, M.: Emerging mobile virtual work. In: Andriessen, J.H.E., Vartiainen, M. (eds.) Mobile Virtual Work: A New Paradigm?, pp. 3–12. Springer, Heidelberg. (2006)
7. Väätäjä, H.: Mobile work efficiency: balancing between benefits, costs and sacrifices. Int. J. Mob. Hum. Comput. Interact. 4(2), 67–87 (2012)
8. Ross, J., Irani, L., Silberman, M.S., Zaldivar, A., Tomlinson, B.: Who are the crowdworkers?: shifting demographics in mechanical turk. In: Proceedings of the CHI EA 2010, pp. 2863–2872. ACM (2010)
9. Väätäjä, H., Vainio, T., Sirkkunen, E., Salo, K.: Crowdsourced news reporting: supporting news content creation with mobile phones. In: Proceedings of the MobileHCI 2011, pp. 435–444. ACM (2011)
10. Jumisko-Pyykkö, S., Vainio, T.: Framing the context of use for mobile HCI. Int. J. Mob. Hum. Comput. Interact. (IJMHCI) 2(4), 1–28 (2010)
11. Forsberg, K.: Navigating in the NewsSpace. In: Proceedings of the CSCWD 1999, pp. 329–336 (1999)
12. Bergstrand, F., Landgren, J.: Visual reporting in time-critical work: Exploring video use in emergency response. In: Proceedings of the MobileHCI 2011, pp. 415–424. ACM (2011)
13. Kristoffersen, S., Ljungberg, F.: "Making place" to make IT work: empirical explorations of HCI for mobile CSCW. In: Proceedings of the International ACM SIGGROUP Conference on Supporting Group Work, pp. 276–285. ACM (1999)
14. Straus, S.G., Bikson, T.K., Balkovich, E., Pane, J.F.: Mobile technology and action teams: assessing BlackBerry use in law enforcement units. CSCW 19(1), 45–71 (2010)
15. Fagrell H., Forsberg, K., Sanneblad, J.: FieldWise: a mobile knowledge management architecture. In: Proceedings of the CSCW 2000, pp. 211–220. ACM (2000)
16. Yuan, Y., Zheng, W. 2009. Mobile task characteristics and the needs for mobile work support: a comparison between mobile knowledge workers and field workers. In: Eighth International Conference on Mobile Business, ICMB 2009, pp. 7–11, IEEE (2009)
17. Gebauer, J.: User requirements of mobile technology: a summary of research results. Inf. Knowl. Syst. Manage. 7(1), 101–119 (2008)
18. Gebauer, J., Shaw, M.J., Gribbins, M.L.: Task-technology fit for mobile information systems. J. Inf. Technol. 25(3), 259–272 (2010)

19. Perry, M., O'hara, K., Sellen, A., Brown, B., Harper, R.: Dealing with mobility: understanding access anytime, anywhere. ACM TOCHI 8(4), 323–347 (2001)
20. Karlson, A.K., Iqbal, S.T., Meyers, B., Ramos, G., Lee, K., Tang, J.C.: Mobile taskflow in context: a screenshot study of smartphone usage. In: Proceedings of the CHI 2010, pp. 2009–2018. ACM (2010)
21. Chatterjee, S., Chakraborty, S., Sarker, S., Sarker, S., Lau, F.Y.: Examining the success factors for mobile work in healthcare: a deductive study. Decis. Support Syst. 46(3), 620–633 (2009)
22. Streefkerk, J.W., Van Ench-Bussemakers, M.P., Neerincx, M.A.: Balancing costs and benefits of automated task allocation in mobile surveillance. In: Proceedings of the 28th Annual European Conference on Cognitive Ergonomics (ECCE 2010), pp. 99–106, ACM (2010)
23. Sadler, K., Robertson, T., Kan, M.: It's always there, it's always on: Australian freelancer's management of availability using mobile technologies. In: Proceedings of the 8th conference on Human-computer interaction with mobile devices and services, pp. 49–52. ACM (2006)
24. Pascoe, J., Ryan, N., Morse, D.: Using while moving: HCI issues in fieldwork environments. ACM Trans. Comput.-Hum. Interact. (TOCHI) 7(3), 417–437 (2000)
25. Yuan, Y., Archer, N., Connelly, C.E., Zheng, W.: Identifying the ideal fit between mobile work and mobile work support. Inf. Manage. 47(3), 125–137 (2010)
26. Sørensen, C., Gibson, D.: Ubiquitous visions and opaque realities: professionals talking about mobile technologies. INFO: J. Policy Regul. Strategy Telecommun. Inf. Media 6(3), 188–196 (2004)
27. Oulasvirta, A., Tamminen, S., Roto, V., Kuorelahti, J.: Interaction in 4-second bursts: the fragmented nature of attentional resources in mobile HCI. In: Proceedings of the CHI 2005, 919–928. ACM (2005)
28. Jumisko-Pyykkö, S., Utriainen, T.: A hybrid method for quality evaluation in the context of use for mobile (3D) television. Multimed. Tools Appl. 55(2), 185–225 (2011)
29. Lin, M., Goldman, R., Price, K.J., Sears, A., Jacko, J.: How do people tap when walking? an empirical investigation of nomadic data entry. Int. J. Hum Comput Stud. 65(9), 759–769 (2007)
30. Hassenzahl, M., Tractinsky, N.: User experience – a research agenda. Behav. Inf. Technol. 25(2), 91–97 (2006)
31. Väätäjä, H.: Framing the user experience in mobile newsmaking with smartphones. Doctoral dissertation, Tampere University of Technology, Publication 1196 (2014). http://URN.fi/URN:ISBN:978-952-15-3270-2
32. Itule, B.D., Anderson, D.A.: News Writing and Reporting for Today's Media. McGraw-Hill, New York (2007)
33. Sissons, H.: Practical Journalism: How to Write News. SAGE, London (2006)
34. Harcup, T.: Journalism: Principles and practice, 2nd edn. SAGE, London (2009)
35. Creswell, J.W., Plano Clark, V.L.: Designing and Conducting Mixed Methods Research. SAGE, Thousand Oaks (2007)
36. Bryman, A.: Why do researchers integrate/combine/mesh/blend/mix/merge/fuse quantitative and qualitative research? In: Bergman, M.M. (ed.) Advances in Mixed Methods Research, pp. 87–100. SAGE, London (2008)
37. Väätäjä, H. User experience evaluation criteria for mobile news making technology: findings from a case study. In: Proceedings of the OZCHI 2010, pp. 152–159. ACM (2010)
38. Wigelius, H., Väätäjä, H.: Dimensions of context affecting user experience in mobile work. In: Gross, T., Gulliksen, J., Kotzé, P., Oestreicher, L., Palanque, P., Prates, R.O., Winckler, M. (eds.) INTERACT 2009. LNCS, vol. 5727, pp. 604–617. Springer, Heidelberg (2009)

39. Väätäjä, H., Koponen, T., Roto, V.: Developing practical tools for user experience evaluation: a case from mobile news journalism. In: Proceedings of the ECCE 2009. VTT, pp. 240–247 (2009)
40. Väätäjä, H.: User experience of smart phones in mobile journalism: early findings on influence of professional role. In: Proceedings of the OZCHI 2010, pp. 1–4. ACM (2010)
41. Väätäjä, H. Männistö, A.A.: Bottlenecks, usability issues and development needs in creating and delivering news videos with smart phones. In: Proceedings of the MoViD 2010, pp. 45–50. ACM (2010)
42. Väätäjä, H. Egglestone, P.: Briefing news reporting with mobile assignments: perceptions, needs and challenges. In: Proceedings of the CSCW 2012, pp. 485–494. ACM (2012)
43. Väätäjä, H., Vainio, T. Sirkkunen, E.: Location-based crowdsourcing of hyperlocal news: dimensions of participation preferences. In: Proceedings of the GROUP 2012, pp. 85–94. ACM (2012)
44. Jokela, T., Väätäjä, H., Koponen, T.: Mobile Journalist Toolkit: a field study on producing news articles with a mobile device. In: Proceedings of the MindTrek 2009, pp. 45–52. ACM (2009)
45. Koponen, T., Väätäjä, H.: Early adopters' experiences of using mobile multimedia phones in news journalism. In: Proceedings of the ECCE 2009, VTT, 4 pp. (2009)
46. Väätäjä, H., Männistö, A., Vainio, T., Jokela, T.: Understanding user experience to support learning for mobile journalist's work. In: Guy, R. (ed.) The Evolution of Mobile Teaching and Learning. Informing Science Press, pp. 177–210 (2009). https://books.google.fi/books?isbn=1932886141
47. Yurdusev, A.N.: 'Level of analysis' and 'unit of analysis': a case for distinction. Millennium-J. Int. Stud. 22(1), 77–88 (1993)

From Transactions to Relationships: Making Sense of User-Centered Perspectives in Large Technology-Intensive Companies

Petra Björndal[1,2(✉)], Elina Eriksson[2], and Henrik Artman[2]

[1] ABB Corporate Research, Västerås, Sweden
Petra.bjorndal@se.abb.com
[2] KTH Royal Institute of Technology, Stockholm, Sweden
{elina,artman}@kth.se

Abstract. In this paper we analyze interviews from four technology-intensive companies, focused on service and service development. All companies have during the last two decades introduced interaction design units, and the corporations were selected due to their interest in also expanding the service share of their business. This service shift has been a top-down initiative. However in only two companies, the initiatives have led to the establishment of enterprise wide service development processes, and in the other two companies, the service development is more ad hoc. It is argued that even if interaction design has close theoretical relation to service design such combination has so far been limited. We discuss the shift from product to service view of the offerings within these companies, and relate this to user-centered perspectives. We argue there is a window of opportunity within technology-intensive and engineering focused industries to include user-centered design when formalizing service development.

Keywords: User-centered design · Service design · Service development · Usability · Technology intensive companies

1 Introduction

Today, technology-intensive product manufacturers go through a shift that addresses fundamental parts of their economy, when business models go from transaction based to relationship based. This transition process is called servitization and create organizational, structural as well as process challenges [1]. To some degree, the servitization process seems almost inevitable for the technology intensive product manufacturing companies, and in management literature, powerful arguments are put forward to integrate service into their core offerings along three lines, economic arguments, customer demands and competitiveness (ibid.). Taking a service perspective put a focus on how the processes are deployed and for whom, rather than focusing on the technology in itself. One might say that service has a focus centered on the experience and fluency relative the business customer. This resembles in a sense imperatives of user centered design and interaction design where the user and user experience are in focus. Put into

© IFIP International Federation for Information Processing 2015
J. Abdelnour-Nocera et al. (Eds.): HWID 2015, IFIP AICT 468, pp. 114–124, 2015.
DOI: 10.1007/978-3-319-27048-7_8

comparison, the concurrent drive for service in part mirror how businesses adopted and incorporated the user centered design (UCD) and usability movement. The UCD and usability movement started academically as early as 1940's but it was through the extended use of computers in industry during the 1980's and forward that made companies employ usability experts. Today larger companies often have at least smaller units with UCD and interaction designers. The process of introducing UCD and usability departments in companies has been slow, in most cases bottom-up and customer demanded [2]. This UCD shift has been playing out differently in different domains. The engineering heavy industries, well-grounded in the industrialization, have put much pride in their technology and few engineering companies have until recently been advertising their products as user friendly or with similar connotations. Instead the excellence of their technology has been focused on the product; the technology itself.

While UCD and interaction design brings focus to user needs and task decomposition relative computerization, service offerings put focus on a higher level of experience which include all forms of aspects relative the business that the industries are offering. Neither UCD nor service development ignores or diminish the technological part, but both put more emphasis on aspects which more or less presuppose that the backend of the technology is there and is (excellently) functional. It is interesting to compare such perspective shifts in general but specifically it is interesting to see if and how the two perspective shifts can be combined.

This work explores the view on service and service development among people working in-house in four global industrial companies and is based on interviews and observations. With help of the empirical material we discuss central concepts in UCD and compare it to the ongoing perspective shift in these companies.

2 Background

The companies within which we have done interviews, are industrial and technology-intensive. However, the focus of the technology is to solve a particular problem in a certain setting and to center technology around certain contexts implicitly include an understanding of a person that use the technology. Below we will present two different approaches which explicitly focuses on this addressed person.

2.1 Evolving User-Centered Approaches

Although human-computer interaction (HCI) is a relatively young research field it has undergone rapid changes and new sub areas have emerged in a fast pace. The perspectives within the field has evolved and is reflected in various user focused practices. HCI has it origin in the disciplines ergonomics and human factors, which are experimental approaches and treats the interaction as an isolated phenomenon. The focus is the machine performance and the unit of analysis is user actions of one person in front of a display. Human factors is criticized for isolating actions from the complex context in which they take place [3].

As a result of the increase in number of computers in working life, demands for ease of use emerged as well as for practical, not so costly, methods to develop usable systems.

Usability emerged as a topic and in the end of the 1980's the user-centered approach evolved as an emphasis for the designer to focus more on the user and to give users an active role [4]. Usability was defined by an international standard as "The extent to which a product can be used by specified users to achieve specified goals with effectiveness, efficiency and satisfaction in a specified context of use" [5]. Furthermore, the computer supported computer work (CSCW) research community grew out of the need to extend the user concept into involving groups of users as well as a multitude of computers. Further on, the technical evolution of a networked society resulted in new challenges and concerns. Earlier clear boundaries between work and leisure have become vague and the significance of the physical location has been altered. Bødker points to the need in HCI to extend the view of context to also include settings outside the physical work-place and she outlines new interests in culture, emotion and experience growing from the shift from always designing purposeful and rational solutions [8]. Such perspectives on HCI have been coined interaction design which have a more design oriented, in contrast to analytical, view on HCI and UCD.

2.2 Evolving Marketing Approaches

Studies of service development started as early as in the 70's marketing research [9], and the evolvement of this subject has mainly been done within the marketing and management disciplines. Service marketing has a history of breaking out of marketing research, i.e. the goods marketing perspective, and has thus reinforced the differences between service and goods to justify the sub discipline.

In the 2000's new arguments was formulated on how to describe and conceptualize service. Vargo and Lusch presented their service dominant logic describing service in a value creation perspective [10]. They are arguing for an interpretation of value as "value in use" contrarily "value in exchange". They defined business processes as service and argue to not distinguish goods and service, instead goods are means for service delivery. A central theme in their arguments is that customers are integrating knowledge and capabilities with the service provider's personnel and artifacts in a co-creation of value. This way of describing value has changed how market research characterizes customers, from passive to active co-creators, and puts an emphasis on the importance of involving customers in the development process [11]. So far, the discussion in market research has been on a conceptual level, with little result on how to put these ideas into practice [12].

2.3 Where the Strands Meet

Branching out from the HCI field in the 2000's, service design became a new interdisciplinary movement with a root in design thinking [13]. It was based primarily on two drivers; firstly the growing service sector supported by experience focused and knowledge-intensive solutions, and secondly initiatives in user-centered disciplines where people recognized the benefit of combining user-centered practices with service development and innovation. For example, Holmlid discusses how service design can help to open up the earlier sometimes impeding focus on computer mediation and the computer as a tool perspective in HCI [14]. The argument is that this movement can give complementing views to earlier approaches, using multiple channels and a diversity in possible ways to create user value. Wetter-Edman has researched the contribution of design practice and design theory in realizing the service dominant logic ideas [15, 16]. She shows how user-centered methods are complementary for user involvement and co-creation and can open up new perspectives on value. She also shows that the valuable role of the designer as an interpreter and intermediator between customer and company, is lacking in marketing research approaches. The possible connection between user-centered approaches and service development points towards positive future concurrence.

Since the implementation of user-centered methods has been slow and gained relatively little impact in industrial product development, we approached service practitioners within these companies. These service practitioners do not always have an outspoken task to realize their respective organizations demand on an increased share of service. With an underlying interest in seeing where user-centered perspectives can meet service development, we aimed to investigate how these practitioners talk about service, how they perceive their role and how the servitization process has been played out within these companies.

3   Method

The material for this paper has been collected from four large international companies selling business to business solutions in different domains, here denoted company A, B, C and D. All four companies are global, with a history in traditional engineering fields, and they all have operations in at least Africa, America, Asia, and Europe and more than 35 000 employees each worldwide. At company A, 7 interviews were conducted, labeled 1:A to 7:A. To further broaden the picture, 5 additional interviews were done with representatives from company B, C and D, i.e. 8: B, 9:B, 10:C, 11:C, and 12:D. The sample of interviewees have been chosen in consultation with contact persons with a good knowledge of their companies view on service, and where based on two criteria. (1) perceived long experience of service delivery/development within the company and (2) some kind of responsibility in regard to this. The 12 semi-structured interviews took place between April 2013 and June 2013.

All interviewees had some kind of management role; concerning projects, methods and/or personnel. 9 out of 12 worked close to or in relatively close connection to customers. Two worked with technical development enabling service delivery, and one worked on a strategic level. 11 out of 12 had an engineering background, and one had training in service management. One of the persons mentioned knowledge of UCD. The interviews took around one hour each, and 14.5 h of recorded material were transcribed verbatim. 7 of the interviews were done in Swedish and 5 in English. The original Swedish quotes were translated to English by the authors. Moreover, to gather more information, 3 on-site observations were conducted in company A. The observations were focused on delivering value to customers; two cases of remote service and onsite service delivery. Additional material was also collected from respective companies' web site.

The transcribed material was collected in Atlas.ti, a common qualitative data analysis software. Furthermore the data analysis were made primarily by the first author, using techniques from grounded theory, specifically inspired by the constructivist grounded theory approach described by Charmaz [17]. During the initial coding the transcribed material was worked through in detail, followed by a more focused coding phase were some key issues was followed up and further explored. These key issues formed emerging themes that were in an iterative process, revisited and refined, together with the field material and information from the web sites.

4   Results and Analysis

In this section we will both recount what status service development have in these four companies and contrast service development with user-centered design and usability through some key concepts.

4.1   Service Status in the Studied Companies

The companies studied for this paper are all mainly technology-intensive organizations with a prevailing engineering culture and have all a long tradition of developing and selling products, where providing spare parts for the products have been their main service business. In line with this prevailing engineering attitude, the format and the specifications of the products produced becomes noticeably important. This is reflected in the organizational structure where different parts of the organizations are dealing with specific product families. When service packages are created, our interviewees explained that these are often seen as separate components added on to the products. In the same vein, service departments have been added as isolated entities into the existing organization. Budgets, tools, and resources often follow these organizational boundaries, which contribute to silo thinking and complicate collaboration between different departments.

Frequently, you find several pieces of equipment from the same producing company at one customer site, but with limited coordination between the departments delivering these products or service. Our interviewees explain that there is a tension between adding service components onto existing products, and by so reinforce the silos, and the wish to solve the customer's problem regardless whether it is a motor or a robot that stopped the production for the customer. This is similar to what Winter et al. have observed, where the organizational set up created conflicts of interest between departments, and giving cause to breakdowns in communication [2]. Hence, there are budding service initiatives within the studied companies, but their organizational belonging is still under construction.

4.2   Top Down Incentives for Service

Within all the studied companies, the top management have emphasized the importance of increasing the percentages of revenues coming from service which is manifested e.g.

in strategies and policies. Hence, these companies are compelling examples of the current servitization process as exemplified by the following quote from company C: *"As times goes on, the greater scope service will get, I'm quite sure [...] it is more and more important you have value-added service. There is probably a stated goal [...] we should have a certain proportion of service. We will be more service oriented as a company" [10:C].*

However, these top down encouraged initiatives does not necessarily mean there is a widespread knowledge about service and service development within the companies we have studied. Hence there is a frustration among people working with service, they are encouraged, or even prompted to develop service revenue, but they seem to be lacking clear goals on what this would be as in the following quote: *"The closest they [the middle management] has come to service may be that they have purchased a TV subscription as a service, they have poor understanding of what service is all about, so now when they get this directive from the top management, 'now, work with service', of course, they do not know what to do" [11:C].*

Not only is there a lack of knowledge, our interviewees also express a concern that support for those supposed to implement the service initiatives are also largely lacking: *"they expect the most and put the least in the service organization" [7:A].*

Service in these organizations could be more than something on top of their products, it could include also the knowledge base of what and how the products may provide value in specific contexts. Still as the quotes above indicate this has not yet become a central position of their business-possibly a consequence of a firm grounding in a product focused mindset. The top-management initiatives have not been that thoroughly grounded in the practices of the organization and their employees which may hinder the servitization process.

4.3 Service Development

All of the studied companies had standardized and clear product development processes, but only two of the organizations had at the time for the interviews defined the processes for service development. Some of the interviewees from companies with defined service development processes, describes that it is difficult to diffuse the process: *"the difficulty that I've seen anyway, is how we roll out the stuff and get this to work practically out there" [10:C].*

Worth noting is that despite there being defined processes in two of the companies, most services in all four organizations were actually developed ad-hoc. As a consequence of this, service is developed in different ways in different parts of the organization, and the resulting solutions are often not coordinated. There are initiatives to mitigate this problem and to create company-wide offerings out of these ad hoc solutions, as explained in this quote: *"the service is created out there, sold and delivered a couple of times before it is washed off a little before it is introduced into the global portfolio" [8:B].*

Reports of the ad-hoc development process are mixed, mentioning both positive as well as negative aspects. There is a pride in the solutions that have been made, but at the same time people feel out of control and without any overview, as exemplified in the following quote: *"there is a mentality to fix things, an entrepreneurship, and this has created very good stuff, what is worse then is that you might not know what you have done, and what opportunities are available"* [1:A].

At this point in time it is difficult to elaborate on the role of a service process in these companies since they are in two cases nonexistent and in the other two cases not widely spread. What can be deduced though is that the interviewees express a wish to have a more structured way of working.

4.4   Use of the Concept Service

The word service, is not well-defined and agreed upon in these organizations. Even if the interviewees worked with service in their daily work, they had difficulties explaining the concept. This was common in all companies, the interviewees expressed a confusion about what other people working in the same organization meant by service, as indicated by these two quotes: *"it is all context dependent, of course, talking internal [A] how I see it, it [service] is very wide and very unclear"* [6:A], *"the service concept is so unclear [...] it means that there are lots of people who develop this who does not understand it is service they develop"* [12:D].

Also the very different categories of service can complicate the communication, especially since maintenance and spare parts are viewed by many as being equal to service in this context. As of today service in these companies can cover for example; agreements, training, spare parts, software, maintenance, consulting, analyzes and financing. This complicate things as this interviewee explains: *"if you talk to people, they will mix all those things together [...] if you talk to some people, they talk about the services needed to get the system going, a bunch of people see services to operate [x], so it is a confusing picture to people"* [9:B].

From the interviews, it is clear that the term service must be defined and grounded in the organization, in order for the service development to work satisfactorily.

4.5   The Customer in Focus

Traditionally, service in these companies has meant maintenance and spare parts tightly coupled to particular products but the perspective oriented towards more product transcended knowledge has begun to gain some support. The former is firmly based on a technological orientation, where the product has a central role, while the latter case is focusing more on what the customer wants to be done, more or less independent of what products might be used. These two views have different implications as the former will focus on one form of equipment while the latter will focus on how different equipment can be combined and integrated in order to fulfill a certain objective. Our interviewees talk about their offerings in terms of a whole, with a certain goal to make the clients work process work smoothly and it is this system that delivers the value for the receiver: *"We handle both our own products that can be installed there and our competitors, we handle maintenance of automation products, systems, electrical equipment, mechanical equipment and everything else, so we take total responsibility for the maintenance. For a production site [...] we have a common goal together with the client"* [4:A].

This perspective puts the customer in the center, and this is a strength the interviewees point to, the tradition of long term relationships to the customers. Previously this has been due to the long life time, sometimes decades, of the equipment they are selling. However, the use of the term customer by the interviewees can be problematic to interpret as a customer is not necessarily the same person as a user [5]. The ISO definition of a user is "a person who interacts with the product" [6], and a customer "organization or person that receives a product or service" [7]. In the transcribed material the term customer is used much more frequently compared to user (512 times, vs. 12 times).

Although some interviewees seems to employ customer and user as synonyms, *"We have a large group of customers that is not a homogeneous group, to truly understand the essence of what they need to achieve, and for us to be able to find something that fits quite a few, not all, but many" [6:C].*

Others show awareness of this problem *"First, there are different types of customers, we start with that, one of the most important things is to actually understanding who the customer is, as the concept of customer is very very difficult, so we have even begun to talk about customers and end users, as two different" [12:D].*

Consequently, a shift towards services seem to put the customer, and perhaps the user, more readily in mind in the developers of services. Since the users are the main focus within an HCI perspective this is an interesting correspondence between service and UCD.

4.6 Service Over Time

An important aspect shared between HCI and service development is that the value of the result is created over time. In contrast to a product perspective where the product is finite and defined at the very moment of construction, both a HCI and service perspective presuppose a user who becomes acquainted with the system and becomes more skilled over time. Both HCI and service perspectives values long relations and the learning process which the users or customers provides. When it comes to services, this long relationship also involves a continuous development as in this quote: *"One of the challenges for us is to find other service opportunities that enables us to have a more continuous contact with the customer, so we can have that ongoing relationship, and [remote] services are very good, very good area that makes sure we have a more continuous contact with those who actually use the services, first we get to know our customers better, they can tell you continuously what are the problems, it becomes a more natural contact with them because they understand, well they can actually help me with something" [12:D].*

It even seems like the service perspective, at least from our interviewees point of view, naturally includes a life-cycle awareness: *"you need a life-cycle view, you can not only have development because then you miss the big maintenance an end of life part of service" [8:B].*

This would imply that at least for these interviewees, a within the HCI field sought after perspective of longevity comes naturally when working with services and service development.

5 Discussion

This paper has elaborated on results from interviews with people working with service at four global technology-intensive companies. The interviews showed that the increased focus on service is an initiative from top management, but also that new ways of thinking is hard to implement. This is due to, on one hand, that the product oriented view reinforces a silos structure of the organization, while services to some degree need to transcend several departments, and on the other hand, service as a concept has so far been ill-defined and can connote different things. Note that both size of the company and the market probably is of importance for servitization and this analysis do not claim to inform the situation for smaller companies.

Furthermore, the large range of service types and the rapid technical development leads to the introduction of new types of services, e.g. software-supported services, and it also increase the confusion. What is referred to as service or product depends on your perspective, or viewpoint [19], often related to what view the company want to market.

One consequence of the concept confusion is that it makes service difficult to relate to during service development [20]. It is important that everybody involved in development has a similar idea of the service and it is likewise interpreted by all [21]. Rexfelt et al. found in an industrial context that a non-agreed upon definition about service turned it into a concept with no real meaning for the participants taking part in the studied service development project [22]. There were negative consequences for development of new service in this case.

Analytically we have scrutinized how service as a contemporary perspective is related to UCD and usability. We can see many similarities such as a focus on the client's needs and goals, as well as how the value of the result is created over time. However the focus on the client or customer can differ somewhat between service and UCD, since UCD as a systems development process is focusing on the actual user of a computer system. In contrast, service perspectives fluctuate between different roles with responsibility for certain processes within the recipient organization, as well as the actual user of a system or several systems. To complicate things even more, these systems might not originate from the delivering organization. Consequently, the service organization of a supplier company must then also have knowledge of the client organization and how they can be integrated in with the supplied products and services. This kind of value creation on a higher hierarchical level for the organization as a whole is lacking in definitions of usability [5], where the goal is met as long as the end-user is satisfied. Taking a service perspective on the other hand, thus makes one not only focus on the actual product, but also the value and enablement of the product for the client. A service perspective in the organization may impose more focus on the value of the reliability of the product than on the constitution of the product. Service thus is value-sensitive rather than product sensitive, interestingly such perspective have also been advocated within the UCD community [18].

The move towards an increased number of service solutions puts a focus on the experience of the receiver. In turn, this places new requirements on the delivering organization, which has to act in harmony and give the impression of acting as one entity towards the beneficiary. To make this possible, the people involved, their tools and policies, as well as their tasks needs to be understood and related to each other as a larger system. Development of solutions adapted to this reality, calls for a multi-level approach, taking tasks, tools as well as organizational aspects into account.

In the interviews, we have noted an understanding of key concepts important for UCD, among people working with service. At the same time, there are economic incentives for upper management in these companies to invest in service. We argue that this is an opportunity to build on already established practices for user-centered design applied within these organizations for service development, a development currently done to a large extend by engineers. The access to professionals with UCD competence is limited today in these types of companies, and will be during a foreseeable future. Hence, a pre-understanding of these concepts will possibly facilitate introduction of a new way to approach service development building on experiences and learnings from the UCD tradition.

When shifting the focus from the product and hence the transaction, to service, there is also a shift to the relationships. Consequently, we see the opportunity for the usability community to take advantage of an increased attention on shared interests. Following this shift in perspective, we feel the hope for an increased perceived significance of what is considered foundations of UCD.

Acknowledgments. We would like to thank those we have been in contact with within these companies. We would also thank the anonymous reviewers for their input.

References

1. Oliva, R., Kallenberg, R.: Managing the transition from products to services. Int. J. Serv. Ind. Manage. **14**(2), 160–172 (2003)
2. Winter, J., Rönkkö, K., Rissanen, M.: Identifying organizational barriers–a case study of usability work when developing software in the automation industry. J. Syst. Softw. **88**, 54–73 (2014)
3. Bannon, L.: From human factors to human actors: the role of psychology and human-computer interaction studies in system design. In: Greenbaum, J., Kyng, M. (eds.) Design at Work: Cooperative Design of Computer Systems, pp. 25–44. Lawrence Erlbaum Associates, Hillsdale (1991)
4. Gould, J.D.: How to design usable systems. In: Helander, M., Landauer, T.K., Prabhu, P. (eds.) Handbook of Human-Computer Interaction, pp. 757–789. Elsevier, Amsterdam (1988)
5. Law, E.L-C, Lárusdóttir, M.K.: Whose experience do we care about? analysis of the fitness of scrum and kanban to user experience (UX). Int. J. Hum. Comput. Inter. just-accepted (2015)
6. International Standard, ISO 9241-11 Guidance on Usability (1998)
7. International Standard, ISO/IEC 12207-2008 Systems and software engineering – Software life cycle processes (2008)
8. Bødker, S.: When second wave HCI meets third wave challenges. In: NordiCHI 2006, Oslo, Norway (2006)
9. Shostack, G.L.: Breaking free from product marketing. J. Mark. **41**(2), 73–80 (1977)
10. Vargo, S.L., Lusch, R.F.: Evolving to a new dominant logic for marketing. J. Mark. **68**(1), 1–17 (2004)

11. Ostrom, A.L., Bitner, M.J., Brown, S.T., Burkhard, K.A., Goul, M., Smith-Daniels, V., Demirkan, H., Rabinovich, E.: Moving forward and making a difference: research priorities for the science of service. J. Serv. Res. **13**(1), 4–36 (2010)
12. Morelli, N.: Designing product/service systems: a methodological exploration. Des. Issues **18**(3), 3–17 (2002)
13. Stickdorn, M., Schneider, J.: This is Service Design Thinking: Basics, Tools, Cases. BIS Publishers, Amsterdam (2011)
14. Holmlid, S.: Participative, co-operative, emancipatory: from participatory design to service design. In: First Nordic Conference on Service Design and Service Innovation, pp. 1–14 (2009)
15. Wetter-Edman, K.: The concept of value in design practice-an interview study. In: Second Nordic Conference on Service Design and Service Innovation, pp. 87–100 (2010)
16. Wetter-Edman, K.: Design for Service: A framework for articulating designers' contribution as interpreter of users' experience. University of Gothenburg (2014)
17. Charmaz, K.: Constructing Grounded Theory: A Practical Guide Through Qualitative Analysis. SAGE Publications, London (2006)
18. Friedman, B., Kahn, P., Borning, A.: Value sensitive design: Theory and methods. Technical report, pp. 2–12, University of Washington (2002)
19. Norman, D.A.: Living With Complexity. MIT Press, Cambridge (2010)
20. Menor, L., Tatikonda, M., Sampson, S.: New service development: areas for exploitation and exploration. J. Oper. Manage. **20**(2), 135–157 (2002)
21. Clark, G., Johnston, R., Shulver, M.: Exploiting the service concept for service design and development. In: Fitzsimmons, J., Fitzsimmons, M. (eds.) New Service Design. Sage, Thousand Oaks (2000)
22. Rexfelt, O., Almefelt, L., Zackrisson, D., Hallman, T., Malmqvist, J., Karlsson, M.: A proposal for a structured approach for cross-company teamwork: a case study of involving the customer in service innovation. Res. Eng. Design **22**, 153–171 (2011)

Specific Contexts

Human Work Interaction Design of the Smart University

José Abdelnour-Nocera[1(✉)], Samia Oussena[1], and Catherine Burns[2]

[1] School of Computing and Technology, University of West London,
London W55RF, England
{jose.abdelnour-nocera, samia.oussena}@uwl.ac.uk
[2] Department of Systems Design Engineering, University of Waterloo,
200 University Avenue West, Waterloo N2L3G1, Canada
catherine.burns@uwaterloo.ca

Abstract. In this paper we present human work interaction design challenges and opportunities for the vision of the Smart University as a platform that provides foundational context data to deliver the university of the future. While learning analytics have enabled access to digital footprints of student activities and progress in terms of data such as demographics, grades, recruitment and performance, they cannot provide information about activities and interaction in the physical study and work spaces in a university. The smart university proposes a novel platform that will provide context aware information to students through the integration of learning analytics with data sensed using cyber-physical devices in order to provide a holistic view of the environments that universities offer to students. However, designing the interaction of students and staff in the smart university ecology of information and sensing devices requires an understanding of how they work as individuals, as members of teams and communities. Through two use cases we illustrate how insights obtained from social cognitive work analysis can be used for the design guidelines of the different interfaces part of the smart university ecology.

Keywords: Smart university · Human work interaction design · Cognitive work analysis · User interface design

1 Introduction

The Smart University is a vision where the university, as a platform, provides foundational context data to deliver the university of the future. As higher education funding in Europe continues decreasing, universities are more reliant on income generated from students. Thus, understanding student progression and identifying ways to improve the students experience are vital to any institution. To improve their students' experience, universities are increasingly reliant on technology to improve and expand their services to students. In this paper we present our proposed version of the smart university and how human work interaction design (HWID) [1] can support the implementation of this platform at design level. Although, as part of Smart university ecosystem, some applications have been already implemented [2, 3], the discussions in the paper refer to a conceptual design of the Smart University platform.

© IFIP International Federation for Information Processing 2015
J. Abdelnour-Nocera et al. (Eds.): HWID 2015, IFIP AICT 468, pp. 127–140, 2015.
DOI: 10.1007/978-3-319-27048-7_9

Smart campus platforms have been researched and reported in the literature and some aspects have been also implemented in some universities. For example, Lei et al., [4] propose the design of a smart laboratory that measures, analyses and regulates the thermal comfort by use of cyber-physical devices. The University of Southern California implemented smart buildings management in the building. A more holistic vision has also been proposed; iCampus, as envisioned by EBTIC[1], is an initiative that proposes that the university of the 21st century be composed of six functional areas or pillars, designed to enrich students' experiences throughout their learning lifecycle: iLearning, iGovernance, iGreen, iHealth, iSocial, and iManagement. Although this is inline with our perspective, this initiative is still at a developmental stage and has a very broad scope. Our proposed platform is different in that our emphasis is on the design of the software platform that will allow the delivery of the vision. The implementation of the platform will take a data-oriented architecture approach. The focus is on how to develop a high-quality platform that will allow the use of cyber-physical devices and data analytics for the university of the future. Students' interactions with university systems are leaving an increasing amount of digital footprint which can be harnessed to understand behaviour and activities of students as well as help them become more effective in their studies and preparation of their career. Learning analytics have used these digital footprints left by students to gain insight on the students' progress and to build a personalised learning environment. However, most of Learning analytics projects have been looking at the monitoring of the digital environment that the institution offers to the students. The smart university vision is to provide a novel platform that will provide context aware information to students through the integration of learning analytics with data sensed using cyber-physical devices in order to provide a holistic view of the environments that universities offer to students. Additionally, this will augment the traditional learning analytics with data related to the physical environment and allow the investigation of these intelligent buildings and their effect on the learning processes.

Designing the interaction of students and staff in the smart university ecology of information and sensing devices requires an understanding of how they work as individuals, as members of teams and communities. HWID approach studies how to understand, conceptualize, and design for the complex and emergent contexts in which information and communication technologies (ICT) and work are entangled. In this paper, through two use cases we illustrate how insights obtained from HWID analysis can be used for the design guidelines of the different interfaces part of the smart university platform.

2 Learning Analytics

Students' interactions with university systems are leaving increasingly large digital footprints which can be harnessed to understand the behaviour and activities of students as well as help them become more effective in their studies and preparation of

---

[1] http://www.ebtic.org/pages/the-intelligent-campus.

their career. Learning analytics have used these digital footprints left by students to gain insight on the students' progress and to build a personalised learning environment. However, most of these projects have been looking at the monitoring of the digital environment that the institution offers to the students. Data that is used for these analytics rely on management data, such as student demographics, grades, recruitment figures and the traces left by the students as they use the university IT systems such as virtual learning environment (VLE) or Learning management system (LMS).

Masses of data can be collected from different kinds of student actions, such as solving assignments, taking exams, online social interaction, participating in discussion forums, and extracurricular activities. This data can be used by Learning Analytics to extract valuable information, which might be helpful for lecturers to reflect on their instructional design and management of their courses. Usable Learning Analytics tools for lecturer that support cyclical research activities are still missing in most current VLE or are far from satisfactory [5]. Data mining tools are usually designed for power and the flexibility of the analytics rather than for the simplicity. Most of the current data mining tools are too complex for educators to use and their features go well beyond the scope of what they might require [6] If tracking data is provided in a VLE, it is often incomprehensible, poorly organized, and difficult to follow, because of its tabular format. As a result, only skilled and technically savvy users can utilize it [7]. Many lecturers, using learning analytics are motivated to evaluate their courses and they already have questions related to their teaching in mind.

3 The Smart University

Over the past decade, innovation in design and manufacturing throughout the industry has enabled the cost, size, power consumption of sensors and the associated networks to improve dramatically. Consequently, sensor-based systems have been proposed for a broad range of monitoring applications; more recently, these technologies have allowed the integration of the cyber world to physical world and effectively blurring the gap between the two.

The smart university proposed a novel platform that will provide context aware information to students through the integration of learning analytics with data sensed using cyber-physical devices in order to provide a holistic view of the environments that universities offer to students. Additionally, this will augment the traditional learning analytics with data related to the physical environment and allow the investigation of these intelligent buildings and their effect on the learning processes. The platform aims to combine a responsive architectural environment with an intelligent virtual environment in order to offer a truly personalised learning environment. The responsive architectural buildings will be providing optimal heating, ventilation and lighting based on the requirements of the learning environment (i.e. chemistry lab or ICT lab), the learning models and the behaviour of the occupant of the environment. The behaviour of the occupant (learner or tutor) can be monitored by their interactions with the IT systems as well as some wearable devices. Sensors measuring temperature, humidity, noise and air quality would be used to monitor the behaviour of the building. Figure 1 illustrates the platform that could be used collecting, processing and visualising the data in a smart university. The platform will need to be scalable, data oriented and distributed with a friendly usable interface while, at the same time, being powerful and flexible enough for the repository of data of heterogeneous sources, integration of data sources in real-time, providing real-time exploration and interventions.

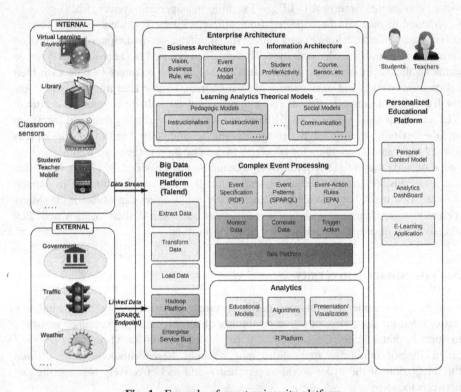

Fig. 1. Example of smart university platform

The platform will need to provide the following capabilities:

- Pre-process data sensed from cyber-physical devices, aggregate sensor data based on pre-determined contexts.
- Use data mining and machine learning techniques to identify patterns, trends and anomalies on the general physical environment of university facilities and usage of those facilities.
- Diagnostics and prognostics capabilities.
- Student engagement based on facilities usage.
- Lab/classroom/building capacities.
- Attendance of events.
- Learning analytics.
- Integrating influence of intelligent buildings on student learning.

- Location-based information useful to students/tutors.
- Interventions based on alarms, diagnostics, prognostics of student experience level based on usage of university facilities, student's study load and requirements, etc.

4 Human Work Interaction Design

Human work analysis is focused on user goals, user requirements, tasks and procedures, human factors, cognitive and physical processes, and contexts (organizational, social, cultural). For instance, Hierarchical Task Analysis [8] and Work Domain Analysis [9, 10] are used to study goal-directed tasks and to map the work environmental constraints and opportunities for behaviour. The study of HCI has historically adapted work analysis methods such as hierarchical task analysis to the design of computer artefacts. Ethnographic methods [11] with a sociotechnical perspective have also been used in HCI (e.g.,[12]). These approaches focus on work as end-user actions performed collaboratively with other people in a field setting: the worker activity is seen as a social and organisational experience. In this context, human work analysis and HCI are interlinked in such as a way to form a distinct field of knowledge, namely HWID.

HWID studies how to understand, conceptualize, and design for the complex and emergent contexts in which information and communication technologies (ICT) and work are entangled. Several aspects influence the way humans work and the work itself. For humans, language, culture, education, skills, knowledge, emotions and cognitive abilities contribute to define the profile of users and their approach to individual and collaborative work. For work, its goals, functions, available tools and content contribute to delineate its characteristics and challenges. In this paper, we illustrate the use of Cognitive Work Analysis (CWA), a well known work analysis technique, to support design considerations for the Smart University system. This technique is driven by a framework that supports and structures the analysis needed when designing a flexible and adaptive system [9, 13]. The framework focuses on analysing the limitations and constraints on workers behaviour; and mapping these constraints is the design of the system that will support the workers.

The CWA framework comprises five different phases; work domain analysis, control task (or activity) analysis, strategies analysis, social organisation and co-operation analysis, and worker competencies analysis. Using CWA has two distinct advantages. First, CWA is a multi-dimensional analysis that incorporates the physical and the social environment to provide a rich description. Secondly, CWA can be paired with Ecological Interface Design (EID) [14] to generate designs for new information systems. EID has shown success in the design of analytic information displays in power plant displays [15]; social systems [16], healthcare decision support [17] and community building [18]. For these reasons, CWA may be a promising approach in cyber physical systems like the smart university.

5 Applying HWID to Smart University Scenarios: Two Examples

In this paper, HWID concepts and tools will be applied to two types of activities in high education domain; exemplifying two aspects of the smart university platform; the learning analytics aspect and cyber-physical devices. The analysis that is discussed in this paper will shape the guidelines of the user interface of the smart university platform.

One of the activities examines a lecturer using learning analytics to provide support to students when preparing for an exam. The lecturer uses Virtual learning platform (VLE) as the main medium for communicating with the students. Past exams, revision notes and other supporting exercises are uploaded on the VLE. The lecturer, might also initiate a special discussion board for exam support. Here we envisage that the learning analytics will allow the lecturer to monitor the effectiveness of the support that is being provided, helping him/her to adapt the materials accordingly.

The other activity is related to the smart campus; i.e. equipping the campus with cyber-physical devices that help provide responsive environment. An example of such environment is an ICT lab. The lab is equipped with a number of sensors; Students usually take a 2 h practical session in this ICT lab. Each student has a set of exercises that they have to complete using the computer. The session is typically supported by an academic staff and an assistant; typically a PhD student.

In this section we present two possible scenarios for the Smart University platform analysed from a HWID perspective. This involves applying CWA and then translating insights from this process into interaction design guidelines for the different interfaces on this platform.

5.1 Scenario A: Supporting Exam Preparation

A lecturer, who offers weekly online exercises has the intention to help his/her students to prepare for an exam. But she is not sure if the currently available exercises are helpful enough for this purpose. Therefore, he/she would like to know if those students who practice with her online exercises on a weekly basis are better in the final exam than students who do not use them. A Learning Analytics toolkit could help him/her to do research on this hypothesis by automatically collecting, analyzing, and visualizing the right data in an appropriate way. The smart university platform should allow for interactive configuration in such a way that its users could easily analyze and interpret available data based on individual interests.

We now look at this scenario through the lens of the different phases of CWA.

Work Domain Analysis: Work Domain Analysis (WDA) provides an overview model of the work environment with a view to understanding what kinds of information should be included in the user interface and how this should be presented. The learning analytics toolkit is part of a sociotechnical system whose main goal is maximising learning outcomes and the learning experience for students. The following presents an Abstraction Hierarchy (AH) typically used for WDA [17]. This is made of five levels, which are now described in terms of the learning analytics scenario:

Since education is a core goal of this scenario, learning needs to be present in the functional purpose and generalized function levels. The scenario indicates that there is a concern that weekly exercises might improve learning, as evaluated through exam results, or might not be helpful. This is why we have chosen to describe at the abstract function level that there must be a balance between evaluation and learning, e.g. you cannot evaluate 100 % of the time, but you also need to evaluate at some level. The functional purpose is to find the sweet spot where learning outcomes and student experience are maximised at optimum levels Table 1.

Table 1. Work domain analysis for learning analytics scenario

WDA: supporting exam preparation	
Physical form	For student (type, program, year of admission, status, performance level); for learning material (type, date available); for evaluation material (type, date of evaluation, grades achieved), for lecturer (level, name, availability); for student record system (type, data available, dates accessed)
Physical function	Student, VLE, Lecturer, university student record system, material to be learned, evaluation material
Generalized function	Student accessing material, lecturer creating and uploading new material, contributing to discussion board, monitoring and evaluation of student's progress
Abstract function	Balance the ratio of evaluation to learning
Functional purpose	Maximize learning outcomes, Maximize student experience

WDA will allow us to identify the analytics data needed for designing components of the system. For instance, a key goal derived from this WDA is to enable the instructor to move that sweet spot between evaluation and learning to maximize outcomes and experience. Those are the drivers, i.e. decisions to be made with the analytic system.

Control Task Analysis: This is done to determine what tasks are being carried within the system and under what conditions. In this learning analytics scenario, control task analysis (ConTA), based Rasmussen's decision ladder [18], the analysis would look like in Fig. 2. Is there uncertainty and ambiguity on the possible goal state? Quite possibly, if the instructor is following a new evaluation approach for students, she may move into knowledge based behavior [7] trying to figure out what is wrong. Analytics could play a role here. Instructors can then 'define a task', i.e. choose to modify their instruction approach. This implies setting a new 'procedure', more or less exercises in this case, which would then be 'executed'.

Strategies, Social and Worker Competencies: This level of analysis can facilitate the discussion of different teaching strategies (traditional, flipped, blended learning). This could also reveal different evaluation strategies (short quick frequent evaluations, longer midterm/final, or project based evaluation).

The identification and description of social competencies could represent values and intentional constraints being conveyed by the institution. It could also consider the culture and cooperation of the students in this. As a worker, the instructor must have competency in teaching, the material being taught, and the use of the smart learning system. Skills, rules and knowledge is the base for all of these [7].

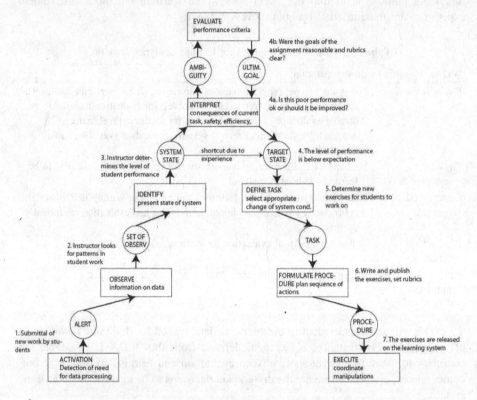

Fig. 2. Decision ladder for learning analytics scenario.

5.2 Scenario B: Monitoring Room Temperature in the Smart Campus

In this scenario, the ICT lab at the university is equipped with an number of sensors and a display at the lecturer station with dashboard and message board for information about the room. Once the students have entered the room and started working, the information about the room is updated with an estimate of the number of people in the room and the ideal temperature for the ICT lab activity. The lecturer had a quick look at the dashboard and noticed that the room was empty for the morning and he/she understood that it will take about 5 min to get the ideal temperature. He/she also noticed that the noise was higher than what is expected for an ICT session and he/she first closed the windows and the door before asking students to work more quietly.

The students with wearable devices capable of giving ambient temperature readings also noticed that the temperature adjusted to the ideal temperature within 5 min of being in the lab.

Work Domain Analysis: As with the scenario A, we now illustrate a possible WDA for the scenario of controlling temperature in the classroom:

Control Task Analysis: This is done to determine what tasks, data, and messages are being processed within the system and under what conditions. In this monitoring ICT lab temperature scenario, inspired in Rasmussen's decision ladder [18] the analysis would look like in Fig. 3. The objective here is to define and implement contextual, multi-sensory inference strategy services that are able to derive contextual information from aggregating different sources data. This will allow us to model user-based energy profiles and user behaviours in the ICT sessions. Based on the contextual models defined and considering the constraints related to comfort, it will be possible to identify diverse energy awareness rendering messages providing adequate feedback on various personalized display (wearables) or the instructor dashboard Table 2.

Table 2. WDA Monitoring Room Temperature in the Smart Campus (the Smart Campus)

WDA: monitoring room temperature in the smart campus	
Physical form	Student (type of clothing, course studying); for ICT lab (size, nb of machine, nb of windows, ideal climate); sensors(type), for lecturer (level, name); session (activity, nb of students, duration), for display (type (dashboard, wearable), data available, messages/alert)
Physical function	Student, ICT lab, sensors, snapshot of climate, ICT session, display
Generalized function	Student attending the ICT session, lecturer receiving messages about the room, adjusting the room, adjusting own clothing/noise, student receiving personalized message, evaluation process
Abstract function	Balance the ratio of climatic comfort to learning
Functional purpose	Maximize learning outcomes, Maximize student experience

Strategies, Social and Worker Competencies: Two strategies are apparent; first, to be energy efficient (i.e. suggestion of taking piece of clothing, opening a window or closing a door) or second, to emphasis on the comfort and make more use of the heating or cooling system. Ultimately, a smart university system will aim to use thermal comfort to change the expectation from largely invisible centralized control of the environment into a more active and responsive approach. Furthermore, the system will implement a 2-way information exchange between occupants and buildings.

In terms of social competencies, students and staff awareness of, and responsibility for, environmental issues is variable. How can we facilitate and encourage sharing of thermal comfort strategies and learning from others? For example what are the alternative ways to keep cool or warm, or how to generate reflection on clothing and its role in thermal comfort? As a worker, the instructor must have the competency to

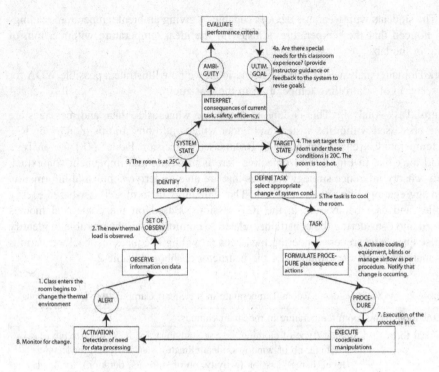

Fig. 3. Monitoring room temperature in the smart campus scenario.

understand the correlations between climatic comfort and student performance and make the right type of decisions about the required behavior.

6   CWA Moderated Interface Design

A Looking at two scenarios through the CWA approach facilitates the decision on which usability and user experience goals that should drive the interaction design of the different interface components of the smart university sociotechnical system. This also applies for the type of user interface design guidelines and levels of representation required at conceptual design level.

The CWA of the learning analytics scenario clearly points to importance of effectiveness and utility [21] as main usability goals driving the design of the user interface of the lecturer trying to establish the optimum level of exercises that should be set for students to meet learning goals in a satisfactory way.

In terms of design guidelines feedback and mapping become core objectives in the presentation of the student performance data. Good user interface design meeting these goals and principles will support the overall functional purpose of the learning analytics systems, i.e. Maximize learning outcomes, Maximize student experience. Similarly, in the ICT lab monitoring scenario, the effectiveness of the adaptive comfort messages is an essential goal since the underlying objective is to change the students environmental behaviour.

It can be illustrated how specific interface design decisions on relevant guidelines and heuristics can be derived from looking at the WDA and ConTA for both scenarios: Table 3 links key tasks to user behaviour, user interface components, design concepts and design principles and heuristics.

Table 3. Mapping CWA to choose relevant user interface design concepts, principles and heuristics.

Generalised function task:	Behaviour type required	User interface components	Design concepts	Design principle and heuristic
Monitoring and evaluation of student's progress	Skill-based behaviour	Learning Analytics Dashboard: Messages/alerts	Visualise information on student performance as well as the level of instructor support.	Feedback: lecturer should receive immediate, intelligible alert if performance falls below expected levels. Mapping: data visualised should map naturally to student's activity record. Any non-technical user should be able to understand the student's position in relation to her cohort.
Lecturer creating and uploading new material	Knowledge-based behaviour	VLE content creation module	Supports the creation and upload of new exercises	Visibility: lecturer should be able to view historical performance data on exercises attempted and overall module performance while setting exercise levels. User Control and Freedom: enable lecturers maximum control of creation and uploading of as many exercises as required.

(*Continued*)

Table 3. (*Continued*)

Generalised function task:	Behaviour type required	User interface components	Design concepts	Design principle and heuristic
Lecturer monitors temperature and noise levels	Rule-based behaviour	Temperature and noise charts in classroom based control panel	Visualising the required information quickly and in a non-disruptive form	Throughput: monitoring temperature and noise levels should not disrupt the core teaching tasks and should be done as quickly as possible. Feedback: lecturer should receive clear indication of temperature and noise levels, with clear indication of acceptable thresholds.

7 Conclusions

This paper introduces a proof of concept attempt to illustrate how HWID can be a useful framework in the design of the smart university platform as sociotechnical ecology of information sharing actors and devices. Through the application of CWA to two different scenarios we have identified the nature of work, artefacts and interactions in which smart university users will engage.

The smart university scenarios have been focused on the common functional purpose of maximizing learning outcomes while maximizing the student experience. CWA has enabled an understanding of the different task requirements in each scenario in order to achieve this: in the first scenario on learning analytics, it has been uncovered how finding the right balance between learning and evaluation is a critical goals; on the second scenario on the use of temperature sensors in the smart campus it is clear that the visualization of relations between climatic comfort and learning experience is a critical goal. Looking at these scenarios through ConTA provides an understanding of behaviours according to skills, rules and knowledge in the context of task goals. Identifying the type of behaviour the user is engaged in will provide useful information on cognitive and material elements of the tasks that should be supported. For instance, it is evident to see how in the learning analytics scenario the teacher is likely to be engaged in knowledge based behaviour more often trying to establish the optimum level of exercises for a particular group, while in the smart campus scenario a rule based behaviour is likely to be more frequent as the relation between climatic comfort and student experience will tend to be more stable.

We were then able to illustrate how this analysis of work in these two smart university scenarios can feed the interaction design of user interface components in the different points of interaction with the platform. There will be a need to prioritize different types of usability and user experience goals in terms of the functional purpose and desired goal states in identified in CWA.

Even in the present examples, it is easy to predict that supporting the instructor with analytics on student performance would be a more extensive design challenge than providing monitoring of the thermal conditions of the classroom. This also has implications on data visibility, information accessibility, and information architecture. In the case of monitoring student performance, the instructor needs a deeper architecture, more data accessibility and more control latitude to develop the view he or she may want. In contrast, the thermal comfort situation may require quite straightforward information display and limited control to the instructor and students.

HWID models also provide considerations for nation, geographic, cultural, social and organizational factors shaping the activities being supported through design [22]. The smart university does not escape these considerations and any of the models and design principles and heuristics shaping the interactive points in these platforms will have to be moderated by them. For instance, Northern European universities will have challenges for design very different from those in the Southern Europe due to cultural, political and climatic factors.

In summary, we have illustrated a case for HWID in the context of the design of the smart university. Work analysis and interaction design can be integrated to support important design decisions affecting the ecology of devices and information repositories in the smart university with a clear focus on its users, their contexts and interactions.

Reference

1. Clemmensen, T., Campos, P.F., Katre, D.S., Abdelnour-Nocera, J., Lopes, A., Orngreen, R., Minocha, S.: Human work interaction design (HWID) SIG: past history and future challenges. In: CHI 2013 Extended Abstracts on Human Factors in Computing Systems, pp. 2537–2540. ACM (2013)
2. Sauer. C., Oussena S.: Approaches to the use of sensor data to improve classroom experience, eChallenges e-2014 Conference, Belfast
3. Oussena, S., Kim, H., Clark, T.: Exploiting student intervention system using data mining. In: The First International Conference on Advances in Information Mining and Management, IMMM 2011 (2011)
4. Lei, C.-U., Man, K.L., Liang, H.-N., Lim, E.G., Wan, K.: Building an intelligent laboratory environment via a cyber-physical system. Int. J. Distrib. Sens. Netw. **2013**, 1–9 (2013)
5. Hijon, R., Velázquez, Á.: E-learning platforms analysis and development of students tracking functionality. In: World Conference on Educational Multimedia, Hypermedia and Telecommunications, pp. 2823–2828 (2006)
6. Romero, C., Ventura, S., García, E.: Data mining in course management systems: Moodle case study and tutorial. Comput. Educ. **51**, 368–384 (2008)

7. Mazza, R., Dimitrova, V.: CourseVis: a graphical student monitoring tool for supporting instructors in web-based distance courses. Int. J. Hum. Comput. Stud. **65**, 125–139 (2007)
8. Annett, J., Duncan, K.D.: Task analysis and training design (1967)
9. Vicente, K.J.: Cognitive Work Analysis: Toward Safe, Productive, And Healthy Computer-Based Work. CRC Press, Boca Raton (1999)
10. Salmon, P., Jenkins, D., Stanton, N., Walker, G.: Hierarchical task analysis vs cognitive work analysis: comparison of theory, methodology and contribution to system design. Theoret. Issues Ergon. Sci. **11**, 504–531 (2010)
11. Button, G., Sharrock, W.: Studies of work and the workplace in HCI: concepts and techniques. Synth. Lect. Hum. Centered Inf. **2**, 1–96 (2009)
12. Abdelnour-Nocera, J., Dunckley, L., Sharp, H.: An approach to the evaluation of usefulness as a social construct using technological frames. Int. J. Hum. Comput. Interact. **22**, 153–172 (2007)
13. Lintern, G.: The foundations and pragmatics of cognitive work analysis: a systematic approach to design of large-scale information systems. 1 March 2009 (2009)
14. Hajdukiewicz, J., Burns, C.: Strategies for bridging the gap between analysis and design for ecological interface design. In: Proceedings of the Human Factors and Ergonomics Society Annual Meeting, pp. 479–483. SAGE Publications (2004)
15. Burns, C.M., Skraaning, G., Jamieson, G.A., Lau, N., Kwok, J., Welch, R., Andresen, G.: Evaluation of ecological interface design for nuclear process control: situation awareness effects. Hum. Factors J. Hum. Factors Ergon. Soc. **50**, 663–679 (2008)
16. Hajdukiewicz, J.R., Burns, C.M., Vicente, K.J., Eggleston, R.G.: Work domain analysis for intentional systems. In: Proceedings of the Human Factors and Ergonomics Society Annual Meeting, pp. 333–337. SAGE Publications (1999)
17. Burns, C.M., Enomoto, Y., Momtahan, K.: A cognitive work analysis of cardiac care nurses performing teletriage. In: Applications of Cognitive Work Analysis, pp. 149–174 (2008)
18. Euerby, A., Burns, C.M.: Improving social connection through a communities of practice–inspired cognitive work analysis approach. Hum. Factors J. Hum. Factors Ergon. Soc. **56**(2), 361–383 (2013)
19. Rasmussen, J.: The role of hierarchical knowledge representation in decision making and system management. IEEE Trans. Syst. Man Cybern. **15**(2), 234–243 (1985). 0018720813494410
20. Rasmussen, J., Pejtersen, A.M., Goodstein, L.P.: Cognitive Systems Engineering. Wiley, New York (1994)
21. Rogers, Y., Sharp, H., Preece, J.: Interaction Design: Beyond Human-Computer Interaction. Wiley, New York (2011)
22. Katre, D., Campos, P., Clemmensen, T., Orngreen, R., Pejtersen, A.M.: Human work interaction design for e-government and public information systems. In: Campos, P., Graham, N., Jorge, J., Nunes, N., Palanque, P., Winckler, M. (eds.) INTERACT 2011, Part IV. LNCS, vol. 6949, pp. 730–731. Springer, Heidelberg (2011)

Contextual Personas as a Method for Understanding Digital Work Environments

Åsa Cajander[1](✉), Marta Larusdottir[2], Elina Eriksson[3], and Gerolf Nauwerck[1]

[1] Uppsala University, Box 337, SE-75105 Uppsala, Sweden
asa.cajander@it.uu.se, gerolf.nauweck@uadm.uu.se
[2] Reykjavik University, Menntavegur 1, 101 Reykjavik, Iceland
marta@ru.is
[3] KTH – Royal Institute of Technology, Lindstedsvägen 3, 10044 Stockholm, Sweden
elina@kth.se

Abstract. The role of IT at the workplace has changed dramatically from being a tool within the work environment to include all aspects of social and private life. New workplaces emerge where IT becomes more and more divergent, embedded and pervasive. These new aspects of IT at work need to be addressed with new or adapted human centred activities. This paper present and discuss a modified version of personas called contextual personas developed to better address the new working life. The contextual personas were developed using contextual inquiry, and focus groups as well as argumentative design. From the process of developing the contextual personas we learned that they are indeed a promising tool to understand the new work situations, and especially the holistic view of IT at work as they bring the whole working-life of the personas into focus. Finally, we discuss in what way the contextual personas could give developers extended understanding of the users' future office work environment.

Keywords: Personas · Digital work environment · Usability

1 Introduction

Working life has been changing for many with a move towards goal oriented tasks, informal communication and virtual collaboration. Moreover, the use of IT has moved from being an isolated tool within the work environment to becoming pervasive through for example mobile apps and social media. Hence this shift has led to work that blurs the borders to social and private life, which is related to definition of one's identity as a digital person in a technical world. Often these changes of working life are enhanced through technology with the technical solutions available. It is common that people use various computer systems, including various equipment to use those such as mobile phones, tablets and laptops. Moreover, they are at different places while using the software systems. This creates complexities that are new and challenging. Other new ways of managing private life and working life has emerged, and one can note trends like for example BYOD (Bring Your Own Device) where the company policy allows employees to bring their own technology to the workplace. This shift makes systems development

© IFIP International Federation for Information Processing 2015
J. Abdelnour-Nocera et al. (Eds.): HWID 2015, IFIP AICT 468, pp. 141–152, 2015.
DOI: 10.1007/978-3-319-27048-7_10

ever more complicated and there is an increasing need for illustrating this new work situation in order to better understand all the variations in the work environment that has emerged.

In this study we made extensive contextual interviews with administrative staff at university offices to gather information on their current work situation from a computer supported work environment perspective. In the paper, we explain a new method for describing results of such contextual interviews called contextual personas. These personas are developed to explain the various work contexts of the workers. Our results show that the employees are willing to give rich information about their work context, when prompted through the persona descriptions. Through the focus group discussions of the contextual personas real life was brought into the conversation.

In this paper we describe how contextual personas can be used to elicit IT based administrative work as one method to understand the digital work environment. Firstly the personas can be used as a tool to describe the work situation and the users within this work situation, which also extends to social life. However, we also argue that the contextual personas can be used as a reflexive tool that lets the respondents further reflect on their own work situation. Hence in our study, the contextual personas gave us information on the work environment and potential health hazards when looking at the holistic work situation including IT based tools and the overarching workload. On concrete finding from our interviews has implications for pervasive and smart workplaces, since the perceived connectedness of these administrators led to an always on status which made it hard for them to feel that they were ever free from work. Furthermore we discuss how the personas can be used in pervasive and smart workplaces such as future office spaces presented below.

2   Background

When creating the contextual personas, the healthy work model by Karasek and Theorell [1] was used. Hence the first section below presents this model. This is followed by a presentation of future offices and the emerging trends in this area. Finally, we present a short description of research on the personas method.

2.1   Digital Work Environment and Healthy Work

As work has become more digitalised the digital work environment becomes more central for employees productivity and also wellbeing. The digital work environment is here defined broadly as the work environment that is the result of digital tools and work support systems. The digital work environment consists of physical, psychosocial and cognitive problems and challenges. It encompasses all cognitive work situations where people interact or are dependent on computer systems. In this definition of the digital work environment we also include aspects of integrity, control and surveillance.

When analysing the data from the contextual interviews, the Demand-Control-Support model is used. In the 1970's Robert Karasek developed a model for analysing work-related stressors associated with cardiovascular illness. His demand and control model was thereafter further developed together with Töres Theorell [1] and is now one of the most widely used models for explaining psycho-social work conditions and their effects on health. This model suggests that the combination of perceived demands and perceived control at work is a determining factor for stress. This model was used since our previous research, see for example [2, 3] that have shown that the model is easily understood and applied in organisations when the digital work environment has been discusses. The figure below illustrates the Demand-Control-Support Model (Fig. 1).

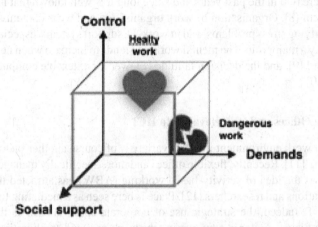

Fig. 1. The Demand-Control-Support Model of stress in a work situation. High job strain, i.e. high demands in combination with low decision latitude, and low social support are associated with the highest risks for health problems.

The figure above illustrates how healthy and sustainable a work is, in relation to the experienced demands, control and social support. High demands are normally not a problem, if combined with high self-control over work situation and tools and strong social support from management and colleagues. A skilled worker can experience this as a challenging situation. She has full control over the work conditions and planning and gets full support when needed. The work is efficient and sustainable. On the other hand, if high demands are not met by strong self-control and social support, the situation will soon become dangerous health wise. If the worker does not have control over work conditions and planning, does not have usable tools and feels totally exposed if things go wrong, the work will be very unhealthy. Such work situations are associated with high stress. In this extreme, different health risks are common and people do not withstand the situation for long. Research shows that subjective control and support factors often decrease when new IT systems are introduced, as did Åborg, [4, 5].

In this research project we have focused on administrative work. The main health problems in such computer-supported work situations are: Users are bound to use the computer for a major part of their working hours entailing constrained, static work postures for long periods. The computer controls the work pace and task order, leaving the users little or no control over their work. Users suffer from stress, caused by excessive workload, time pressure and poorly designed computer support [6, 7].

Traditionally, occupational health experts work in isolation from the software development process. They evaluate and suggest improvements to existing workplaces and tools [3]. It is, however, often too late to do something about poorly designed software tools once they have been installed and are running. Thus, poor and inadequate design leading to health problems cannot be sufficiently modified post-hoc of systems development when the computer system is in use. Instead, occupational health and ergonomics experts must be involved in the actual software development process. Work-related stress has increased in the past years and since long it is well known that it is a growing health problem [8]. Organisation of work organisation and work content are important factors underlying stress problems, and in work, IT support systems, especially computer software, play a major role. The mental workload tends to increase when new IT systems are introduced [9], and the decision latitude is lower for extensive computer users than for others [10].

2.2   Future Offices and its Relevance to HCI

The physical work environment in all its variety is of course another factor influencing office workers [11]. Recently, flexible offices and more specifically management philosophies such as the idea of activity-based working (ABW) has attracted the interest of both organisations and researchers [12]. Place is here seen as a mediating factor between people and IT. Indeed, the strategic use of corporate space is seen as the necessary, though not sufficient, factor in empowering the workforce and ameliorating many of the downsides of computer-supported work [13]. A part of the concept is increased use of IT in support of both mobility and monitoring, and not surprisingly, the IT industry itself is one of the major proponents of this new way of work [14]. Yet, while ABW is proposed as a solution to the problems associated with open plan offices, not least cognitive stress, research is inconclusive [15]. In a seminal paper [16] traces the origins of this seemingly new–anywhere, anyplace–work rhetoric and exposes some its inherent paradoxes, not least how these images of newness contribute to the conservation of old work patterns.

As IT in the workplace thus becomes more and more embedded and pervasive the scope for HCI broadens. The pioneering works of [17] have already argued for the application of usability concepts in the field of facility management, yet the field seems to have attracted limited attention so far [18]. Instead, the most common tool seems to be variations on the model developed by [19]), where the amount of face-to-face interaction is contrasted with the amount of job autonomy (resulting in a matrix of four basic office types: the hive, the cell, the den and the club). While this broad categorisation of work can aid planning, other techniques, such as personas, could provide a deeper understanding on how to improve the quality of work and the work environment.

2.3   Personas

Within development of IT-based systems, the persona method has become frequently applied tool and is used extensively in both industry and in research. The persona method is a user-centred way of representing users in situations where users cannot be available; the idea is that the overall focus and awareness of the users in development projects are heightened when working with personas [20]. However the use of the method can be manifold for example, the personas are described both as a communication tool and as a design aid. However, [21] argues that by trying to separate the different ways to use the method will help the usability practitioner to more skillfully use the personas, as well as being open for alternative applications.

Within the field of Human-Computer Interaction, the persona method was originally introduced by Cooper [22], and he argued for hypothetical archetypes of real users in order to avoid designing systems that become too generic and in the end does not fit anyone. According to Cooper [22], the personas should be based on actual users and the personas should be precise and specific since it is more difficult to ignore a detailed persona than aggregated user data. The ideas is that numerous personas initially are created through an iterative process, and then these are condensed, according to their goals, into fewer but more precise, personas. One more important claim from Cooper is that even though multiple personas can be created, the developers should focus on one primary persona [22].

The extensive use of personas result in different views on what should be the basis of the personas. The most common argument is for collecting qualitative data through for example interviews and observations of real users [21–23]. However, the data underpinning the personas does not need to be based on ethnographic studies of real users; for example [24] describe personas within secure systems design based on assumptions. Quantitative data from for example surveys can also be used to statistically render personas, although these can later be refined by interviews and observations [25]. Moreover, the widespread usage of the method in disparate settings and contexts has made the resulting personas in different shapes and forms. [26] outline in their paper a loose typology of personas, however, the persona kinds that are described in their paper are not exhaustive; for example, other possibilities are assumption personas [24] or a collaboration persona [25]. The persona method is also criticised, where the most alarming critique is that the personas are being misused and that this leads to designers distancing themselves from real users [28]. [28] argues that it is better to engage with users directly than to create a façade of user-centeredness [28]. Other types of critique are that the method is difficult to verify as (more) beneficial compared to other method [29] or that it is inevitable that designers will create stereotypes [30]. Furthermore there is literature that shows when personas have failed to work, such as the case that [31] present. The reasons for this was mainly because the design team was not familiar enough with the method and the interaction designers were not involved in the creation of the personas. [32] present a case where the persona method was abandoned in the context of developing software for mass-market mobile devices, although this mainly was because of the power and dominion of stakeholders outside the development organisation. Some recent studies have shown that the probability of personas being used is higher if the designer has participated in the creation of them [27, 33]. (Furthermore, [34] presents a case where personas were used outside the development project in which they were developed. In their case the educational department adopted the personas as a way to introduce newly employed to different clusters of customers.

3   Using Contextual Personas to Define Current Work Situation

In this section the background of the study is presented as well as the data gathering method used.

3.1   The Case Uppsala University

Uppsala University is a large Scandinavian research university with about 40 000 students and 6000 employees. The business administration department of the university handles the overall strategic economy at the university, whereas the different business administrators at the departments work with the daily economical work.

The majority of the business administrators at the departments are women. The work of the business administrators at the different departments at the university are however organised in many different ways. Some work both with economy, human resource matters and study administration since they belong to very small departments, whereas others are very specialized in one area such as EU project economy and work with that full time with the support of a larger group of business administrators. Today, computers constitute the primary working tool for the business administrators at the universities, and hence comprise a major part of the work environment and procedures.

The study presented in this paper was a part of a collaborative project (KiA) between a research group of Human-Computer Interaction and the university administration [35]. The KiA project ran for two years, 2012–2013, and was coordinated by the university administration whereas the researchers did most intellectual contributions. It should be noted that the project was not a research project as such but the researchers were allowed to use the findings for scientific work beyond the project. The researchers worked within a participatory action research tradition [36, 37] meaning that they were used to work closely with organisations, rather than observing without interfering.

3.2   Data Gathering

3.2.1   Contextual Inquiry

The data gathering was conducted from May to late August 2013. Field studies and interviews were conducted with 12 economics administrators at four different institutions in Uppsala University lasted approximately 2–3 h. The field studies followed the method Contextual Inquiry and its four principles [38]:

Studies of the Work in its Context. Field studies were conducted on site. Researchers are studying the users who do their tasks and discuss the systems used to solve them.
Cooperation. The user and researcher work together to understand the user's work. The researcher alternate between observing the user when they work and discuss what the user was doing and why.
Interpretation. The researcher share their interpretations and insights with the user during the interview. The user can expand or correct the researcher's understanding.
Focus. The researcher focus the conversation on topics that are relevant to the survey.

During the field studies the researcher took notes using pen and paper. The first field studies were made with an open mind to understand the work and the situation, but eventually the researcher asked the business administrator more specific questions as for example to show some particular parts of the systems or tasks.

3.2.2   Data Analysis and Sketches of Contextual Personas

The collected data was analyzed based on four categories from Karasek and Theorell's model of work [1], and the fourth category was the general working environment problems. Three researchers (three of the authors), analysed the data together in a workshop in August 2013 and wrote the first descriptions of the three personas together during the workshop which resulted in rough contextual personas. The researchers worked visually with the personas and made use of large white boards where the dimensions of healthy work were visualised together with descriptions of personas. After the workshop, the descriptions were reviewed individually by the researchers and modified. The illustrations of the personas were just modified images from Clip Art at this point.

3.2.3   Focus Groups

One researcher revisited two of the business administration departments, and arranged focus groups with four and three business administrators to discuss and reflect upon the presentations made in the personas. After the focus groups the personas were revised according to the reflections made by the business administrators. An illustrator was asked to draw the faces of each persona according to the descriptions at this point.

4   Results

4.1   Three Contextual Personas

Three personas were made based on the interviews and analysis of those. Each description was about one page of text describing the personal life, one day at work and the goals of the persona. Additionally, the need for control, support and the demands that the persona has are described. Each persona had a figure, illustrated by a professional illustrator. One example of a persona can be seen in Fig. 2.

4.2   Reflections on the Contextual Personas

Some really interesting points emerged during the focus group discussions that did not occur in the earlier interviews. The business administrators really liked the job descriptions made, and could identify themselves with the personas. Someone said, "It really feels like this person is working here".

One of the things that one of the groups wanted to add was how life was affected by their work. In their mind private life and work forms one whole, and they wanted that to be better represented in the personas. They also gave concrete examples of situations where they need to adapt their working hours, their vacation and their weekends to meet the goals of different business administration deadlines. As a business administrator at the university in their opinion, you need to adapt life to work, and they often worked long hours before deadlines. One person described that new deadlines might occur in

Fig. 2. An example of a persona that was created using the contextual personas method

the calendar if researchers receive new research projects, and that these have individual deadlines for reporting. Especially EU projects mean a lot of work for the business administrators, who adapt their working hours according to the schedule of the projects.

Some business administrators also complained about the current systems at the university that does not support flexible work, and some systems require that you are on the university network to be able to work. They also wanted more possibilities to work using their mobile devices.

Another interesting discussion that emerged was the lack of a persona that would represent the elderly generation of business administrators. This persona would describe the situation that technology has changed work so much that it is not the same at all. The persona would illustrate an elderly lady who has had problems understanding the new technology, and being terrified with the changes even though they are at the very core of their work. This persona has the feeling that her knowledge is not valid any more.

5 Discussion

The contextual personas were based on the theory of healthy work by Karasek and Theorell [1]. The theory was used in a very concrete way when designing the personas, and each aspect (control, support, demand) were discussed separately to ensure the quality of the descriptions. However, during the discussions it became clear that some aspect of the workplaces were not fully covered by the theory such as for example the aspect of interruptions and doing things in parallel. Other aspects that are not covered by the model that emerged in the discussions were the personality of the persona and how that affects the perceived stress. The contextual personas method could hence be further improved in the future to cover all aspects of working life through an conceptual development of the theoretical foundations of the process. One possible theoretical model that could be relevant to use to enhance the personas is the Effort-Reward Imbalance theory that was developed by Johannes Siegrist [39]. This model is widely used in work environment research and would add aspects of intrinsic and extrinsic motivation, and overcommitment which is highly relevant in the context of new ways working.

In our contextual personas we describe the holistic work environment as it is today for the business administrators. The main difference in our way of describing personas compared to how Cooper defined personas [22] is that Coopers personas are used for improving one particular software system. The descriptions of these personas are aimed to describe their way of working solving the goals that the software system being developed will support in solving. Contextual personas are not focused on the usage of one system, they are focused on describing the whole context of work, so contextual personas could typically be using 20 software systems for solving various tasks at work. The usage of personas in new contexts is also argued in [40] where the author elaborates on how the users in the study started to more readily talk about their work situation when confronted with the personas that depicted themselves. This could be interpreted as the personas as a reflexive tool to be used as trigger material when talking with users, which in our cased highlighted the diverse and multifaceted work of the business administrators.

Contextual personas describe the current work situation, similar to Cooper's personas [22] and to Hackos and Redish's [41] scenarios. [41] describe two types of scenarios, "task scenarios" that describe the current situation for a persona and "use scenarios", that describe: "the future use of a computer system". Contextual personas could also be used in a similar way, using the contextual personas to give insights into future work environments. Previous research has show that user feedback is often informal and limited [41]. The contextual personas could work as a new human centred activity that would improve the quality of usability work for developers. In that case, the personas should be based on data from brainstorming sessions with users, so the descriptions will not be too hypothetical and superficial. [22, 38] have emphasised that personas are grounded in interview data from users and are not based on designers imagination.

There is a need to develop and adapt current human centred activities to better address the future workplaces, and contextual personas shows promising results in this context. One should note that contextual personas are not recommended to be used in isolation, but together with other human centred activities to fully incorporate the essence of future work places. We conclude that the personas need to be complemented with a vision work concerning the future needs and visions of the users as well as other user centred activities.

Acknowledgments. This study was made with financial support from Uppsala University Administration through the KiA project (Quality in Use). We would like to thank everyone that participated in the interview study, and those who have given valuable input to this paper. We would also like to thank the illustrator, Maria Osk Jonsdottir, for her professional work on illustrating the faces of the personas.

References

1. Karasek, R., Theorell, T.: Healthy Work: Stress, Productivity and the Reconstruction of Working Life. Basic Books, New York (1992)
2. Cajander, Å.: Usability–who cares? the introduction of user-centred systems design in organisations (2010)
3. Sandblad, B., Gulliksen, J., Åborg, C., Boivie, I., Persson, J., Göransson, B., et al.: Work environment and computer systems development. Behav. Inf. Technol. **22**(6), 375–387 (2003)
4. Åborg, C.: How does IT feel@ work? And how to make IT better: Computer use, stress and health in office work (2002)
5. Åborg, C., Sandblad, B., Gulliksen, J., Lif, M.: Integrating work environment considerations into usability evaluation methods—the ADA approach. Interact. Comput. **15**(3), 453–471 (2003)
6. Bergqvist, U.: Visual display terminal work—a perspective on long-term changes and discomforts. Int. J. Ind. Ergon. **16**(3), 201–209 (1995)
7. Punnett, L., Bergqvist, U.: Visual display unit work and upper extremity musculoskeletal disorders Ergonomic expert committee document/National institute for working life (Solna), Solna, p. 16 (1997)
8. Marklund, S., Arbetsmiljöverket, S.: Worklife and health in Sweden 2000. Arbetslivsinstitutet (2001)
9. Aronsson, G.: Dimensions of control as related to work organization, stress, and health. Int. J. Health Serv. **19**(3), 459–468 (1989)
10. Tornqvist, E.W., Eriksson, N., Bergqvist, U.: Risks factors at computer and office workplaces. In: Worklife and Health in Sweden 2000, p. 189 (2000)
11. Danielsson, C.B.: The Office–an explorative study. Architectural design's impact on health, job satisfaction and well-being. (Doctoral thesis), KTH Royal Institute of Technology, Stockholm (2010). http://urn.kb.se/resolve?urn:nbn:se:kth:diva-24429
12. Appel-Meulenbroek, R., Groenen, P., Janssen, I.: An end-user's perspective on activity-based office concepts. J. Corp. Real Estate **13**(2), 122–135 (2011). doi: 10.1108/14630011111136830
13. van Koetsveld, R., Kamperman, L.: How flexible workplace strategies can be made successful at the operational level. J. Corp. Real Estate **1**(4), 303–319 (2011)
14. Gates, B.: The New World of Work. Accessed 17 October 2014 (2005). https://www.microsoft.com/mscorp/execmail/2005/05-19newworldofwork.mspx

15. Too, L., Harvey, M.: "TOXIC" workplaces: the negative interface between the physical and social environments. J. Corp. Real Estate **14**(3), 171–181 (2012). doi: 10.1108/14630011211285834
16. Humphry, J.: Visualising the future of work: myth, media and mobilities. Media Cult. Soc. **36**(3), 351–366 (2014). doi:10.1177/0163443713517730
17. Alexander, K.: The application of usability concepts in the built environment. J. Facil. Manag. **4**(4), 262–270 (2006). doi:10.1108/14725960610702947
18. Rasila, H., Rothe, P., Kerosuo, H.: Dimensions of usability assessment in built environments. J. Facil. Manag. **8**(2), 143–153 (2010). doi:10.1108/14725961011041189
19. Laing, A., Duffy, F., Jaunzens, D.: New Environments for Working: The Re-Design of Offices and Environmental Systems for New Ways of Working. Construction Research Communications Ltd., Watford (1998)
20. Grudin, J., Pruitt, J.: Personas, participatory design and product development: an infrastructure for engagement. In: Paper presented at the PDC 2002 (2002)
21. Guðjónsdóttir, R.: Personas and Scenarios in Use (Doctoral thesis Trita-CSC-A), KTH, Sweden (2010)
22. Cooper, A.: The Inmates are Running the Asylum. SAMS publishing, Indianapolis (2004)
23. Pruitt, J., Grudin, J.: Personas: practice and theory. In: Paper presented at the Designing for User Experiences (2003)
24. Faily, S., Fléchais, I.: The secret lives of assumptions: developing and refining assumption personas for secure system design. In: Paper presented at the Human-Centred Software Engineering (2010)
25. Sinha, R.: Persona development for information-rich domains. In: Paper presented at the CHI 2003 Extended Abstracts on Human Factors in Computing Systems (2003)
26. Floyd, I.R., Jones, M.C., Twidale, M.B.: Resolving incommensurable debates: a preliminary identification of persona kinds, attributes, and characteristics. Artifact **2**(1), 12–26 (2008)
27. Matthews, T., Whittaker, S., Moran, T., Yuen, S.: Collaboration personas: a new approach to designing workplace collaboration tools. In: Paper presented at the CHI 2011 (2011)
28. Portigal, S.: Persona non grata. Interactions **15**(1), 72–73 (2008)
29. Chapman, C.N., Milham, R.P.: The personas' new clothes: methodological and practical arguments against a popular method. In: Paper presented at the Human Factors and Ergonomics Society Annual Meeting (2006)
30. Turner, P., Turner, S.: Is stereotyping inevitable when designing with personas? Des. Stud. **32**(1), 30–44 (2011)
31. Blomquist, Å., Arvola, M.: Personas in action: ethnography in an interaction design team. In: Paper presented at the NordiCHI 2002 (2002)
32. Rönkkö, K., Hellman, M., Kilander, B., Dittrich, Y.: Personas is not applicable: local remedies interpreted in a wider context. In: Paper presented at the Participatory Design Conference (2004)
33. Friess, E.: Personas and decision making in the design process: an ethnographic case study. In: Paper Presented at the CHI 2012, Austin, Texas, USA (2012)
34. Markensten, E., Artman, H.: Procuring a usable system using unemployed personas. In: Paper presented at the Third Nordic Conference on Human-Computer Interaction, Tampere, Finland (2004)
35. Cajander, Å., Nauwerck, G., Lind, T.: Things take time: establishing usability work in a university context. EUNIS J. High. Educ. IT **2**(1) (2015)
36. Heron, J., Reason, P.: The practice of co-operative inquiry: research 'with' rather than 'on' people. In: Handbook of Action Research, pp. 144–154 (2006)

37. McKay, J., Marshall, P., McKay, J., Marshall, P.: The dual imperatives of action research. Inf. Technol. People **14**(1), 46–59 (2001)
38. Holtzblatt, K., Wendell, J.B., Wood, S.: Rapid Contextual Design: A How-to Guide to Key Techniques For User-Centered Design. Elsevier, San Francisco (2004)
39. Siegrist, J., Starke, D., Chandola, T., Godin, I., Marmot, M., Niedhammer, I., et al.: The measurement of effort–reward imbalance at work: European comparisons. Soc. Sci. Med. **58**(8), 1483–1499 (2004)
40. Eriksson, E.: Situated Reflexive Change : User-Centred Design in(to) Practice (Doctoral thesis), KTH Royal Institute of Technology, Stockholm (2013). http://urn.kb.se/resolve?urn=urn:nbn:se:kth:diva-116403
41. Hackos, J.T., Redish, J.: User and Task Analysis for Interface Design. Wiley, New York (1998)
42. Larusdottir, M.K., Cajander, A., Gulliksen, J.: Informal feedback rather than performance measurements – user centred evaluation in scrum projects. Behav. Inf. Technol. **33**(11), 1118–1135 (2014). doi:10.1080/0144929X.2013.857430

The Work and Workplace Analysis in an Elderly Centre for Agility Improvement

Arminda Guerra Lopes[1,2](✉)

[1] Instituto Politécnico de Castelo Branco, Castelo Branco, Portugal
[2] Madeira Interactive Technologies Institute, Funchal, Portugal
aglopes@ipcb.pt

Abstract. The mission of elderly services is to enable elders to live in dignity and to provide necessary support for them; to promote their sense of belonging, sense of security and sense of worthiness. The goals of the Portuguese social security system are to oversee the activities of non-public institutions for social solidarity and to improve the quality of operations and services. Conversely, it demands the alignment of the interaction process' collection, requirements and information system with those of the social centers for elderly. In this paper, we describe a workplace environment, a social center for elderly, and our strategy was, firstly, to understand the information flow in and out of the institution. We concluded that it needed to redesign and reconfigure his business process components, combining individual tasks and capabilities, in response to the environment (other social solidarity centers and the social security system) in order to improve agility. Secondly, we proposed a prototype interface, as new tool, to serve the communication process among the social centers for elderly and the national social security institution. This attempt may contribute to improve the interaction among the whole partners and to address organizations' agility and innovation.

Keywords: Work analysis · Workplace · Agility · Information systems · Information technologies

1 Introduction

The long-term care system, in Portugal, until recently, was not integrated in the public sector. The Misericórdias (Holy Church), independent non-profit-making institutions with a religious background, provided the service. In order to expand services, a new private/public mix centered on the public subsidizing of non-profit institutions was created in the late 1980s. It was implemented through a new legislation on the legal status of non-profit provider institutions (designated as PISS – Private Institutions of Social Solidarity). In 2006, due to the increasing number of elderly persons and the reduced offer of these services, the National Network for Continuous Integrated Care was implemented, based on the existing structure. The Ministry of Labor and Social Solidarity, in each Portuguese region, provided the social services. Health and social care services were, mainly, provided by private non-profit-making institutions (subsidized by the State) and by Misericórdias. Nowadays, there are various services and facilities available for the elderly: day-care

© IFIP International Federation for Information Processing 2015
J. Abdelnour-Nocera et al. (Eds.): HWID 2015, IFIP AICT 468, pp. 153–167, 2015.
DOI: 10.1007/978-3-319-27048-7_11

centers, home-based services (home help and integrated home care that includes health care), nursing homes (long-term and palliative care) for highly dependent persons, and also residential care (protected flats) and family accommodation. However, the last two solutions are still very poorly developed.

In terms of information systems and technologies these institutions face several problems. The new technologies are not used properly for management, and conversely, the software development enterprises have single applications for each purpose: staff management, accounting management, vehicle management, and so on. Platforms that cover the whole information do not exist. Consequently, staff spends several hours filling and finding forms. On the other hand, the social security institution demands several reports to those institutions, which are difficult to prepare since information is spread over offices. For PISS, the quality management systems are outlined by the institutions of social solidarity as an important functioning guideline with all the rules that must be accomplished. However, there are bureaucracies to follow each time an intervention is made with the client. This takes an out-sized amount of information to deal with.

Facing this situation, and in order to contribute to sort specific problems of a private institution whose concerns were to increase its service quality, we proposed a technological solution, which was implemented, and later, tested and validated by the client. To arrive to the solution several steps were carried on such as the work and workplace analysis. The workplace analysis was determinant to improve quality of services, either for the employees or other stakeholders. It permitted to increase the levels of employees' motivation, and engagement. We questioned several factors to change the workplace environment - the intervenient requirements, needs, and workflow, in and out of the institution. Our methodology approached methods and techniques of human work interaction design.

The changes that occurred with our proposal contributed to improve institution agility. The institution's agility was addressed to increase institution and customers' services satisfaction. Conversely, the internal and external business processes were beneficiated by agility. Gartner stated that the main contributions considered by agility are customer service, security, knowledge management, asset management and cost efficiency [3].

2   Theoretical Background

The context for our study is the Portuguese Social Security System and the interactions with the private institutions of social solidarity. Those interactions are established either by paper format documents or by digital media of communication. We introduce, briefly, the Portuguese social security system its aims and relationships. We outline, also, the information systems and technologies as a tool to achieve organization agility.

2.1   The Portuguese Social Security System

The literature is scarce about Portuguese studies in the presented field. We found some references about the third sector and the imperative of professionalization. Non-profit organizations are defined and their objectives [23]; the social and solidarity environment is presented by [24], third sector dimensions in Portugal are described in the report "Portugal's Nonprofit Sector in Comparative Context" [25]. The information found was important to help to understand the functioning of these institutions and the interactions among the stakeholders.

In Portugal, the origins of several non-profit organizations were connected to the church, like Misericórdias [24]. The Misericórdias (holy houses of mercy) are an example of the strong cooperation between state and church, which has marked the history of Portuguese society in general. The statute of PISS is granted to organizations that are constituted "without a profit motive, on private initiative, with the purpose of giving organized expression to the moral duty of solidarity and justice among individuals" [25]. The social security system in Portugal is managed by the state and in principle, it applies to all individuals working in Portugal, either as employees or self-employed. It provides benefits for health care, sickness, retirement, disability, death, elderly, maternity, paternity and adoption. PISS helps children, young people and families. They support social and community integration, assist the elderly and disabled, promote and safeguard health, education and vocational training, and resolve housing problems.

The relationship between the social security system and the private institutions of social solidarity (PISS) is extremely important for their functioning. The social security makes, annually, agreements among institutions, the cooperation protocols, in order to answer the institution's demands. Besides these protocols, the social security elaborates quality manuals with guidelines to help institutions to create their own quality manual. The quality manuals are organized into validities: familiar housing, residential home, center of occupational activities, home of infancy and youth, residential center of temporary housing, structures for elderly, day-care centers, and domiciliary services support.

These models are an instrument of good practices to help the auto-evaluation of the social answers, permitting to review systematically its performance and to support the development and implementation of a quality management system to improve the functioning of each organization. Conversely, they are a normative referential for the requirements to a social reply, independently of the legal nature of the institution.

In Portugal, at reference point 31st December 2010, there were 5,800 owners' entities of social solidarity. Around 70 % had non-profit goals. Among these, 61,4 % were private institutions of social solidarity (which included the social services of enterprises and the 'Misericórdia' (Holy Church of Lisbon); 1,4 % were official entities, 2,1 % other private non-profit organizations and 3 % were entities equivalent to PISS [26, 27].

In comparison with the residential care provided by the public sector, the nursing homes run by Misericórdias and other non-profit institutions are usually of better quality and only request a nominal contribution from patients and their families. Nursing homes in the private sector are very expensive and the majority of the population cannot pay for them.

Home care is expanding in Portugal and in some regions infrastructures to deliver support to the elderly have been developed in partnership with municipalities, regional health administrations and non-profit institutions. Apparently, the establishment of social care networks is becoming a priority.

The Portuguese government recognizes the relevance of PISS in the provision of social services to the population through the establishment of cooperation and financial agreements. In fact, the family support has been decreasing and the state considers the PISS a strategic part in the care system.

Afterwards, after understanding the main goals of these institutions, we analyzed, in loco, the communication forms and interactions among social solidarity institutions, and social security system to design a solution that would permit communication, easily, of the information shared among them.

2.2   Information Systems and Technologies to Achieve Organizational Agility

According to literature, the definition of agility is very broad, although its semantics converge. Along the last twelve or thirteen years we found that this concept started to be a common sense necessity between the academy and industry. However, agility is defined from different points of view and according different focus: Oosterhout et al. define agility focusing on business process unpredictable changes beyond flexibility levels [4]. Overby et al. describe agility as an ability that firms should have to sense environmental change and respond readily [5]. The response to the challenges posed by business environment dominated by change and uncertainty is the main aspect of agility. It helps the firm to be able to generate the required information for management decision-making. The speed in responding to variety and changes is the attempt to improve organizations' systems and architectures [6].

Considering agility within manufacturing, Jin et al. define it as the capability of surviving and prospering in a competitive environment of continuous and unpredictable changes by reacting quickly and effectively to changing markets, driven by customer-defined products and services [7]. Liu et al. refer agility emphasizing the supply chain as a form's ability to effectively collaborate with channel partners to respond to market-place changes in a rapid manner [8]. Kalbande focus on business process agility high-lighting e-procurement as the solution [9]. Sletholt gives another perspective: he emphasis agility practices in software development, and defines it as the responsiveness to change and collaborate [10].

Agility is very important since every organization must build agility to perform effectively in unstable environments. A set of processes that allow an organization to send changes in the internal and external environment, responding efficiently and effectively in a timely and cost-effective manner, and learn from the experience to improve the competencies of the organization is defined as organization's agility [11].

In order for information systems (IS) to act as an enabler of organizational agility, increasing the positive sides of information systems while minimizing the opaque sides, firms need to evaluate their information systems thoroughly, understand their dynamic environments, modify, and implement their suggestions [12]. Seo et al. identified several factors to minimize the called dark side of IS: standardization, buying, leasing or outsourcing, management skills, individual agility, organizational structure and culture. Once organizations analyze their own situations following the proposed factors, they will be agile since they learn in every cycle and it becomes their competency and flexibility.

Information Technologies (IT) is an important agility concern of many enterprises. The main reason for this is because the agile enterprise is collaborative since it communicates among its collaborators and stakeholders. Once IT is agile, several resources such as new tools, technologies and solutions including: cloud computing, collaboration technology, application portfolio management, and IT outsourcing will empower the agile enterprise [13]. Liu et al. studied the impact of IT capabilities on firm performance [14]. They underline the importance of supply chain agility, which is all about customer responsiveness in the uncertain market [15] and is essential in ensuring the firm's competitiveness because it enables effective and efficient responses to operational changes [16–18].

IT capabilities are deemed as enablers to firm performance and the alignment between IT capabilities and strategy is increasingly important [19]. In fact, performance effects not only are affected by responding to environmental change, but also may be contingent upon the congruency between design choices and strategy [20].

Organizational and technical solutions help to achieve agility. However, besides the information technology sector being fundamental either for enterprise infrastructure, or for business process implementation and management it is not sufficient. The solution should fit with the enterprise agility needs and its specific situation. Information technology could be a barrier to business agility, the existence of inflexible systems is supposed to be a very important disabler in achieving more business agility. However, information technology enabled innovations, in general, and enterprise resource planning systems in particular, have contributed to the simplification, standardization and automation of business processes in the past [21].

3   The Study

This study adopts case study methodology to unveil the how questions in delving into the process of developing strategic Information Systems (IS) application. The process of unveiling strategic IS application is complex and multi-faceted, connected to each specific organizational context, comprises technological, complex human and social components [23].

The case study selection emerged from two conditions posed by our research questions. First, the case study had to have aimed to improve its workflows to interact with social security system. Second, the design process of our solution proposal should engage the whole intervenient to participate along the design process, in order to achieve a higher institution's agility practice.

Considering the prevailing situation about the interaction difficulties among the social solidarity institutions and the Portuguese social security system we attempted to fill the void to operationalize the agility practice by selecting as a case study, a small social center for elderly identified as SCLF.

The main goal of the SCLF, a private institution of social solidarity, is to help the clients who do not succeed to have, in their homes, the support conditions for the necessary care for a good quality of life. The SCLF offers several different services namely, residential structure for elderly, domiciliary support services, center of day, physiotherapy services and leisure activities for children until ten years old. The institution has a kitchen to prepare meals and is also responsible to supply and feed children of the village's school.

The center is organized as presented in Fig. 1. Two main groups can be distinguished, both having in charge the technical and services directors. The technical director area is divided into the technical bureau and the valences that the nursing house gives, namely the leisure center activities (LCA), day care center (DCC), domiciliary support service (DSS) and the residential structures for elderly (RSE). These services have different types of workers: direct help providers and service auxiliaries; the technical bureau has the health office with a physiotherapist, a doctor and nurse. The social office has a sociologist and in the leisure office there is a social educator. In the area supervised by the service director we have stocks management activities and the secretariat whose tasks are developed by the director. The kitchen has six cookers and the laundry is where service auxiliaries realize the tasks.

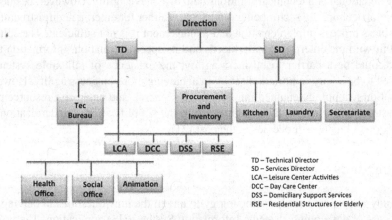

Fig. 1. Organogram SCLF

In order to explore the interactions context among the whole partners (users, collaborators, customers), we analyzed institutional documents and software applications; we use analysis and interviews and observations to understand the information flow among these organizations types, the employees, and user's needs. The interviews were recorded and additional notes were taken to provide more detail. To maintain interview originality and integrity, we conducted verbatim transcriptions. All the informants were provided with an assurance of confidentiality.

In the first phase, twelve semi-structured interviews were made to allow the interviewees a space of freedom to comment and/or present their concerns. The interviews were in a person-to-person interaction form. They were conducted in three social centres, (private organizations). (Table 1)

Firstly, we prepared the text for the interviews and we selected the staff members of each institution according to a defined profile. After each set of interviews with people from the same profile (technical and/or services director & IT specialist) in each of the three institutions, we analyzed the data and started to design first

Table 1. Total number of Interviews (Phase I)

Institution	Interviewees	Interviews	Follow-ups	Total
A	Technical director IT specialist	1	1	4
B	Technical director IT specialist	1	1	4
C	Technical director IT specialist	1	1	4
Total			12	

sketches of our prototype. Then, we interviewed the information systems technician of each institution. Another phase of interviews with the previous members of staff was made to consolidate and correct the gathered information.

Table 2. Total number of Interviews (Phase 2)

Institution	Interviewees	Interviews	Follow-ups	Total
SCLF	Technical director IT specialist	2	1	3
	Technical bureau management	2	1	3
	Service auxiliaries	1		1
	Physiotherapist	1	1	2
	Doctor	1	1	2
	Nurse	1	1	2
	Sociologist	1		1
	Social educator	1	1	2
	Service director	2	1	3
	Staff manager	2	1	3
	Cookers	1		1
	Administrative staff	2	2	4
	Secretary	2	2	4
	IT specialist	2	2	4
Total			35	

In the second phase, at the SCLF, we undertook face-to-face interviews, which were conducted over a period of two months – a total 35 interviews. We used the same methodology, presented for first phase. We interviewed different staff members (directors, administrative staff, nurses…) (Table 2).

Questions asked were exploratory in nature, open-ended, and tailored to the role of each interviewee. The first step was to sort the interview data into an initial set of themes. Sixteen questions were designed to gather information from the interviewees, either to understand the procedures and interactions in and out the institutions or to know the type of complains about the work situations experienced. We were interested, namely, to identify the kind of information that was necessary for users' management; the compulsory information to be exchanged between the institution and the social security system; the access points to consult information; people that should be involved in the process and the output documents that should be created.

The goal was to understand the difficulties that staff, in nursing homes, had when dealing with the whole amount of information that is spread all over the institution.

Finally, we interviewed the administrative people that will be in charge of the application's use. We also did a questionnaire to verify if the functionalities of our application were in consent with users. We intend to have suggestions about our layouts, functionalities, usability, and user's own comments.

4   The Work Analysis

The backgrounds of work analysis came from the analysis of the process of collecting information about jobs [1]. Dierdorff and Rubin refer the theoretical issues associated with the work-related information to come to the term work analysis [2]. The change of the focus from jobs analysis to work analysis admits that the methods and concepts being applied in the workplace changes, as well as, the different situations that can be found. Work analysis can be approached within different perspectives: either as a methodology, a resource tool or a process. Work analysis data can be obtained from a widely collected type of human resources data in different organizations and/or during artifacts development. We used both as a process and resource tool.

The early focus on our interactive design process was the investigation about the workplace, the people, the technology, and the interactions among them. (To simplify we use the work 'people' meaning the whole individuals or groups that are involved in a process, being an employee, a customer, a staff, a patient or an institution). The workplace was analyzed considering the institution's characteristics: mission, goals, people, and different resources (technical, technological, finances, social, cultural). We tried to understand the different perspectives and aspects of the institution. The output gave us some of the information about the workplace environment. This process is what we consider the first contact with the work analysis in-between people and technology (Fig. 2).

The work analysis are tasks, subtasks, activities, procedures, complains, needs, etc. The technology is the tangible or intangible output as the result of the interaction design process: it can be physical devices, information artifacts, software systems and other

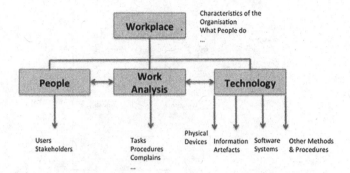

Fig. 2. Initial Data Analysis Framework

methods and procedures. The approaches to gather information about situations, users, customers, collaborators and other stakeholders were institutional documents, attitudes from the community (nursing houses and institutions of social solidarity) and software applications in use.

The data was, initially, collected following Fig. 2 and filling the information on Table 3, which served as a guideline support to organize and objectivize the gathered information about the known and unknown situations. This table allowed ensuring a complete and holistic understanding of the institution's architecture.

Table 3. Data Collection Table

	What	How	Where	Who	When	Why
Scope						
Business						
Information Systems for Elderly Care						
Technology						

Table 3 is a four by six classification schema. The four rows represent different perspectives of the institution: its scope (vision, mission and objectives); the business characteristics and services; the main information systems and technologies used for elderly care and their features.

5   The Results and Discussion

After the institution first picture, obtained from the first interviews data, we refined our analysis and we organized the data according the information on Fig. 3.

According our research we concluded that, in general, information was spread by different means of communication in a mixed of digital and paper forms. Social solidarity institutions do not interact, efficiently and effectively with the social centers for elderly due to the disaggregation of information systems and technologies. Almost all the institutions use different information technologies systems for management, accounting and

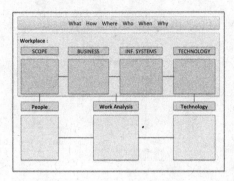

Fig. 3. Data collection framework

other services. The human resources were scared for the amount of activities that social security demands. The human resources of these institutions had different backgrounds and experiences and, in general, they had few appetencies and were not motivated for technology use. In situations where they needed to exchange information, a diverse number of forms and documents were exchanged. They were also scared with the amount of activities that social security demands.

5.1 Information Systems and Technologies

Concretely, in the SCLF center, there were two software programs: one responsible for the accounting management and the other for user management. The former could only be functional for an accountant with some experience. The software had specific features, which do not permit a person who was not familiarized with accounting concepts, to use it properly. The software was divided into several areas; each one had its particular characteristics (Table 4). Several features needed constant updates according the new law decrees; and conversely, the compatibility issues with the supervisory bodies were not easy to make. In parallel with the difficulties of operating the software, users dealt with information exchange in paper format, which was not aligned with those in the software.

Table 4. Accounting management software issues

Clients control	User accounting control
Waiting list to set properties	Automatic calculation (monthly)
User registration (Documents Control)	Receipts issued from users
User Registration per valence (Documents Control	Receipts issued from users with bar codes
Payments monitoring
Documents attachment (Various formats)	Maps (IRS, current account, etc.)
Users misconduct control	General receipt control

The other software, the management software, was extremely complex due to its virtual use. Through this software users could create and record all parameters of the institution receipts and they could make the calculations about what each customer spends. A list with all the people on the waiting list could be drawn.

The main problems encountered with the information systems use were based on the absence of customization hypothesis, the lower experience and background of the institution's workers, and conversely, on the frequent legislation changes.

5.2 Proposed Solution

In order to help the social center (SCLF) to interact either with their stakeholders or with the social security system we proposed a prototype implementation for innovation in the organization. Staff took part sharing their personal knowledge with other stakeholders. We analyzed the characteristics of the environment, characteristics of the organization, characteristics of the people (staff and stakeholders) and the interactions along the processes as well as the needs of the people involved.

Table 5 summarizes the main issues we found and the proposed solutions to improve agility practices at SCLF.

Table 5. Issues and solutions

Issues	Solutions
• Information systems disaggregation • Support conditions delivery • Different software packages • Procedures/Interactions • Information management: • Access points to consult information • Information exchange among institutions • Complains • ...	• New layouts • New functionalities • New application design • New output documents • Training with IT • Reduction of paper use • Management tool for the communication process • Optimisation of human resources skills • Software customisation • Framework design as a guideline for communication • Interactive application to manage intern information • ...

Considering the issues that were a concern for the institution and the solutions we found more suitable to achieve best agility practices, we proposed a prototype of an interactive application. This application integrates the whole information to be shared among institutions and users: administration, patient management, social care, doctors, nurses, the other help care providers and even the information about meals and food management. The information about each person's process, namely, the medical information, nursing information, social services information, physiotherapy, accounting, among others is organized and different users, those with permission, can consult it in an efficient way (Fig. 4). The integration of services was highly complicated and controversial. The changes were progressively made with the collaboration of the staff. The information concerning the social area (social security services) was also included. Each month the system will deliver information maps about the different institutions interaction (waiting lists, client's allocation without institution place, etc.) Presently, the problems of mixed forms of communication were sorted. The difficulties we had with the communication among institutions and the social services were, almost, settled.

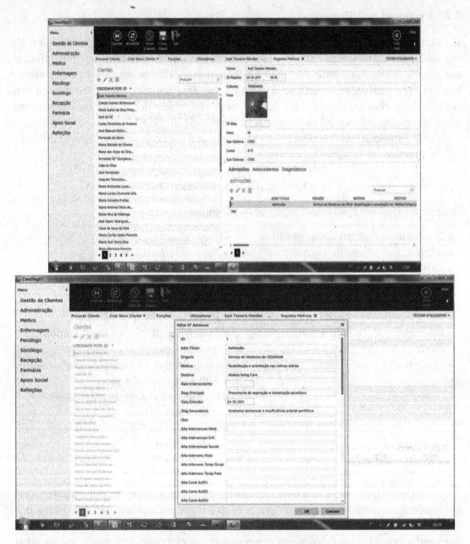

Fig. 4. Application Design

Afterwards, we designed a framework which could answer some of the problems, and the encountered needs (Fig. 5). Firstly, it must be able to congregate all the areas and information necessary to center the whole necessities that can be performed in the institution.

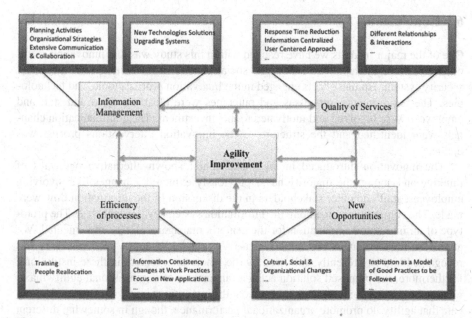

Fig. 5. Framework for agility improvement

5.3 Pursuing Agility

The proposed approach contributed to introduce innovation on the social center through the alternative pathways of thinking and acting. The achieved changes permitted the organization to be agile. Every organization needs agility. An agile organization is one that senses change in the environment and responds efficiently and effectively to those changes in a timely manner. Moreover, to be agile is not straightforward, new systems, new business processes; even ways of working must be designed and implemented.

This study provided some design guidelines for building and applying interventions to increase agility in the described institutions. Many practices that promote agility already existed in the organization, but they needed to be deeply identified, improved where necessary and then aligned within an overall capacity-building strategy. Change-management practices were designed to promote agility, which were concentrated on creating an openness to change and assuring immediate execution of strategy by ending structural or cultural barriers that impeded the flow of work, people, resources and ideas.

The prototype solution was implemented on the SCLF center and then replicated on three other centers, until the moment. Information technology could generally be a barrier to business agility [28], and information technology may inhibit or allow agility [4]. We consider that these social centers are satisfied with the prototype proposal since they validate it. However, some improvements will be considered for the final application development. Agility was achieved through the organizational and technical solutions suggested.

6 Conclusions

One of the major insights we have reached within this study was that innovation methodologies were implemented across the social centers in interaction with the social security system. Human efforts engaged in the innovation process, tools, and technologies. The requirements, processes and outcomes were clearly defined and staff and employees were involved and motivated to this investment. The communication channels were identified and the structure of the innovation interventions process was defined.

The innovation introduced in the social center shown alternative pathways of thinking and acting; the majority never previously explored. Changes like involving employees, staff and other stakeholders in the discussion of the information flow were made. The communication among the information systems was established. The prototype of an interactive application for the center's management was implemented. We attained a final product development phase. As a result, a set of good practices was recognized and is, presently, followed by the whole intervenient in these institutions. Furthermore, the proposed solution acted as an enabler of organizational agility maximizing the gaps of communication in and out the institutions involved. Our results indicate that agility do promote organizational performance, though in somewhat different ways.

Acknowledgments. The author would like to acknowledge the work of Andre Alves. We would also like to thank all the interviewees and involves partners on the study.

References

1. McCormick, E.: Job Analysis. American Management Association, New York (1979)
2. Dierdorff, E.C., Rubin, R.S.: Carelessness and discriminability in work role requirement judgments: influences of role ambiguity and cognitive complexity. Pers. Psychol. **60**, 597–625 (2007)
3. Gartner: Will web services standards ever happen? In: Pezzini, M. (ed.) Gartner report (2002)
4. Oosterhout, M., Waarts, E., Hillegersberg, J.: Change Factors requiring Agility and Implications for IT. Eur. J. Inf. Syst. - Including a special section on business agility and diffusion of information technology **15**(2), 132–145 (2006). Macmillan Press Ltd. Basingstoke
5. Overby, E., Bharadwaj, A., Sambamurthy, V.: Enterprise agility and the enabling role of information technology. Eur. J. Inf. Syst. **15**, 120–131 (2006)
6. Gong, Y., Janssen, M.: From policy implementation to business process management: Principles for creating flexibility and agility. Gov. Inf. Q. **29**, S61–S71 (2012)
7. Jin, K., Wang, T., Palaniappan, A.: Improving the agility of automobile industry supply chain. In: Proceedings of the 7th International Conference on Electronic Commerce, pp. 370–374. ACM (2005)
8. Liu, H., Ke, W., Wei, K.K., Hua, Z.: The impact of IT capabilities on firm performance: the mediating roles of absorptive capacity and supply chain agility. Decis. Support Syst. **54**, 1452–1462 (2012)

9. Kalbande, D.R., Thampi, G.T., Deotale, N.T. E-Procurement for Increasing Business Process Agility. In: Proceedings of the International Conference & Workshop on Emerging Trends and Technology (ICWET), Mumbai, 25–26 February 2011. ACM (2011)
10. Sletholt., M., a literature review of agile practices and their effects in scientific software development. In: SECSE, Waikiki, Havai. ACM (2011)
11. Dongback, S., la Paz, A.: Exploring the dark side of IS in achieving organizational agility. Commun. ACM **51**, 11 (2008)
12. Seo, D., La Paz, A.I.: Exploring the Dark Side of IS in Achieving Organizational Agility. Commun. ACM **51**(11), 136–139 (2008)
13. Gartner IT Glossary – Enterprise Architecture (EA). http://Gartner.com. Accessed 29 Jul 2013
14. Liu, H., Ke, W., Wei, K.K., Hua, Z.: The impact of IT capabilities on firm performance: the mediating roles of absorptive capacity and supply chain agility. J. Decis. Support Syst. **54**(3), 1452–1462 (2013)
15. Van Hoek, R., Harrison, A., Christopher, M.: Measuring agile capabilities in the supply chain. Int. J. Oper. Prod. Manage. **21**(1–2), 126–147 (2001)
16. Agarwal, A., Shankar, R., Tiwari, M.K.: Modeling agility of supply chain. Ind. Mark. Manage. **36**(4), 443–457 (2007)
17. Sambamurthy, V., Bharadwaj, A., Grover, V.: Shaping agility through digital options: reconceptualizing the role of information technology in contemporary firms. MIS Q. **27**(2), 237–263 (2003)
18. Swafford, P.M., Ghosh, S., Murthy, N.: The antecedents of supply chain agility of a firm: scale development and model testing. J. Oper. Manage. **24**(2), 170–188 (2006)
19. Hevner, A.R., March, S.T., Park, J., Ram, S.: Design science in information systems research. MIS Q. **28**(1), 75–106 (2004)
20. Huang, P.-Y., Ouyang, T.H., Pan, S.L., Chou, T.C.: The role of IT in achieving agility: a case study of Haier, China. Int. J. Inf. Manage. **32**, 294–298 (2012)
21. Seethamraju, R., Seethamraju, J.: Enterprise systems and business process agility - a case study. In: 42nd Hawaii International Conference on System Sciences, HICSS 2009, pp. 1–12 (2009)
22. Tyrell, S.: Using Information and Communication Technologies in Healthcare. Radcliff Medical Press, Oxford (2002)
23. Balonas, S.: The third sector and the imperative of professionalization. In: European Social Marketing Conference, Lisbon, Portugal, 27–28 November 2012
24. Azevedo, C.; Franco, R., Menezes, J.W. (eds.) Gestão de Organizações Sem Fins Lucrativos - o desafio da inovação social. Imoedições, Porto (2010)
25. Salamon, L.M., Sokolowski, S.W., Haddock, M., Tice, H.S.: Portugal's Nonprofit Sector in Comparative Context 2002–2012. Johns Hopkins Center for Civil Society Studies in cooperation with Instituto Nacional de Estatística (2012)
26. Almeida, V.: Capitalism, Institutional Complementarities and the Third Sector, The Private for Social Solidarity (IPSS) in Portugal (2008). http://dspace.ism.pt/xmlui/handle/123456789/346
27. Carta Social, Rede de Serviços e Equipamentos, Relatório 2010. Gabinete de Estratégia e Planeamento, Ministério do Trabalho e da Solidariedade Social (2010)
28. Seethamraju, R., Seethamraju, J.: Enterprise systems and business process agility - a case study. In: Proceedings of the 42nd Hawaii International Conference on System Sciences. IEEE Computer Society (2009)

A Multi-Perspective View on Human-Automation Interactions in Aviation

Monica Samantha Quercioli[✉] and Paola Amaldi

Psychology Department, University of Hertfordshire, College Lane, Hatfield, UK
samtorrens@yahoo.com, p.amaldi@herts.ac.uk

Abstract. Control mechanisms for the evolving potential of autonomous systems are not yet sufficiently established. However, there is a need for control to be allocated throughout organisational and institutional levels of society in order to manage increasing complexities. This study, which applies to the domain of Air Traffic Management (ATM), aims s to gauge stakeholders' attitudes at an organisational level in order to lay the foundations for an easier identification of the challenges and paths to improvements in this industry. Using Grounded Theory (GT), the study maps and interprets workshop data and questionnaires gathered to elicit professionals' views on automation in the aviation industry. The themes identified, which resonate with all those reviewed in the literature, will form the basis for the construction of a checklist and survey of automation issues expressed at an organisational level of control.

Keywords: Automation · Regulation · Systems-orientated design · Human-automation interaction in socio-technical systems

1 Introduction

Control mechanisms for the evolving potential of autonomous systems are not yet sufficiently established. However, there is a need for control to be allocated throughout organisational and institutional levels of society in order to manage increasing complexities At the same time, training seems to lag significantly behind the level of technological complexity in automated system. This study seeks to highlight current automation/autonomy issues as represented by stakeholders positioned at various echelons of those institutions involved in civil ATM. The study will first review how these concerns are expressed in different domains (such as rail, civil aviation and the military) supported by reviews in cognitive and resilience engineering literature.

As automation increases the degree of *coupledness* (defined as the interdependence of one element on another), the impact and interaction with other system components cannot be satisfactorily anticipated. This is why increased automation contributes to those accidents/incidents where components' behaviour, while within the range of expected variability, creates the condition for the breakdown. In order to better appreciate the effects of multiple dependencies, Feary and Roth (2104) emphasise that new information from the context is needed when designing for complex interactions. Much too often safety risks associated with the introduction of new technologies, such as safety

© IFIP International Federation for Information Processing 2015
J. Abdelnour-Nocera et al. (Eds.): HWID 2015, IFIP AICT 468, pp. 168–179, 2015.
DOI: 10.1007/978-3-319-27048-7_12

nets, are examined without an explicit definition of the system's strategic goals, objectives and constraints. Contextual information should include a model of the system and operations viewed as subcomponents in the context of a larger system in order to allow for potential interactions/dependencies among sub-components to be identified. In particular, goal conflicts, resource shortages, double-bind situations and coordination/communication issues should be considered for their impact on the success of the new human-automation subsystem.

Operational issues raised by the introduction of automation have been documented by Balfe et al. (2012) in a study about the consequences of an Automatic Route Setting (ARS) on signallers' management of train routing. Some of the issues raised were: (i) lack of appropriate co-ordination mechanisms now needed as new dependencies were created between remote teams; (ii) lack of contextual, up-to-date traffic info requiring operators to monitor for inappropriate ARS decisions on routing; (iii) decision-making by ARS is based on a narrower set of criteria, making it inadequate to reflect the regulating task complexity; (iv) lack of focused training that would allow signallers to understand and predict ARS; (v) poor feedback preventing signallers knowing what the system is doing (no matter the degree of technical complexity); (vi) sparse knowledge of how the system works; (vii) effects caused by 'automation surprises' due to a inadequate understanding of underlying ARS logic; (viii) bending the use of a safety net to cope with the design deficiencies of ARS; (ix) workload is not reduced *tout court;* rather, its pattern has changed; and (x) responsibility allocation is not clearly defined. All of the items on this list resonate with issues raised in cognitive engineering literature dating back to the 1990 s and make those recommendations by Feary & Roth about contextual framing of automation even more compelling.

The US Defense Science Board (DSB) published a review of major automation issues and assumptions in 2012. In this review, the role of 'autonomous' systems in US Department of Defence (DoD) operations is critically appraised. Although autonomy technologies – which presume even less human involvement than automation - are recognised as having significant impacts on warfare worldwide, their potential contribution not only to vehicle and platform control but throughout all echelons of the command structure is hampered by a lack of a proper conceptual framework for the design and implementation of autonomous systems. Two points are worth noting. First, the widely accepted notion of 'level of automation' does not seem to be adequate as it emphasises the tasks each agent is made responsible for without highlighting the fundamental need to coordinate the management of different aspects of the mission. Second, it tends to imply that throughout a mission planning and execution at these levels are fixed and there is no guidance as to how to switch among different levels throughout. If the potentialities of these intensive technological environments are to be realised, then a more comprehensive framework for design and deployment needs to be developed. The proposed framework extends the scope of autonomous systems by including the echelons of the mission structure from the mission commander to the section leader, and on down to the pilot or sensor operator. The autonomous system framework outlines three criteria that design decisions should meet:

[1] Ensure clear allocation of functions and responsibilities to achieve specific capabilities;

[2] Understand that allocations might vary within the same mission and through echelons; and

[3] Make explicit the high level system trade-offs that are inherent in any autonomous
capabilities.

It is important to emphasise the need to ensure coordination across echelons and
roles as autonomous components increase. In particular, : design trade-offs should be
explicitly considered. Often autonomous systems are introduced without considering
the wider consequences and adjustments required once fully deployed. As a consequence
there is a risk that new sources of errors are introduced and the autonomous technology
is not typically used to its full potential.

In a recent review of automation issues as raised by the two fratricide incidents in
the second Gulf War, Hoffman et al. (Hoffman et al. 2014) report and comment on an
investigation commissioned to the Army Research Laboratory (ARL) on Patriot-human
system performance. (Patriot - an example of intensive technology deployed during the
second Gulf War - is a missile system that launches advanced-technology ammunition
capable of neutralising multiple air targets.) A fairly broad range of issues emerged,
mainly related to what is called an "undisciplined insertion" of autonomous technology
where very little, if anything at all, was done to anticipate downstream consequences.
Undisciplined automation might involve some of the following: *software failures* not
being adequately addressed during software upgrades, and not made known to operators
through training or standard operating procedures (SOPs); emphasis on *software development*: does not address software failure and possible human coping strategies but it
emphasises development of more autonomous technology with less and less apparent
need for human intervention. Front line remains uninformed about the issues; *failure to
train* for expertise while encouraging a 'blind' trust in the autonomous weapon system;
thus training emphasised rote drill rather than the highly specialised technical skills
needed to master the complexity of the monitoring and control process; technology-
intensive systems require considerable operator expertise for effective use; complexity
cannot be reduced by progressively designing the human out of the loop. Already the
current trend is to characterise human-*on*-the-loop rather than human-*in*-the-loop, which
indicates a trend towards monitoring the autonomous system rather than controlling
it - such a function requires a new set of skills which have not received adequate attention
from developers, commanders and higher up in the echelons of organisations; *inadequate administrative procedures* for job allocations such that crew member staff are
rapidly rotated out of the battle positions on to other jobs. It turned out to be difficult to
keep operators and crews in the same position long enough for them to reach a satisfactory level of competence. The result is a fairly inexperienced crew that learns and
adapts to the new complexities in a somewhat haphazard fashion.

The autonomous system should be the subject of analysis, testing and costing in its
organisational context, including infrastructures and training requirements.

A report on the interfaces of modern flight deck systems in the current aviation
industry prepared by the Federal Aviation Administration (FAA) described it as "very
safe" (FAA, 1996). However, a separate review of the data identified vulnerabilities in
flight crew management of automation and their functional understanding of the situation. To address these concerns, the Performance-based Aviation Regulatory Committee

(PARC) and the Commercial Aviation Safety Team (CAST) established a joint working group comprising representatives from the industry (including individuals drawn from both the authorities and research communities) to update the 1996 report. The working group identified several factors that may have an impact on future operations:

- Growth in the number of aircraft operations;
- Evolution in the knowledge and skills needed by crew and air traffic personnel; historically low commercial aviation accident rates that make the cost/benefit case for further safety measures and regulatory change more challenging to argue;
- Future airspace operations that exploit new technology and operational concepts for navigation, communication, surveillance and air traffic management.

The list above is a departing point of the FAA report to illustrate current issues of automation (the focus is mostly on flight crews) interaction, design, and training. Two recommendations and two (combined) findings from the report follow: these summarise some of the most commonly debated problems, such as the need to model interactions and dependencies and to develop up-to-standard training programmes and training skills.

Recommendation 6 and 14 - Flight Deck System Design and training: flight crew *training* should be enhanced to include [...] system relationships and interdependencies during normal and non-normal modes of operation[...].Instructor/Evaluator Training and Qualification. Review guidance for [...] training and qualification for instructors/evaluators. This review should focus on the development and maintenance of skills and knowledge to enable instructors and evaluators to teach and evaluate flight path management, including use of automated systems.

Recommendation 18 – Methods and Recommended Practices for Data Collection, Analysis and Event Investigation that address Human Performance and Underlying Factors: Explicitly address underlying factors in the investigation, including factors such as organisational culture, regulatory policies, and others.

Findings 27–28. Interactions and Underlying Factors in Accidents and Incidents and mitigation to risk factor. Current practices for accident and incident investigation are not designed to enable diagnoses of interactions between safety elements and underlying or "latent" factors [...] there is a lack of data available addressing such factors. When developing safety enhancements, such factors (e.g. organisational culture or policies) are just as important to understand as the human errors that occur. [Interaction among latent conditions might imply that] mitigations to one risk factor can create other, unanticipated risks.

Historically, there has been a somewhat unhelpful human-centric approach, where automation issues revolved around the one-to-one (human – automation interface) interaction; future debate should no longer place humans - viewed as being disconnected from influences and roles of societal pressures, at the centre, of a far too impoverished 'universe' of dynamic interactions.

There are considerable challenges posed for humans by technology in complex work systems (Hoffman et al. 2014). These challenges need to be better understood so as to provide the more appropriately skilled workforce that emerging technologies now require. It is thus vital to embrace the concept of human-machine inter-dependence and collaboration (Bradshaw et al. 2013). It is also necessary to acknowledge the role of human expertise in the implementation of such systems. As Hawley (2011) notes, it is a mistake to believe that we can achieve optimal performance levels through technology alone (Hoffman et al. 2014).

These and other concerns have moved the UK Air traffic National Service Providers (ANSP) NATS and the Civil Aviation Authority (CAA) UK to elicit views and concerns within the air transport industry through a number of workshops held to keep up to date with the continuous changes taking place within the industry. The workshops were intended to contribute to the theoretical and practical body of reference material that can be used by industry specialists (such as regulators) to understand safety attitudes at an organisational and managerial level. In one such workshop held by the NATS/CAA in February 2014, 66 industry professionals (including pilots, engineers, regulators and air traffic controllers) were asked a series of questions, each designed to explore the present and future implementation designs that use advanced human-system integration, i.e. automation and the need for further regulation. Questions and answers were written in bullet point form and placed within a matrix. Using Grounded Theory (GT), this study will map and interpret the workshop data and questionnaires gathered to elicit professionals' views on automation in the aviation industry. The GT method is used in order to analyse the factors affecting automation at an organisational level - that is, roles and responsibilities as identified by the analysis. The aim of the study is to gauge stakeholder attitudes at an organisational level.

{The 2014 workshop and industry surveys held in 2015 provide a critical reflection of industry professionals' views, including: how confident stakeholders feel; what they believe; issues that need to be addressed; and the changes that could be made to improve aviation safety. The GT process interprets the characteristics of the data gathered by describing, categorising and developing themes before applying theoretical foundations to them.}

Two important features of the GT method which make it particularly suitable for this study are that that the themes are traceable to the data and are 'fluid' – meaning that emphasis is placed on process and the temporal nature of the theory. This production process helps to build a story or an "account" and becomes the building blocks of a hypothesis.

In doing so, the method draws out observations of reciprocal changes in patterns of action/interaction between humans and automated systems as well as among humans themselves. Seen at the organisational level, these interactions highlight the needs, behaviours and actions of humans within a consistently changing environment.

2 Study Objective

This study builds on previous research commissioned by NATS to elicit critical views from all parties involved in the design, implementation, regulation and use of existing or planned automated systems (Amaldi and Smoker 2013). It will also analyse views from major stakeholders in civil aviation/air traffic management environments about the current status of automation and the roles that each stakeholder group can play in addressing areas of concern. The study will lay the foundations for an automation survey to gauge stakeholder attitudes at an *organisational* level. This will differ from previous automation surveys which historically have been largely limited to the level of human-machine interaction at an individual (operator) level. In doing so, it will identify the challenges and paths for improvements in the field.

The study comprises three key stages:

(a) Carrying out a thematic analysis of the statements issued during the workshop.
(b) Elaborating on 2014 workshop statements through surveys with stakeholders to gain a thorough understanding of issues; checking that study themes constitute an accurate synthesis of individual stakeholder through a survey.
(c) Testing the relevance and significance of statements at an organisational level by asking the group to score the relevance of statements on a scale – thus capturing the group view.

Results from stage (a) will be reported in what follows.

3 Thematic Analysis

Systems thinking is about non-linearity and dynamics rather than linear cause-effect-cause sequences. In ultra-safe industries, "accidents come from relationships, not broken parts (rules)" (Dekker 2011). These "relationships" comprise "soft", difficult-to-define issues such as the nested layers in complex interactions between human agents (engineers, pilots, ATCs and regulators), between human agents and procedures (flight plans, rules and procedures), and between operators and technical systems (radar systems, aircraft navigation systems, traffic alert and collision avoidance system).

Using GT, sixteen themes that can be integrated into six broad interaction-related themes have been identified, all of which appear to have some relation to the overarching concept of safety culture:

1. Feedback loops within stakeholder interactions. Generally speaking, there is an assumption that feedback will assist stakeholders to: (1) increase their knowledge of the system and thus (2) improve awareness of individuals within the organisation. (Amalberti 2013). More importantly, it is also assumed that through such interaction stakeholders can better understand and anticipate the impact of their actions so as to prevent system failures. Regulators, in particular, are required to rely on feedback gained from industry experts in order to gain a broader perspective of the potential interactions that anticipate failures within the system. However, because regulators do not conduct actual operations and have different educational background from other stakeholders (engineers, pilots and ATCs), they may not fully understand the broader perspective of the organisational system. The best they can do is to rely on the knowledge base of other stakeholders causing them to gain only partial knowledge, which may lead to either misinterpretation or bias on their part when creating s regulatory structures. As a result, regulator group interactions that rely on feedback can be inadequate because regulation becomes more opaque and difficult to manage (Amalberti 2013). This raises the question of whether the system is unmanageable.

2. System not designed to optimise socio-technical interactions. Designers cannot foresee all possible scenarios of system failure and are thus not able to provide automatic safety devices for every contingency. Automation therefore becomes limited with regard to dealing with multiple failures, unexpected problems and situations requiring deviations from Standard Operating Procedures (SOPs). Furthermore, unanticipated situations requiring human agents to manually override automation are difficult to understand and manage. For instance, too much time spent trying to understand the origin, conditions, or causes of an alarm or several alarms may distract pilots from other priority tasks, such as the value of pitch, power and roll when flying the aircraft. This may cause adverse circumstances due to the pilot's surprise as well as induce peaks of workload and stress. Furthermore, interactions of this kind may foster human agents' feelings of distrust, dis-use of automation in future (Woods 2006).

3. Interactions with automation can undermine confidence/trust. Human distrust of automation undermines confidence in it (Gao et al. 2006). Operators also lose confidence in their own ability because the use of automation contributes to the lack of manual skills practice and can cause skills degradation (Gao et al. 2006). This may make them more reluctant to be proactive when interacting with automation.

4. Degree and delegation of control, autonomy, authority and responsibility between human and automated agents need to be better understood. There is a poor understanding of the mechanics behind automation and how to manage human interaction with it. How much should we grant to automated systems? Which stakeholders should have authority for which tasks? How are decisions taken to empower automation, and to what extent? Too much authority, autonomy and control in the hands of the human agent can be seen as not optimising automated systems (Sheridan and Parasuraman 2006). On the other hand, too much authority, autonomy and control given to automated systems can give rise to an over-reliance on automation (Thackray and Touchstone 1989; Wiener 1981). Over-reliance on automation can lead to interaction challenges when operators need to transition back to manual or degraded modes, Furthermore, new technologies can complicate or change the operator's tasks, altering the situations in which tasks occur and even the conditions that affect the quality of the operator's, work and engagement in such tasks (Carroll and Campbell 1988; Dekker and Woods 2002). For example, pilots today "monitor screens" rather than fly planes. The building of interactions based on trust, cooperation, and coordination between human agents and automation needs to be better understood and managed. (Dekker and Woods 2002; Hancock 2014).

5. Organisational "Just Culture" undermined by legal realities. This refers to "good practice" principles that reduce finger-pointing and encourage individuals to report near-misses (Dekker 2007). While Just Culture is an admirable goal (and one that would shed more light on potential safety improvements), legal realities are such that individuals may be reticent about reporting incidents for which they might be held liable for fear of the legal consequences. These contradictions and the lack of transparency can create blind spots within the organisation, which may subsequently obscure sound decision-making.

6. Human interaction and the ETTO PRINCIPLE. Acknowledging the Efficiency–Thoroughness Trade-Off principle - balancing the trade-off between efficiency or productivity/profits/business realities on the one hand, and thoroughness (such as safety assurance and human reliability) on the other (Hollnagel 2009). In an ideal world, corporate governance and ethical management practices would be of paramount importance, particularly in high-risk industries such as aviation. However, market forces encourage productivity, incentivising stakeholders to focus on increases in production/workload without foreseeing the impact on safety (Hollnagel 2009). As the ETTO principle demonstrates, the reality is that management's prioritisation of production over safety will have financial benefits on the one hand, but also a negative impact on safety that only becomes clear in the future - by which time a manager could have left the organisation. Such a "bad decision" is rarely traced back to the manager once time has passed and he is no longer with the organisation. As a result, short-term financial gain (such as a significant bonus) may prevail over long-term safety considerations (for which there is no trail of responsibility). It can therefore not be assumed that companies will prioritise safety when making strategic decisions. Business leaders are under pressure to be productive/competitive/efficient, and thus may run the risk of encouraging an organisational culture where productivity is favoured over safety.

4   Integration with Previous Study

The web of connected themes in Fig. 1 constitutes the articulated views and perspectives of the stakeholders interviewed in the February 2014 workshop.

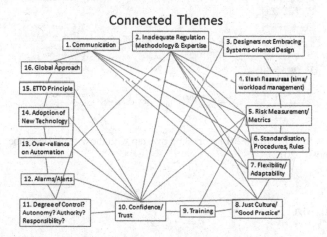

Fig. 1. The 'web' of connections and links between themes are displayed above.

The outcome of this workshop is compared with that of two previous workshops (Amaldi and Smoker 2012) to check for thematic overlap and consistency. Figure 2 shows a number of statements extracted from the previous workshops. Figure 3 shows where themes from previous workshops overlap with those from the 2014 workshop.

Main reflections about automation	
Lack of definition/vision	Lack of definition/vision Different expectations about what the automation will deliver. What 'levels' of automation
Responsibility and role allocation	No clear vision about responsibility for decision making. Define roles and appropriate training
Safety and effectiveness of automation	Safety relies on effective human- automation interaction. Manage the cost/benefit of automation. Automation needs to be focused upon removing key risks from the operation and exploiting the different strengths of the human and the machine.
Role/responsibility under unexpected circumstances	How tasks and roles will shift
New skills required	What skills need 'un-learning' and what the new are
Validation of effective co-operation and co-ordination	Automation as 'user friendly'

Fig. 2. Main reflections about automation taken from December 2011 survey (Amaldi & Smoker, 2012).

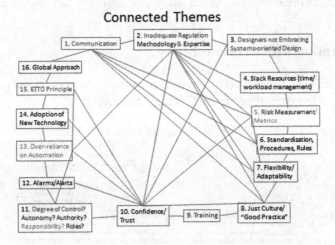

Fig. 3. Themes from February 2014 workshop overlap with those from December 2011 survey (Amaldi & Smoker, 2012).

5   Conclusion

The focus of the study is ultimately on the interactive processes between technology and humans as conceived within and across the domain of expertise, from front line operators to regulators. Emerging technologies lead to inadequate understanding, control and management of the increasing complexities faced by stakeholders (Bradshaw et al. 2013). As automation/autonomous systems make their way into safety critical systems, the dependencies of interactions that impact on other system sub-components cannot be satisfactorily anticipated (Perrow 1984). Thus, socio-technical interactions, particularly in times of crisis, become poorly understood (Hancock, 2014). Furthermore, it makes training for these for these technologies inadequate (Hancock 2014). Therefore, the challenges of emerging technologies need to be better understood in order to provide control and a more skilled workforce (Bradshaw et al. 2013). Recent research views human-machine inter-dependence and collaboration as key to improve effectiveness in a work system (Hancock 2014). For this to happen, human expertise needs to be recognised as key since optimal performance levels can not be achieved through technology alone (Bradshaw, et al. 2013; Hancock 2014). The themes developed through GT assisted in viewing the emerging patterns of the relationships, intent, behaviours and actions of individuals interacting with each other as well as with automation. These patterns help to provide a clearer picture of what expertise stakeholders believe is needed in order to perform at optimal performance levels, and where potential pitfalls lie. Human-machine teamwork is seen as vital to allow "virtues" to emerge and propagate – chief among these being the wisdom to understand "how to work smarter" (Johnson et al. 2014). Mapping the patterns of interactions between team members in socio-technical systems may be a step in the right direction to gain such wisdom Fig. 4 .

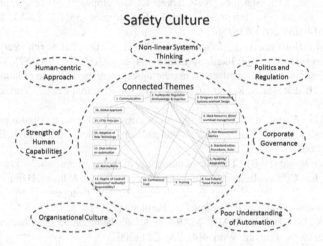

Fig. 4. Connected themes appear to be influenced by pervasive external themes within the organisational environment; the over-arching theme seems to be safety culture.

The findings of the study are intended to contribute to the theoretical and practical body of reference material that can be used by industry specialists (such as regulators) to understand safety attitudes with respect to automation within management and organ-isations.

Using these findings, current regulations will be tested for their suitability in future operating environments. Assessments will also be made as to whether any further requirements are needed both nationally and globally.

This study also aims to lay the foundations for an automation survey to assess measure stakeholder attitudes at an *organisational* level - automation surveys have historically mostly been limited to the level of human-machine interaction at an individual (operator) level. Further this study is part of an ongoing CAA/NATS-initiated project whose aim is to provide guidance material to help create, design and deploy systems for safe and effective operation, while recognising business drivers for the industry as a whole.

Acknowledgments. We thank all participants in the study, including those from the CAA and NATS, as well as various other organisations.

References

Amalberti, R.: Navigating Safety: Necessary Compromises and Trade-Offs Theory and Practice. Springer, Amsterdam (2013)

Amaldi, P., Smoker, A.: An Organizational Study into the Concept of Automation in a Safety Critical Socio-technical System. In: Campos, P., Clemmensen, T., Nocera, J.A., Katre, D., Lopes, A., Omgreen, R. (eds.) Human Work Interaction Design. Work Analysis and HCI, pp. 183–197. Springer, Heidelberg (2012)

Amaldi, P., Smoker, A.: An organizational study into the concept of "automation policy" in a safety critical socio-technical system. Int. J. Sociotechnol. Knowl. Dev. 5(2), 1–17 (2013)

Balfe, N., Wilson, J.R., Sharples, S., Clarke, T.: Development of design principles for automated systems in transport control. Ergonomics **55**(1), 37–54 (2012). doi: 10.1080/00140139.2011.636456

Bradshaw, J.M., Hoffman, R.R., Johnson, M., Woods, D.D.: The seven deadly myths of 'autonomous systems'. IEEE Intell. Syst. **28**(3), 54–61 (2013). doi:10.1109/MIS.2013.70

Carroll, J.M., Campbell, R.L.: Artifacts as psychological theories: The case of human-computer interaction. IBM Research Report RC 13454, Watson Research Center, Yorktown Heights, NY (1988)

Gao, J., Lee, J.D., Zhang, Y.: A dynamic model of interaction between reliance on automation and cooperation in multi-operator multi-automation situations. Int. J. Ind. Ergon. **36**(5), 511–526 (2006)

Defense Science Board (DSB).: The role of autonomy in DoD systems. pp. 1– 115 (2012)

Dekker, S.W.: Just Culture: Balancing Safety and Accountability. Ashgate, Hampshire (2007)

Dekker, S.W.A.: Drift into Failure: From Hunting Broken Components to Understanding Complex Systems. Ashgate Publishing Co., Farnham (2011)

Dekker, S.W.A., Woods, D.D.: MABA-MABA or Abracadabra: progress on human automation cooperation. Cogn. Technol. Work **4**(4), 240–244 (2002)

Hancock, P.A.: Automation: how much is too much? Ergonomics **57**(3), 449–454 (2014). doi:10.1080/00140139.2013.816375

Hoffman, R.R., Hawley, K.K., Bradshaw, J.M.: Myths of automation, partsome very human consequences. IEEE Intell. Syst. **29**(2), 82–85 (2014)

Hollnagel, E.: The ETTO Principle: Efficiency-Thoroughness Trade-Off: Why Things That Go Right Sometimes Go Wrong. Ashgate, London (2009)

Johnson M., Bradshaw J.M., Hoffman R.R., Feltovich J.F., Woods D.D.: Seven cardinal virtues of human machine teamwork: examples from the darpa robotic challenge. IEEE Intell. Syst., 1 (2014)

Murphy R.: The Role of Autonomy in DoD Systems, Defense Science Board Task Force Report (2012) http://fas.org/irp/agency/dod/dsb/autonomy.pdf

Perrow, C.: Normal Accidents: Living With High-Risk Technologies. Basic Books Inc, New York (1984)

Sheridan, T.B., Parasuraman, R.: Human-automation interaction. Rev. Hum. Factors Ergon. **1**, 89–129 (2006)

Silva, S., Lima, L.M., Baptista, C.: OSCI: an organisational and safety climate inventory. Safe. Sci. **42**(3), 205–220 (2004)

Thackray, R.I., Touchstone, R.M.: Detection efficiency on an air traffic control monitoring task with and without computer aiding. Aviat. Space Environ. Med. **60**, 744–748 (1989)

Weiner, E.L.: Complacency: is the term useful for air safety? In: Proceedings of the 26th Corporate Aviation Safety Seminar, pp.116–125, Flight Safety Foundation, Inc., denver (1981)

Designing a Demonstrator Virtual Learning Environment to Teach the Threshold Concept of Space Syntax: Seeing from the User's Perspective

Judith Molka-Danielsen[1(✉)], Mikhail Fominykh[1,2], David Swapp[3], and Anthony Steed[3]

[1] Molde University College, Molde, Norway
{J.Molka-Danielsen, Mikhail.Fominykh}@himolde.no
[2] Volga State University of Technology, Yoshkar-Ola, Russia
FominykhMA@volgatech.net
[3] University College London, London, UK
{d.swapp, a.steed}@ucl.ac.uk

Abstract. Space syntax is an important knowledge domain and focus of study for students of Architecture. It centers on the understanding of spaces, tectonics and volumes for the informed design of buildings or outdoor spaces. Space syntax is considered to be a threshold concept in Architecture, in that understanding and interpreting this knowledge domain is something that the learner needs to acquire in order to progress as a professional in this field. The concept of "line of sight" is a specific example of a concept in the space syntax domain. This research investigates a case of systems design of an immersive virtual learning environment to support teaching a concept of space syntax to students of Architecture. Such environments can engage, immerse and guide learners in ways not yet undertaken and may find application in workplace learning. This research explores the systems design requirements through a demonstrator that is tested by a small pilot group. One case scenario to teach the concept of "line of sight" was selected for the target design. Based on the expert feedback we designed a learning module demonstrated at the University College London CAVE-hybrid facility. The demonstrator was trialed in 16 timed trials. Several conclusions for workplace learning on the systems design choices are drawn.

Keywords: Virtual Learning Environments · Space syntax · Threshold concepts · Systems design · Experiential learning · Virtual worlds

1 Introduction

Information Systems (IS) designers have often made analogies between the design of information systems and the design of buildings, saying that IS design is like building design in that, "Architecture, design, construction, furnishings, inhabitants, and location all play major roles in shaping the overall experience" [1]. It is not surprising then that "consideration of the end users first person perspective" would be an important approach to teaching of concepts in Architecture. And we as systems designers of Virtual Learning

© IFIP International Federation for Information Processing 2015
J. Abdelnour-Nocera et al. (Eds.): HWID 2015, IFIP AICT 468, pp. 180–191, 2015.
DOI: 10.1007/978-3-319-27048-7_13

Environments (VLE) would seek to discover and include these requirements in the design of VLE learning module for students of Architecture. In this paper, we describe our approach of systems design of a VLE *demonstrator*. We report on the trials of the demonstrator and discuss the implications that such tools support reflective learning approaches [2] and can be suitable for students at different stages of their careers. This paper explores: What are the systems design requirements for VLEs to support learning of the threshold concept of "line of sight" in the knowledge domain of space syntax.

The remaining paper is presented as follows. In the next section, we clarify meaning of threshold concepts and the role of virtual technologies in practical experiential learning, and we present prior research in these domains. In Sect. 3, we give a description of our methodology for this project describing the systems design approach for the demonstrator. In Sect. 4, we describe our trials and observations. Section 5 discusses implications for VLE design. Section 6 gives concluding remarks.

2 Literature Review

2.1 Virtual Reality Technologies

In recent years, virtual reality (VR) technologies have been applied in teaching and learning. The main motivations for their use have been that VLE based on VR technologies are engaging as media [3] and that use of 3D media facilitates comprehension by means of situating learning materials in a context and exploiting the natural capabilities of humans to interact in 3D space [4]. In particular they investigated user interaction in immersive VR environments and found that the use of virtual content successfully changed the users' conceptual understanding of the content [4]. A key characteristic that motivates the use of VR in training is that participants behave in a way that is similar to their behavior in comparably similar real situations [5, 6]. These studies distinguish immersive VR from desktop VR proving that in the immersive VR the participant acts, to a great extent, as they would in the real physical world. In desktop VR, this level of immersion is limited by the form and structure of the interface. General studies of the capabilities of immersive VR systems on comprehension have shown that these systems are preferred for tasks that are exploratory and interactive [7–9]. One study identifies that for constrained tasks that features of immersive VR are contributing to performance differences [10]. However, these studies are limited in that they have not provided requirements analysis that can predict tasks for which immersive VR environments are superior over desktop approaches.

2.2 In Search for Pedagogical Approaches

Modern pedagogic approaches have emphasized the importance of real life experience, such as in the workplace, for transforming learning objectives into knowledge that can be applied in practice. At the same time, workplace experience needs to be converted into knowledge to enable deeper learning. The information relevant for a master level of performance (aka 'theory'), traditionally, is separated from the immediate experience of competent action (aka 'practice') [11]. In the past, this conversion has been supervised by skilled experts or teachers using shared experience and direct instruction. Various media, such as textbooks or instructional films, have been used as information containers. However, with recent technical advances in virtual and augmented reality, new opportunities arise for training that do not rely on strict separation of knowledge from its application.

Knowledge appears in many forms. Tangible knowledge may be stored as written instructions or in databases. Intangible knowledge appears as activity, practice, relation between participants, and in their shared experience. The former type of knowledge is known as explicit and the latter as tacit [12, 13].

Tacit knowledge can be converted to explicit knowledge through narratives – in addition to iterative training that aim to create embodied experience through activity [14]. Immersive VR as well as augmented reality provides an embodied dimension that makes users interact in the same way they do in a real context [15, 16].

Approaches, such as experiential learning [17] and problem-based learning [18], have been applied in classrooms and have been intended for acquiring workplace skills. While having correct objectives, these approaches often fall short of supports for the transformative process necessary for the learner to capture core concepts within the targeted discipline.

2.3   Threshold Concepts

The core concepts referred to here are identified as *threshold concepts*. Erik Meyer and Ray Land state, "A threshold concept can be considered as akin to a portal, opening up a new and previously inaccessible way of thinking about something. It represents a transformed way of understanding, interpreting, or viewing something without which the learner cannot progress" [19].

These necessary knowledge components represent transitions in understanding [19]. While struggling with a new way of perceiving the practices of a discipline, the learner is in a state of liminality before finally grasping the concept and passing the threshold [20].

Threshold concepts among other qualities are difficult to perceive and comprehend for the newcomers in a community of practice. Experts differ from the newcomers not only by the level of their skills, but by deeper understanding of the discipline, the profession, and, in other words, of the threshold concepts. Such understanding is often connected to tacit knowledge [17]. Access to such knowledge is therefore important and necessary for a professional to achieve the level of expert in a discipline. Land and Meyer state further that threshold concepts are central "core" concepts within a discipline that are essential in the acquisition of creative thinking, learning and communication of understanding within a discipline [19, 21–23].

There is a documented lack of support for threshold experiences in higher education [24]. However, we have recently explored teaching threshold concepts with the support of VR technologies [25] and identified conceptual requirements for systems design [26]. This study extends the research of [26] in that it designs and pilot tests a demonstrator of a VLE that aims to support an exploratory and interactive learning task for Architecture students. The demonstrator is designed with use of immersive VR technologies that are described in the next section.

3 Methodology

This research applies the general steps of Design Science Research (DSR) as an approach to design the demonstrator artifact that is a learning module implemented in a VLE. We selected DSR as recent studies for developing user innovation in virtual world's shows that DSR can be used as problem solving process to develop IS artifacts [27–29]. Through a cyclical process of design of the learning module, a better understanding of the users experience and design requirements are obtained. The general steps of DSR are: problem awareness, suggestion, development, evaluation and conclusion. At each stage of development, evaluation and conclusion, knowledge is gained and fed back into problem awareness, thus influencing suggestions for further improvements. The DSR approach was useful in that it allowed us the designers of the VLE, to study how a trial group learned. We conducted the following steps:

1. *Problem Awareness:* Through interviews with experts in the selected field of learning, Architecture, we recognize difficulties with traditional learning methods.
2. *Suggestion:* The knowledge gained from the interviews and designers knowledge of VLE technologies influence the initial development of the learning module.
3. *Development:* The learning modules are implemented using two software implementations to allow control for the influence of the software interfaces on the trials.
4. *Evaluation:* The demonstrators are evaluated by general users in timed trials.
5. *Conclusion:* The designers draw conclusions based on the observation of the trials.
6. *Cycle-2:* Further cycles are suggested with use of several trial groups of Architecture students at different points in their progression of study.

3.1 Problem Awareness and Suggestion

In September 2013, the researchers conducted interviews with Architecture experts Dr. Sean Hanna (SH, Space and Adaptive Architectures, UCL) and Dr. Sam Griffiths (SG, Urban Morphology and Theory, UCL). The information from these interviews was used to inform the learning module that would be implemented in the VLE. Some of the statements of the interviews are summarized as follows:

- SH: "Space syntax" is a long threshold concept. This is a very broad theme, and the knowledge domain for a master's level program. SH says that students that have mastered the concepts of space syntax make different assessments and decisions as applied to architectural designs. This has been tested in students' responses to school assignments and even in master's thesis.
- SH: Issues such as "lines of sight", "where people are likely to move, gather around objects, meet others", are related to understanding of space syntax.
- SH: The way that students think about "spaces, tectonics, and volumes" is part of a long threshold in Architecture. Students that know about design space syntax are more likely to use those concepts in design decisions.

- SG: Points out that there are some students who you can see that "get it" and that these are distinguishable from those who may struggle with the tools and models. While understanding the tools and models, these can give very delineated responses to questions. However, the questions are sometimes complex and do not have simple responses.
- SG: Most of the tools and visual presentations of their work are done in 2D. The work presented in 2D only is a challenge for students with little work experience to transform that view in a classroom exercise into an integrated analysis of the space syntax. The use of 3D tools in itself offers another perspective that can be helpful in learning.

We concluded at this stage to develop a module that would function in a Cave Automatic Virtual Environment (CAVE), as described in the next section. The aim is that a simulation in the CAVE that provides a real-time feedback would help in the student's integrated analysis.

3.2 Development Components of the Immersive 3D VLE

The platform applied in this research made use of CAVE, an immersive projection technology [30]. A CAVE is typically a cube-shaped display that the user stands inside. The CAVE surrounds the user, thus excluding other distractions and allowing the participant to move about un-constrained by the need to face a specific desktop display. The wide field of view allows natural peripheral observation and gaze control.

More specifically, this research was conducted as part of a visiting scholar research project (see acknowledgements) in cooperation with the Virtual Environments and Computer Group (VECG) of the CS Dept. at University College London. The project applied VECG group computers and immersive visualization facilities. The VECG group of the Department of Computer Science (UCL-CS) has excellent visualization facilities including a four-sided CAVE-hybrid driven by a PC cluster (four client nodes with GeForce Quadro 5600 graphics), a six-camera Vicon motion-tracking system, an eight camera Optitrak system, an Intersense wireless tracking system, head-mounted VR and augmented reality displays, a GRAB haptic interface and various other tracking systems and input devices including bio-signal amplifiers.

This research applied two virtual world technologies that are normally accessed through desktop interfaces. However, the learning modules were instantiated (brought up) in the CAVE. These virtual world technologies were vAcademia™ (vA), a VLE software that was created especially for educational purposes [31], and Second Life™ (SL) a general purpose virtual world software that has been widely adopted also for non-educational purposes. The implications for this study were that the researchers had access to more server side hooks for vA when bringing up simulations in the CAVE. With use of two virtual world technologies we also control for some behavior differences that can be due to perspectives afforded by the different interfaces.

3.3   Demonstrator Design

In the next phase of the project, we developed a learning module that is based on a prior design of Kalff et al. [32]. The demonstrator activity is shopping for items in a food store. In our scenario, the participant is to look for and identify three items on the shelves in a food store. Our model has eight shelves. There are two perspectives of the shelves and in the VLE models and both perspectives are replicated in SL and vA. That is we have made two separate builds for each perspective. The perspectives are with shelves pointing towards the participant ("plus" or A) and with shelves pointing away from the participant ("minus", B).

The 2D overhead view of the VLE scene is depicted below (Fig. 1, left). A person would stand at point A or B. In general, the perspective of B should result in faster times for participants to locate and identify items in the food store. This would be a typical "line of sight" exercise for a new student in Architecture.

For a participant to look at the 2D representation above, it can be difficult to visualize which perspective is more effective. With the help of a 3D representation, the "better" design could be more easily identified. Applying the 3D representation would be seeing from the end user's perspective, that is, the shopper's perspective. A more experienced Architecture student might be given more delineated tasks. For example, they might be asked to determine the best angle of the shelves. This was not asked in these trials.

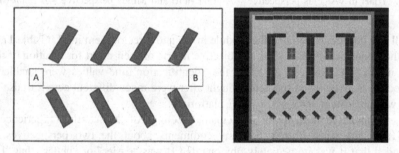

Fig. 1. The Learning Scenario in a VLE (left) and a 2D layout of a food store (right)

4   Trials and Observations

We conducted trials of the learning module with five volunteer participants, using a Think-aloud protocol [33] to gather data. Participants were asked to talk about what they were doing while active in the trials. The trials were video recorded to not interfere with the participants while they completed their tasks. All had prior experience with virtual reality environments. They gave verbal consent for use of video recording of their trials. We first showed them a 2D diagram of a food store (Fig. 1, right) and asked which perspective would be their preferred starting point (A or B). Although everyone did choose B, most of the responders were hesitant and unsure. We then had the participants try out the module in SL (Fig. 2) and in vA (Fig. 3).

Fig. 2. Trials in SL: Plus perspective – A point (left) and Minus perspective – B point (right)

Fig. 3. Trials in vA: Plus perspective – A point (left) and Minus perspective – B point (right)

All five participants trialed the module in vA and three of them in SL (Table 1). We used the 'identification times' as an objective metric of their effort for location of three items in the food store. In all trials, the 'identification'time values were smaller for perspective B, even when the items sought after were made different across trials. This trend was consistent across both VLE platforms.

As an affective measure of participants' feelings of the learning experience we asked after the trials if they had any comments about the two perspectives. All responded that it was immediately obvious that B was "easier" or "better" that "I can see everything in B, but in the other (A) my view is blocked". Some noted that it was also a more pleasant shopping experience with B, as it was so hard to move around in the VLE and with B they did not have to move the avatar so much. Many commented that in real life grocery stores, that store owners want you to walk around, and maybe wanted customers to not find items so quickly. Some participants of the exercise noted that items were easier to see/identify in vA than in SL. We attribute this to the fact that first person perspective functioned in the vA trials, giving a better view. And, only third person perspective functioned in SL in the CAVE. However, some commented that it was easier to move around in SL. In both VLEs, the participants controlled the movement of the avatar using a keyboard. The model in vA had shelves inside a four-walled store; while alternatively, the model in SL had shelves on an open plane. So the reason for some longer identification times in vA may have been the presence of the walls, as sometimes the users' camera view was obstructed when standing too close

Table 1. Trial Times according to VLE and Perspective

VLE	Perspective	Items to Find	User (U); Trial (T) = Time to locate the item
SL	A	• Orange Juice, Tooth paste, Milk • Pasta, Tooth paste, Olives • Tomatoes, Tomato sauce, Yoghurt	U3; T365 = 1 min 42 s U4; T384 = 0 min 50 s U5; T387 = 1 min 15 s
SL	B	• Yoghurt, Pasta, Olives • Milk, Cabbage, Lunch Meat • Milk, Cabbage, Pasta	U3; T366 = 0 min 30 s U4; T383 = 0 min 35 s U5; T388 = 0 min 33 s
vA	A	• Orange Juice, Tooth paste, Crisps	U1; T351 = 1 min 50 s U2; T354 = 2 min 30 s U3; T369 = 1 min 20 s U4; T374 = 2 min 15 s U5; T378 = 1 min 00 s
vA	B	• Yoghurt, Pasta, Olives	U1; T353 = 0 min 30 s U2; T357 = 0 min 50 s U3; T373 = 0 min 26 s U4; T375 = 0 min 42 s U5; T379 = 0 min 35 s

to the walls. While the number of trials is too few to make performance comparisons of the two VLEs, future designs could be created in open spaces to avoid confusions caused by misaligned camera views.

5   Implications for VLE Systems Design

This study gives evidence that VLEs hold potential to support of learning of threshold concepts through experiential learning approach. A demonstrator of one threshold learning scenario was implemented and trialed in the CAVE using two VLE platforms. The primary implications of this research are summarized in Table 2.

We conclude that several VLE design factors were important and can contribute to better workplace learning environments that support experiential reflective learning. These are:

1. First person view is important for achieving realistic lines of vision/sight (Fig. 3). The use of third person view in SL places the user above the scene (Fig. 2). In addition, as one user pointed out, it is harder to get closer (next to) the shelves in third person view, and so it is more difficult to see and identify the items.
2. Choices of interface tools are important. Several commented a joystick would have enabled easier movement as opposed to the application of keyboard for movement. The choice of "easier movement" would represent more accurately the real life ease of walking around in a food store.

Table 2. Implications for VLE systems design

Implications

- Learning with your virtual body – the VLE supported the learning of threshold concepts through the interaction of the learner (through their avatar) with the 3D virtual environment. In brief, walking around in the store in the demonstrator had the feel of walking around a store in real life.
- First person view perspective – was one of the features that was most important in the ability to read items on the shelves and to move naturally around. This was not apparent to an outside observer that views 2D video recordings of movement in the virtual environments. But, it was reported as important by those participating in the trials.
- The students were informed by their experience in the trials that enabled them to "see from the user's perspective" – however, that perspective will depend on who is the user. The trial participants realized during the trials that a customer in a food store will want to find items quickly, while a shop manager will want the customer to spend more time in the shop.
- Learning takes place after becoming familiar with the technical interface and moving around in the VLE – when the users became more familiar with the VLE interface controls, they were able to focus on the cognitive task. The comments then focused more on which architectural perspective was better, rather than on the VLE interface. A pre-task interaction session is recommended for all learning modules.

3. The food items on the shelves in the store models were placed with no specific logic next to each other. For example, refrigerated items (e.g., orange juice) could be on shelf next to dry storage items (e.g., toothpaste). In addition, the color of the shelves were green, indicating dry storage space, and this did not make sense to one participant that was looking for orange juice in a cold refrigeration unit that should be white. Obliviously, the placement of items in the model is not how the items would be located in stores in real life. In brief, during trials the participants could not rely on internalized experience models of normal layouts of food stores. While done purposely for this exercise, course designers and VLE designers might consider multiple layouts when testing learning outcomes.
4. The model of the scene and avatar in the 3D (e.g. CAVE environment) should be built to a 1:1 scale as they would be in real life. That is if the participant is using first person view, the size of the objects should be on a 1:1 scale with the size of the avatar. For example, the shelf height should be designed as in real life, on average about 2–2.5 meters for a 1.6–2 meter tall person. The reason for doing this is, if a shelf height of a three meters is used, the top of the shelf could not be viewed in first person view mode, unless the avatar would take a step away from the object. This was at least what our participants experienced in the CAVE. Alternatively, the issue of scale is not as important for a PC desktop interface. That is because when using a

PC desktop interface the user often uses a third person view to find items. As such, the scales of objects (items and shelves) are often made larger in respect to the avatar than they would be in real life, to take advantage that the objects in the desktop module would fill more screen space.

Regarding the four points above, it is clear that VLE design choices had implications for how the participant saw the environment and solved problems.

6 Concluding Remarks

In summary, this paper explored the systems design requirements for the design of VLE for teaching an architectural threshold concept of "line of sight" within the knowledge domain of space syntax. Our research used a DSR approach to design a demonstrator that contributes to a proof-of-concept, that VLE can be applied to support learning of a threshold concept. This was demonstrated in two different VLEs. We described the implementation and analysis of a demonstrator of a threshold learning scenario in the CAVE and assessed the system elements that would support that environment. We identified some basic factors about the software and hardware components that need to be considered in VLE design to be more supportive of a workplace learning environment. Last, we created a testing environment that can be replicated, modified and applied in future research projects.

For further DSR cycles of the VLE design, we recommend testing of the modules with Architect students at various stages of their career including those with workplace experience. Educators could also change tasks and apply different assessment methods. Future changes to this design should explore the question: can the VLE be a learning aid for those who already "get it". That is, more experienced professionals may already comprehend the threshold concept, but may struggle with it in different contexts.

Finally, we think the DSR approach may be applied to the design of other VLE scenarios for workplace training and for teaching threshold concepts in other knowledge domains. For example, possible scenarios could include re-training for new equipment or settings in industry, continuous training in medicine, and threat detection in emergency management. In such a case, VLEs can be used as tools for vocational training. Creating more learning scenarios and trialing these with expanded target groups is a natural next step.

Acknowledgements. The research leading to these results has received funding from the European Commission's Research Infrastructure Action – grant agreement VISIONAIR 262044 - under FP7/2007-2013. The author wishes to thank Mikhail Morozov, Maksim Tsukanov and Andrey Smorkalov from the support team of vAcademia at Volga State University of Technology, RU, for their contribution of the development of the VLEs.

References

1. Morville, P., Rosenfeld, L.: Information Architecture for the World Wide Web. O'Reilly Media, Sebastopol (2007)
2. Boud, D., Keogh, R., Walker, D. (eds.): Reflection: Turning Experience into Learning. Kogan Page, London (1985)
3. Winn, W., Windschitl, M., Fruland, R., Lee, Y.: When does immersion in a virtual environment help students construct understanding. In: Fifth International Conference of the Learning Sciences, Seattle, Washington, 23–26 October 2002, pp. 497–503. ICLS, Chicago (2002)
4. Roussou, M., Oliver, M., Slater, M.: The virtual playground: an educational virtual reality environment for evaluating interactivity and conceptual learning. Virtual Reality 10(3–4), 227–240 (2006)
5. Sanchez-Vives, M.V., Slater, M.: From presence to consciousness through virtual reality. Nat. Rev. Neurosci. 6(4), 332–339 (2005)
6. Slater, M.: Place illusion and plausibility can lead to realistic behaviour in immersive virtual environments. Philos. Trans. R. Soc. Lond. 364(1535), 3549–3557 (2009)
7. Demiralp, C., Jackson, C.D., Karelitz, D.B., Song, Z., Laidlaw, D.H.: CAVE and fishtank virtual-reality displays: a qualitative and quantitative comparison. IEEE Trans. Visual. Comput. Graphics 12(3), 323–330 (2006)
8. Prabhat, F.A., Katzourin, M., Wharton, K., Slater, M.: A comparative study of desktop, fishtank, and cave systems for the exploration of volume rendered confocal data sets. IEEE Trans. Visual. Comput. Graphics 14(3), 551–563 (2008)
9. Swindells, C., Po, B.A., Hajshirmohammadi, I., Corrie, B., Dill, J.C., Fisher, B.D., Booth, K.S.: Comparing CAVE, wall, and desktop displays for navigation and wayfinding in complex 3D models. In: Computer Graphics International, Crete, Greece, 16–19 June 2004, pp. 420–427. IEEE, New York (2004)
10. Ragan, E.D., Kopper, R., Schuchardt, P., Bowman, D.A.: Studying the effects of stereo, head tracking, and field of regard on a small-scale spatial judgment task. IEEE Trans. Visual. Comput. Graphics 19(5), 886–896 (2013)
11. Fominykh, M., Wild, F., Smith, C., Alvarez, V., Morozov, M.: An overview of capturing live experience with virtual and augmented reality. In: 1st Immersive Learning Research Network Conference (iLRN), Prague, Czech Republic, July 13–14. IOS Press, Amsterdam (2015)
12. Polanyi, M.: The Tacit Dimension. Peter Smith, Glouchester (1966)
13. Lam, A.: Tacit knowledge, organizational learning and societal institutions: an integrated framework. Organ. Stud. 21(3), 487–513 (2000)
14. Jang, S., Black, J.B., Jyung, R.W.: Embodied cognition and virtual reality in learning to visualize anatomy. In: 32nd Annual Conference of the Cognitive Science Society, pp. 2326–2331. Cognitive Science Society, Portland, OR (2010)
15. Mennecke, B.E., Triplett, J.L., Hassall, L.M., Conde, Z.J., Heer, R.: An examination of a theory of embodied social presence in virtual worlds. Decis. Sci. 42, 413–450 (2011)
16. Mennecke, B.E., Triplett, J. L., Hassall, L.M, Conde, Z.J.: Embodied social presence theory. Paper presented at the 43rd HICSS, Hawaii, US (2010)
17. Kolb, D.A.: Experiential Learning. Prentice-Hall, Engelwood Cliffs (1984)
18. Gijselaers, W.H.: Connecting problem based practices with educational theory. In: Wilkerson, L., Gijselaers, W.H. (eds.) Bringing Problem-Based Learning to Higher Education: Theory and Practice, pp. 13–21. Jossey-Bass, San Francisco (1996)

19. Meyer, J.H.F., Land, R.: Threshold Concepts and Troublesome Knowledge: Linkages to Ways of Thinking and Practicing within the Disciplines. ETL Project Occasional Report, No. 4 (2003). http://www.etl.tla.ed.ac.uk/docs/ETLreport4.pdf
20. Meyer, J.H.F., Land, R.: Threshold concepts and troublesome knowledge: linkages to ways of thinking and practicing. In: Rust, C. (ed.) Improving Student Learning - Theory and Practice Ten Years On, pp. 412–424. Oxford Centre for Staff and Learning Development (OCSLD), Oxford (2003)
21. Meyer, J.H.F., Land, R.: Threshold concepts and troublesome knowledge: issues of liminality. In: Meyer, J.H.F., Land, R. (eds.) Overcoming barriers to student understanding: threshold concepts and troublesome knowledge, pp. 19–32. Routledge, Abingdon (2006)
22. Meyer, J.F., Land, R.: Threshold concepts and troublesome knowledge (2): epistemological considerations and a conceptual framework for teaching and learning. High. Educ. 49(3), 373–388 (2005)
23. Meyer, J.H.F., Land, R., Davies, P.: Threshold concepts and troublesome knowledge (4): issues of variation and variability. In: Land, R., Meyer, J.H.F., Smith, J. (eds.) Threshold Concepts Within the Disciplines. Educational Futures Rethinking Theory and Practice, pp. 59–74. Sense Publishers, Rotterdam and Taipei (2008)
24. Perkins, D.: The constructivist classroom - the many faces of constructivism. Educ. Leadersh. 57(3), 6–11 (1999)
25. Perkins, D.: Threshold experience. In: 3rd Biennial Threshold Concepts Symposium, Keynote Address. Sydney (2010)
26. Fominykh, M., Prasolova-Førland, E., Hokstad, L.M., Morozov, M.: Repositories of community memory as visualized activities in 3D virtual worlds. In: Ralph, H., Sprague, J. (eds.) 47th Hawaii International Conference on System Sciences (HICSS), Waikoloa, HI, USA, pp. 678–687. IEEE, New York (2014)
27. Molka-Danielsen, J., Savin-Baden, M., Steed, A., Fominykh, M., Oyekoya, O., Hokstad, L. M., Prasolova-Førland, E.: Teaching Threshold Concepts in Virtual Reality: Exploring the Conceptual Requirements for Systems Design. In: Fallmyr, T. (ed.) Norsk Konferanse for Organisasjoners Bruk av Informasjonsteknologi (NOKOBIT), Stavanger, Norway, November 18–20, pp. 93–106. Akademika forlag, Trondheim (2013)
28. Vaishnavi, V., Kuechler, W.: Design research in information systems. http://DESRIST.org (2004). http://desrist.org/design-research-in-information-systems/
29. Spence, J.: The researcher's toolbox. J. Virtual Worlds Res. 3(1), 91–93 (2010)
30. Hevner, A.R., March, S.T., Park, J., Ram, S.: Design science in information systems research. Manage. Inf. Syst. Q. 28(1), 75–105 (2004)
31. Cruz-Neira, C., Sandin, D.J., DeFanti, T.A., Kenyon, R.V., Hart, J.C.: The CAVE: audio visual experience automatic virtual environment. Commun. ACM 35(6), 64–72 (1992)
32. Morozov, M., Gerasimov, A., Fominykh, M.: vAcademia – Educational Virtual World with 3D Recording. In: Kuijper, A., Sourin, A. (eds.) 12th International Conference on Cyberworlds (CW), Darmstadt, Germany, 25–27 September 2012, pp. 199–206. IEEE, New York (2012)
33. Kalff, C., Kühner, D., Senk, M., Dalton, R.C., Strube,G., Hölscher, C.: Turning the shelves: empirical findings and space syntax analyses of two virtual supermarket variations. In: Dara-Abrams, D., Hölscher, C., Conroy-Dalton, R., Turner, A. (eds.) Proceedings of the Workshop at Spatial Cognition, 2010, Mt. Hood, Oregon, SFB/TR 8 Report No. 026-12/2010. pp. 25-48, Universität Bremen, Bremen, Germany (2010)

Participatory Action Design Research in Archaeological Context

Barbara Rita Barricelli[1(✉)], Stefano Valtolina[1], Davide Gadia[1],
Matilde Marzullo[2], Claudia Piazzi[2], and Andrea Garzulino[3]

[1] Department of Computer Science, Università degli Studi di Milano,
Via Comelico 39/41, 20135 Milan, Italy
{barricelli,valtolin,gadia}@di.unimi.it
[2] Department of Cultural Heritage and Environment, Università degli Studi di Milano,
Via Festa del Perdono 7, 20122 Milan, Italy
matilde.marzullo@outlook.com, claudia.piazzi@hotmail.it
[3] Department of Architecture and Urban Studies, Politecnico di Milano,
Via Bonardi 3, 20133 Milan, Italy
andrea.garzulino@polimi.it

Abstract. This chapter presents an overview of the results of an interdisciplinary collaboration between several domain experts in the frame of archaeological projects. Since 2001, different independent interactive systems have been co-designed, developed, and tested on the field, in the frame of the "Tarquinia Project" carried out since 1982 in the ancient Tarchna, one of the foremost Etruscan cities, by the Università degli Studi di Milano. The adoption of a semiotic approach to a participatory action design research process with the involvement of domain experts led us to a better understanding of the main characteristics but also the challenges of the archaeological practice and helped us to apply technology in a better and efficient way. The currently undergoing work is focused on the co-design of a cloud of services aimed at integrating all the tools into a bigger framework to support the archaeological practice in a more pervasive way.

Keywords: Digital humanities · Archaeology · Cloud of services · Domain experts · Co-design · Interdisciplinary teams · HWID · Participatory action design research

1 Introduction

The reconstruction of a historical and cultural context in Archaeology is a very complex activity where most of the times the collaboration among several scientists from different domains (e.g., geography, geology, architecture, chemistry, anthropology) is needed. Interdisciplinarity in Archaeology aims at studying excavation sites by considering not only the local excavation activity but also by reconstructing the entire historical and cultural context. To support such a comprehensive work, technology can be used in several ways to design and realize innovative digital humanities tools. Today, technology is widely adopted in Archaeology (e.g., Geographical Information Systems

© IFIP International Federation for Information Processing 2015
J. Abdelnour-Nocera et al. (Eds.): HWID 2015, IFIP AICT 468, pp. 192–211, 2015.
DOI: 10.1007/978-3-319-27048-7_14

(GISs), orthophotos, Digital Terrain Models, 3D models. However, despite the use of such variety of technologies, one of the main time-consuming activity for the researchers working on excavation sites is the constantly look up for relationships among the retrieved archaeological evidences and the geographical, architectonic, and anthropological data collected. Another important issue is domain experts' knowledge, both in terms of content and structure, is highly dependent on professional or individual practice and this makes the collaboration among all the stakeholders even harder and critical. All this complexity leads to an overwhelming production of digital documentation that represents the archaeological context from different points of view: landscapes, stratigraphic layers, and artefacts – e.g., mobile findings (organic and inorganic) and architectonic structures. To build a comprehensive knowledge on such extensive mole of data and to integrate the information that stems from it is nearly impossible without the support of further technological efforts.

- In the last 14 years, the two departments of Computer Science and Cultural Heritage and Environment of Università degli Studi di Milano (in particular with Giovanna Bagnasco Gianni, Director of the excavation site of Tarquinia) and the Department of Architecture and Urban Studies of Politecnico di Milano, actively collaborated to develop tools and methods for supporting the archaeological practice in a very pervasive way: on the field (excavation site), in warehouse for data storage and catalog operations, and during the study and collaborative analysis time (back at the University). This collaboration has led all the participants to developer higher awareness of the potentials and challenges that such an interdisciplinary research field may encounter. During this collaboration, the IT in archaeology has positively influenced the archaeological practice of our interdisciplinary group. We have drawn on a wide range of expertise to carry out work in the archaeological analysis, assessment and evaluation, topographical and geophysical survey, historic buildings recording and community research. Specifically, the sites of the Etruscan cities of Tarquinia and Cetamura are the benchmark of an all-comprehensive investigation upon which multiple disciplinary areas applied to Archaeology are converging, such as Geology and Natural Sciences, Archaeometry, Architecture and Computer Science. Thanks to this cooperation, the work done in the field of Etruscan Studies is significant and internationally recognized [2, 3, 9]. This chapter presents both the work done so far and the one that is still under development and that is aimed at furtherly explore new technological solutions to support archaeological practice in all of its aspects.

Section 2 presents the semiotic approach we adopt for the co-design of the tools by involving the domain experts in choosing the more suitable interaction style and visual language to use. In Sect. 3, we give an overview of the archaeological practice, how technology is used to support it, and the relationship of our research work within the frame of Human-Work Interaction Design (HWID). The tools developed so far are presented in Sect. 4, while in Sect. 5 we illustrate the currently ongoing work focused on the creation of a cloud of services for integrating all the existing interactive tools.

2 Semiotic Approach to Co-design with Domain Experts

The complexity and the expanding scale of most collaborative projects that take place in these years require more comprehensive knowledge than any single domain expert can possess. Experts in different disciplines have to share their specialized knowledge, skills and practices in order to work collaboratively and reach common goals. The design of a common knowledge management system to support such collaboration needs to balance different requirements. On the one hand, the information and data need to be organized according to common, generic schemes or ontologies in order to allow the sharing of data and results. On the other hand, different domain experts need to have access to content structured in a way that fit their specific interest and professional practice and expectations. It is however challenging to be able to catch the right way to structure the content has to be organized. However, these structures are often not explicated, since they are tacit knowledge, which users possess and use to perform tasks and to solve problems, yet they are unable to express verbally and might even be unaware of.

The domain experts perform their activities, take their decisions, read and create documents using implicit information, articulatory skills and tacit understanding, which derive from their individual and professional experience and practice. All these factors result in determining what Nardi and Engeström [29] call invisible work. Implicit information – e.g., information embedded in spatial displacement, physical appearance of the text, and graphical elements in a document – is often significant only to users who possess the right knowledge and background to interpret it. Practitioners are often more able to act in a specific way rather than to explain how and why they act so [37]. Therefore, domain experts from heterogeneous technical and scientific communities involved in co-design processes often face cultural clashes and communication gaps [39, 40] due to their different backgrounds and ways of reasoning, solving problems, and making decisions.

Our research work aims at resolving the contradictory requirements that arise in a co-design process with an interdisciplinary team. It addresses the question of how to conceptualize and design knowledge management systems supporting collaboration across multiple heterogeneous domains and at the same time providing each participant with tools that respond to their specific need and expectations. This means to design user interfaces and interaction processes that enable the uses to access shared knowledge bases, flexible enough to be tailored to fit into different domain experts' practices. To this end, an approach framed in computer semiotics [13] is adopted: user interfaces are studied as compositions of graphic elements that reflect their end users' expertise, their reasoning patterns, and their work practices [14, 15]. Such tailoring is a response to the weaknesses of a "one fits all" idea of interactive system design. In fact, the interaction with a same user interface can trigger in different end users very different semiosis processes leading to different meanings assignment, and consequently to different interpretation results. When using an interactive system, a significant portion of the information conveyed by the system is implicit information [11], i.e., embedded in the actual shape of the elements displayed and in the visual organization of the overall user interface. For this reason, it is of fundamental importance that knowledge management systems are provided with user interfaces and interaction styles that have to be flexible enough to adapt to the different professional practices they have to support. A design strategy of this kind is what we apply to the archaeological field, and implies a long-term planning of development and testing that fits in a star software life-cycle [7, 23]. From our experience in this field, such a complex environment calls for evolutive and never-ending process of design and development in that the use of the tools very often suggests new uses: the separation between design time and use time becomes fuzzy and these two stages need to be bridged into a unique "design-in-use" continuum to create open and continuously evolving projects. Therefore, according to [10] we can say that the tools designed and developed with this approach are always in a "perpetual beta" version.

Peculiarity of the star software life-cycle is the central role that is played by evaluation. In the years, to study the validity of the tools and of the semiotic approach we adopted several techniques: ethnography (shadowing), interdisciplinary workshops, focus groups, structured/unstructured interviews and questionnaires, collaborative design of paper prototypes (e.g., CARD, PICTIVE [28]), and End-User Development (EUD) [16, 26] applications for interfaces and systems design. Moreover, we paired cognitive engineering methods of usability evaluation with those defined by semiotic engineering that are directed to investigate the so-called "communicability" of an interactive system. This allowed us to understand if the communication between the different domain experts was effective and efficient and if user interfaces and interaction style responded correctly the end users expectations and needs.

3   HWID: Archaeological Practice and Technology

The archaeological application domain is characterized by strong social and organizational factors and the successful introduction of technology and interactive systems, designed according to our semiotic model, has proved once more the validity of the Human Work Interaction Design (HWID) framework [31].

Theories and Models. We apply our semiotic approach (presented in Sect. 2) to the archaeological domain and put in practice a participatory action design research [8]. We follow all the five stages: (1) analysis of the domain with open problems identifications; (2) detection of opportunities and open challenges to be addressed with a participatory approach; (3) actual design with the use of prototypes and recurrent usability evaluations; (4) measurement of impact evaluation with the active involvement of the members of the interdisciplinary team on the field; (5) generalization of the outcomes in a model that reflects the expertise we developed in this field [41]. This chapter focuses mainly on the first three stages of our research. Presenting the results of evaluation of the tools is not in the scope of this chapter: they can be found in our previous publications cited in Sect. 4.

Environment and Context. Environment and context play a very important role and strongly influence the archaeological practice in all its aspects. Particularly challenging are the distributed nature of the work (on excavation site, in storage rooms, in laboratories, in universities), the interdisciplinarity with the involvement of experts in different domains, and the International collaborations that highlights the existence of often radically different methods, use of different languages (not only in terms of spoken language but also visual notations) and remote interaction (most of the time asynchronous and written).

Human Work. The data collection activity that archaeologists perform in their practice mainly follows two families of methods: non-intrusive and intrusive.

Non-intrusive methods include the analysis of aerial photography for landscape alterations, use of ground-penetrating radar to find buried anomalies, and the systematic, controlled collection of materials from surface contexts.

Intrusive methods include shovel testing (units 40 cm on a side), test units (1 or 2 m on a side) or excavation blocks (anything larger than 2 m on a side). Archaeologists analyze these remains to determine their original purpose and effective role within the overall context of a given site. In turn, archaeologists attempt to understand cultural processes and behaviors, with the primary goal to interpret how and why cultures evolved over time.

Interaction Design. Several technological approaches can be adopted in order to support archaeologists in their analysis and interpretations. For example, mobile or Web applications can be used for collecting information from an archaeological site, while 3D modeling, processing, and visualization technology can be adopted for helping in generating very precise three-dimensional models of any archaeological context, perfect replicas of how the soil layer looked like the exact moment before its removal and the position of artefacts and structures. At the same time, technology such as laser scanners, high-precision survey strategies or systems for managing orthophotos, Digital Terrain Models (DTM), geo-spatial information, and LiDAR data, represent new solutions for studying landscape and monuments from an archaeological, geological, and architectural point of view in order to reconstruct the territorial conformation and its elements. Of course, it is nearly impossible to keep track of every category of documentation produced during the fieldwork without the support of technological solutions and without taking into consideration that the organization structure of the produced documents highly reflects the domain experts' background, knowledge, and expertise. Although there is a growing use and demand for advanced technologies in archaeological resources management, there is still an inherent lack of innovative solutions and methodologies for documenting, combining and managing the vast data sets generated by these technologies and for presenting them to domain experts in effective ways. At the same time, no platforms are available so far for integrating all these data, fostering their dissemination between scholars and researchers through a correct management of the cultural objects contained in the original sources.

4   The Tools

In these years, we co-designed and developed tools for responding to the main needs that arise during all the phases of archaeological (interdisciplinary) work. The tools we co-designed and developed so far can be categorized according to the archaeological activity that they are meant to support: excavation data management, stratigraphic analysis, 3D reconstruction of tombs, geographic analysis, and decipherment of non-verbal markings. In what follows, we present the tools following this categorization.

4.1 Excavations' Data Management

In archeological knowledge creation and dissemination the information overload plays one of the most critical roles. At the beginning, the collaboration between the departments of Computer Science and Cultural Heritage and Environment of Università degli Studi di Milano, took the first steps towards the digitizing of their archaeological collections. Before that, the main problem was that archaeologists acquired data in manual way, without any strategies based on computer databases for storing, making future research difficult. Undocumented changes in data and loss of original organizational strategies could further compromise accessibility and integrity. Based on our experiences in research analysis, we proposed specific methods to make archaeological data management as flexible and useful as possible.

Another problem was that the large quantity of digital material generated by each team (archaeologists, architects, geologists, chemists) was incomplete, inconsistent and often hard to access. Moreover, very often, the teams are geographically distributed and the communication among all the stakeholders becomes challenging. As a possible solution to these problems, we identified a strategy based on a holistic approach for knowledge representation, designed according to widely held community understanding.

We designed and developed an application called "Tarchna DB" (See Fig. 1.) that is meant to collect the categories of evidences predetermined by the archaeologists in order to classify the multifaceted aspects of the findings that are almost always fragmentary (e.g., architectural structures, layers of ground, pottery, different kinds of equipment) [17]. Several problems arise from the integration of different archives, and one of the most important issues is the need of establishing a common knowledge representation to be used to exchange data among all the stakeholders involved in the collaboration. Specifically, our model allows to organize archeological data in a way that is more natural for archaeologists to use. It relies on an ontology (i.e., "a description of the concepts and relationships that can exist for an agent or community of agents" [18, 19]) organized into two levels, and on specialized services for managing it. The top level of the ontology presents a view that is suitable for non-computer experts while the bottom level is suitable for interacting with the computing infrastructure. The top-level ontology exploits the concept of a standard ontology of cultural heritage (CIDOC-CRM [12]) for producing a representation of concepts and relationships suitable for archaeologists. The information core also supports the ability to perform information retrieval and to browse the existing knowledge. This approach uses the knowledge base as a semantic access point to the information that can then be retrieved from databases federated by means of the ontology schema. The knowledge representation model at the base of our framework uses an ontological schema, representing a specific cultural context, as a semantic access point to different types of data sources using suitable mapping strategies.

4.2 Stratigraphic Analysis

Beyond archiving, managing and studying the findings collected during archaeological excavations there is a wide research area that is focused on information visualization.

Fig. 1. Tarchna DB system is used for archiving all archaeological data resulting from the excavation campaigns in Tarquinia.

The way in which the information is represented can deeply impact how it is understood and used [22].

In particular, in Archaeology graph visualization systems can face the problem of facilitating the exploration and analysis of a vast amount of data by means of visual methods and tools able to support needs of a wide range of different research communities involved in the study of an excavation such as archaeologists, architects, geologists, chemists, and biologists. Information visualization strategies are applied for assisting domain experts in the examination and interpretation of the stratigraphy of excavation sites, and identifying both natural and cultural strata.

The British archaeologist Edward Cecil Harris in 1973 invented the Harris Matrix method that is used to graphically represent stratigraphic sequences in a graph-based form [21]. Before the design and development of a dedicated interactive system, Harris' method was used to realize the graphs on paper with the following procedure.

During the excavation phase, each time that a stratigraphic unit is detected, the archaeologists filled in a proper paper form to keep track of its characteristics. A type identifies each unit: layer stratigraphic unit (US) – of natural origins – or structural stratigraphic unit (USS) – a manufactured artifact (e.g., a wall). After this first categorization, the number of the box in which the findings retrieved in the unit were recorded, together with the maximum and minimum altitude of the unit and a description of the unit itself. In the rest of the form, the relationships among the unit and other units were made explicit.

Three types of relationship could exist: active, passive, and neutral. Active relationships are (a) covers, (b) fills, (c) leans, and (d) cuts; passive relationships are (a) is covered, (b) is filled, (c) relies on, (d) is cut; neutral relationships are (a) is equal to, and (b) binds. Once the form was completely filled in, the archaeologists represent the stratigraphic unit in a drawing on paper that was then used in successive data analysis. At the end of the excavation campaign, all this material was collected and studied for creating the correspondent Harris Matrix. The resultant Harris Matrix enabled the archaeologists to determine the chronology of the various units (an example is shown in Fig. 2. The rectangles represented the stratigraphic units, while lines are used to indicate the existing relationships among them (e.g., "copre" means "covers", "taglia" means "cuts", "riempie" means "fills"). After the drawing was complete, the archaeologists tried to determine the historical age to which the stratigraphic units belong to. After this, the next activity is the detection of the overlays, i.e., logical levels that are constituted by the stratigraphic units that belong to the same historical period.

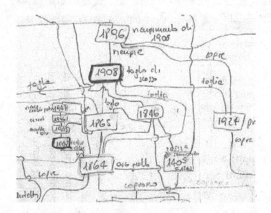

Fig. 2. A fragment of a Harris Matrix.

This entire procedure was performed using paper documents and therefore the quantity of the material related to an excavation site tended to grow very fast and its consultation became extremely difficult. Moreover, the more stratigraphic units are added, the more the Harris Matrix to be drawn became big and exponentially complicated to be modified and extended. Given these difficulties, the main disadvantages that came from the use of a non-digital approach was the impossibility of properly diffuse the knowledge that was gathered through the archaeologists' activity performed on the field and the difficulty of keeping the Harris Matrix documents up to date. In fact, to give permissions to modify the Matrix to more than one person is not so simple, and new problems arise when many people have access and modification permission to the same resource.

Our work aimed to design and development an innovative visualization tool named ArchMatrix [6, 40] able to efficiently store and manage excavation site knowledge so that the data may be visualized and queried in a graph-based environment, and to offer a visual representation of archaeological assets and their relationships in order to support intuitive and useful explorations. To support real-world knowledge construction and decision making by means of a Harris Matrix, the most important challenge was to realize a system able to meet real needs of domain experts in handling content and structures that fit their domain-specific interests and practices. In this context, the paradigm of the map as a support for knowledge organization has been used. This is based on the principle that maps can also be used to spatially represent knowledge about systems and subjects. In fact, the

Harris Matrix system uses a map-based representation to show the stratigraphic units, the relationships between them and other related information. ArchMatrix is implemented as a Web application which uses a graph visualization as tool for knowledge assessment. Through a Harris Matrix and its nodes, relationships and conceptual structure, ArchMatrix offers a solution for collaborative managing shared knowledge among experts of different domains. A screenshot of ArchMatrix is given in Fig. 3.

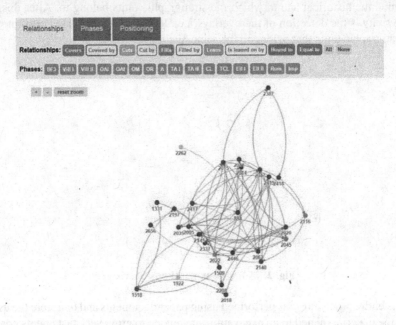

Fig. 3. A screenshot of ArchMatrix system. The nodes in the graph represent the stratigraphic units while the edges are the relationships that exist between the nodes. The color of an edge depends on the type of relationship that it represents.

4.3 3D Reconstruction of Tombs

During the last decade, Virtual Reality (VR) technologies have been the focus of intense developments and applications, mainly because of the increased availability of dedicated cheaper hardware platforms and display technologies. These are some of the domains with respect to which VR techniques have an important potential for the deployment and manipulation of 3D materials, images, sounds, and datasets in order to provide a richer and visually-appealing content presentations. Consider as an example the Archaeological domain. Using VR techniques, heritage which no longer exists, or which must be handled with special care in order to be preserved, can be virtually reconstructed and presented to an audience from perspectives which go beyond what it is possible in the real world. Not only, VR can be used to provide innovative strategies for studying and analyzing features of existing monuments or ancient populations, or for visiting and exploring collections, which elements are physically located at different museums or cultural institutions, and so forth. Although those solutions are very appealing and today many museums and cultural institutions have started investing in such direction, VR solutions are still not widely adopted as a mean for archaeological study and dissemination. The main reason is the high cost of content production and the low reusability and poor portability of infrastructures. In addition, researchers and users are quite sophisticated and have high expectations; therefore, they are not interested in simple walk-through applications. Instead, they ask for formative and interactive experiences that they can personalize on the basis of their preferences.

We adopted this innovative strategy in the field of the VR applied at the Archaeology in the design of the virtual reality simulation of the Etruscan Necropolis of Tarquinia (UNESCO site since 2004) that has been realized not only for dissemination purpose but also for supporting archaeological analysis [33]. The site is an outstanding testimonial of the Etruscan culture, in which so far more than 6200 tombs carved in the rock were discovered. Among them, around 140 are extraordinarily painted, and many hundreds more present traces of paintings [27]. The earliest tomb dates from the 7th century B.C. Most of them are constituted by a room only, while others are more articulated. Currently, 64 tombs are accessible: some of them are protected by glass and always visible, some others are open for visits in rotation, whereas many others are kept closed. Most of the painted tombs were discovered in the second half of 19th century. Across the centuries, many paintings were detached from the walls and then lost or destroyed, while others are currently not visible due to the fading of the original colors. In these cases, our knowledge of those paintings is mainly based on descriptions and paintings made by artists and scholars in 17th, 18th, and 19th centuries. Cultural Heritage experts rely in a relevant way on digital images acquired inside the tombs: natural light is not present (or it is limited to some parts of a small number of tombs whose entrances are adequately oriented), while artificial light is often not adequate to achieve a full and detailed observation of the full painted walls. Therefore, many samples of each area that compose the inner parts of the tombs are collected through several accurate sessions of photographic acquisition. The images are then processed to enhance details, merged using adequate techniques in order to allow an ensemble analysis of the painted walls, and eventually stored in a multimedia database for supplemental studies and for dissemination.

3D models allow to investigate the morphology of the architecture in its completeness and to analyze all the parts of the architecture in detail and as a whole. The VR reconstruction of the Necropolis is based on a modular approach, in order to handle a site composed by a large number of independent tombs. The 3D visualization of the tombs is based on a first-person point of view approach, and the users can rotate their view and eventually move inside the environments. Moreover, we have introduced the possibility to visualize the already mentioned drawings and paintings as superimposed on the original walls (See Fig. 4).

4.4 Geographic Analysis

Over the last two centuries, several more or less scientific archaeological and restoration projects have been carried out, and their merits and defects are still visible today. Given the complexity, the extent and the prolonged use of an excavation site, researchers need

Fig. 4. A screenshot of the reconstruction of a tumb with a painting superimposed on the original wall.

innovative tools for deeper understanding the site and for comparison with archaeological sites in the vicinity. Three-dimensional tools are useful solutions for facilitating the investigation of the sites in their landscape setting, for example on a large scale, exploiting the possibilities offered by LiDAR [35] (Light Detection and Ranging) survey. The cartographic results thus obtained can be used as metrically correct basis for the positioning of all the archaeological sites, thus enabling their comparison and analysis. Precisely because of the prolonged use of sites and their extent, the creation of reconstructive models can be crucial for our understanding and dissemination of the results to non-specialist as well as professional audiences.

A LiDAR survey, by means of an aerial recognition, has been carried out in the area of the Civita of Tarquinia in 2010 (see Fig. 5). The Figure shows how it is possible to pre-process the LIDAR image on the left for identifying buildings/structures, terrain skin, and vegetation, in order to identify only archaeological evidences such as ruins, territorial presence/absence, candidate archaeological items (LIDAR image on the right).

The application of laser scanning and LiDAR technology in an archaeological environment has rapidly established abroad and recently in Italy.

The first output of the aerial survey appears as a dense cloud of points (defined by planimetric coordinates, elevations, intensity, number of returns and other parameters) arranged along the scanning pattern of the instrument. From such raw data, it is possible to reconstruct the territorial conformation and the related elements (vegetation, ground, structures, etc....). Subsequent digital processing produces different elaborations: Digital Elevation Model (DEM), Digital Terrain Model (DTM), high-resolution orthophotos, and elaborations based on intensity and number of returns. These elaborations are recorded in a Geographical Information System to catalog and to systematize the existing documentation about historical cartography and scientific and literary information, in order to grasp persistence and consistence of meaningful traces of the ancient territorial occupation. Therefore, an exhaustive georeferenced documentation, gathered in a diachronic and synchronic atlas endowed with each punctual or areal data, is available in order to compare and contrast the palimpsest of settlement. After the analysis, through the use of metric models previously created, a 2D-3D cartographic archive is

Fig. 5. A LIDAR 3D reconstruction example.

improved to permit the geo-referenced localization of every data set on the territory, giving the possibility to interface information through a shared platform. Such work results useful tools to identify and analyze settlements and to assess cause-effect relationship between their architectural and urbanistic features and the terrain morphology. The GIS cartographic database, with all its interfaces (geological, historical, archaeological), makes it possible to read permanent signs and assess the land use in historical cartography.

4.5 Non-verbal Markings Collaborative Decipherment

In the frame of IESP (International Etruscan Sigla) Project, we co-designed and developed a system aimed at supporting the collaborative decipherment of Etruscan sigla (non-verbal markings) found on objects discovered in different digging sites distributed in the Mediterranean area. The project involved archaeologists from Università degli Studi di Milano and Florida State University, giving us the possibility of studying the two different approaches to archaeological practice, both in terms of methodology and terminology used. A screenshot of IESP system is given in Fig. 6.

Unlike what happens in deciphering verbal languages, in the case of non-verbal signs it is possible to study their elements from a graphical point of view and to apply similarity techniques to support the human interpretation activity. As to Etruscan language, thousands of examples of non-verbal markings exist. Typically, they are referred to as graffiti, a term that is found to be inadequate. Instead, the Latin word siglum (pl. sigla) – corresponding to the Greek one sema (pl. semata) – should be used. Etruscan sigla, composed by one or more symbols, numbers or letters, are dated from around 700 BCE to the first century BCE. They are incised, painted or stamped on different types of objects; e.g., pottery weights, spindle whorls, sarcophagi, burial urns, roof tiles,

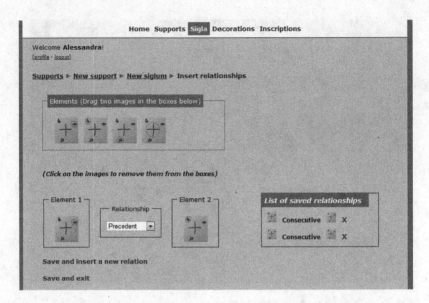

Fig. 6. The IESP System. The archaeologists, using the visual notation they usually adopt on paper, are able to identify relationships between different elements in the same siglum.

architectural terracotta, boundary stones, stone walls, and a wide variety of artefacts in bronze (axes, fibulas, helmets, knives, razors, sickles). The contexts in which the objects have been found include cemeteries, sanctuaries, ports, artisans' quarters and habitations – all spheres of Etruscan life and afterlife. The study of Etruscan sigla is aimed at assessing the real consistency of archaeological indicators according to a deductive method that takes into account a dialectic comparison between the ideas of function and role [2, 20]. The function of an object could be in fact be deduced by its shape. On the other hand, the role of the same kind of object can be determined differently on the basis of the conditions of their discovery and from the comparison of iconographic sources. This means that the meaning of sigla can change widely according to the context in which they have been discovered. An example is the case of V-shape siglum that can be interpreted as a number 5 or letter U. The same uncertainty exists in interpreting a siglum formed by a cross inscribed in a circle: it could mean the Greek letter theta or could be the graphic representation of a sacred space [1, 4]. The experience we developed in the frame of IESP Project led to the design and development of an approach and its software implementation for:

- Analyzing cases of recurrent sigla as cultural indicators of non-verbal communication within their different archaeological contexts.
- Supporting questions about function and role in the field of sigla and according to a multifaceted perspective that takes into account archaeological data to a larger extent.

The main goal of the approach and the final system is to assess sigla with reference to their geographical range and chronology, to the nature of the objects and contexts to which they belong and to the layout of the graphic design. The enormous amount of data, the variety of the cultural background of archaeological experts involved the wide span of different hypotheses about the interpretation of each siglum type and their relationships led to the design of a tool that supports collaborative activities and dialectic comparisons. In our case, the goal is to interpret the meaning of non-verbal markings by means of the comparison of images, the sharing of descriptions, and the collaborative contribution by whole interdisciplinary team.

5   Innovative SOA Architecture for Supporting Archaeological Research

Now that the main tools required by the team to support their practice have been developed, the need of bridging gaps among them represents the new challenge that we are working on. We are currently working on connecting the tools to integrate archaeological data, artefacts and architectural structures (subsoil and over-ground), cartographic and photographic documentation, and scientific content. There is in fact a growing demand for a comprehensive solution in archaeological resources management able to offer a multifaceted and flexible environment for supporting archaeologists' work during all phases of their activities of study.

To this aim, many organizations are looking to cloud computing to reduce their Information Technology costs. Specifically, a cloud-based technology infrastructure is enable the aggregation of digital content and a number of services help to reduce technical, semantic and skills barriers and to render the content more discoverable and interoperable. A cloud of services is definitely needed when no supercomputer or no dedicated hardware infrastructure is available.

Starting from these considerations, the our current activities aim at setting up a cloud platform on top of current public and private repositories (owned by universities, cultural institutions, museums, and archaeological parks either open, private, or subjected to fee). The platform is conceived for extracting and integrating content according to the researchers and scholars' needs, the specific quality criteria, and the sharing policies. The member of the interdisciplinary team of domain experts (archaeologists but also architects, chemists, geologists, anthropologists or others users) are the target of this cloud of service. They are put in the condition to search content to be used either for their personal studies or for supporting their interpretations and ideas in comparison with other colleagues. The idea is to exploit the metaphor of the "Cloud of Services" in order to provide a vision inspired from the Service Oriented Architecture paradigm where services are fully connected to the network and integrated with the cloud. Cloud computing can offer virtually unrestricted capabilities (e.g., storage and processing) to implement services and applications that can exploit data and visualization strategies provided by the cloud of services in different archaeological contexts. The cloud essentially acts as a transparent layer between services and applications providing flexibility and scalability and hiding the complexities between them. The final result is expected to be the development of an innovative authoring Web platform that uses an ontology-based discovery and integration mechanism. The challenge of this environment is to enable the combination of a cloud of services that can support analytical reasoning facilitated by interactive visual interfaces. The design of this ontology is based on our previous research carried in the context of the T.Arc.H.N.A. Project [42]. It will provide a global ontology specifically tailored for the archaeological context able to map concepts and content available in each considered data source in order to establish a kind of *lingua franca*[1] among the different services. The aim of this ontology is to offer a way for mapping services in an integrated manner with well-defined semantics. Through the use of this ontology, the platform will build on a Web-mashups strategy able to integrate interactive components (widgets/gadgets), to represent the services coming from the cloud, to create new consistent and value-adding composite applications. To achieve this ambitious result, we plan to use methods and techniques of End-User Development [5], i.e., a research discipline that studies how to enable users who are not professional developers in create or modify software without forcing them to acquire programming skills. Under this perspective, the platform is designed for supporting the domain experts in detecting, combining, visualizing and analyzing data coming from different services and transforming the data into information, information into knowledge, and knowledge into wisdom. The basic idea aims at enabling domain experts for unwittingly developing personalized mashups according to specific needs via the use of direct manipulation interaction. In Sect. 4, we presented the tools we developed for supporting the archaeological practice. In what follows, we illustrate the services that are currently under development and that will be integrated in the cloud.

5.1 Wrapping Service for Many Original Data Sources

This service is designed to identify the type and format of archaeological content (but also other related data coming from architectural, geographic, geological, and historical archives) available in each repository. This service provides data at three layers.

The first layer offers an access to the (physical) objects belonging to the different institutions. These can be archaeological artefacts, archived documents, cartographies, chemical/geological analysis results or any other type of item that can be of interest.

The second layer allows to access digital objects that somehow represent the physical objects. These can be photographs, scans, transcriptions, 3D models, videos, audio recordings or any other type of digital file. It is important to note that there can be multiple digital objects relating to one physical object.

In the third layer, the service provides descriptive metadata about the digital objects: information about the digital and physical object and factual information such as titles, authors and dates as well as descriptions and relationships to other objects.

The final output of this service will be a semantic representation of the data coming from the distributed repository defined according to the ontology concepts created for effectively expressing the intrinsic characteristics of a specific archaeological context.

5.2 Map-Based Spatio-Temporal Queries and Data-Mining Strategies

This service, receiving as input a set of data-wrapping services, combined by using the ontology-based integration mechanism, provides data-mining functionality for

---

[1] Bridge language, trade language.

searching hidden patterns in collection of heterogeneous data and spatio-temporal queries. This service is designed around a set of classical data mining techniques such as anomaly detection (outlier/change/deviation detection), association rule learning (dependency modelling), clustering, classification, regression, and summarization.

The data wrapping service, when combined with a service able to offer detailed information about geographical regions and sites (such as Google Maps), can provide map-based data visualization functionalities in order to exploit the temporal and spatial nature of the integrated data. Several studies and projects [32, 36] aim at studying some aspects of the design and implementation of map-based applications for managing, querying and visualizing changing locations of moving objects. By exploiting these studies, this service aims at providing a map-based visualization through which to carry out analysis and monitoring of trajectories of objects discovered in an excavation site. These trajectories can concern both documented movements that brought an object towards the place in which it was found, and later movements that brought it from the place where it was discovered to the place where it is preserved. This service will enable to specify typical continuous queries (such as range, distance, and nearest neighbor search) and visual display of objects' trajectories and collection of movement statistics. This service will be endowed with a location intelligence visualization strategy to identify patterns and trends by seeing and analyzing data in a map view with spatial analysis tools such as thematic maps and spatial statistics. This location aware service will help to find data by using spatial relationships to filter relevant data. A temporal condition of this location aware service will be applied for providing spatio-temporal clusters, simulation and visualization, map animation and movement tracking.

5.3 Social Networks Service

The service aims at offering a set of functionalities for creating a social network of domain experts, scholars, students, and researchers. It will promote the creation of communities around the knowledge areas and will support their members in all the phases of the creation, revision, audit, and publication of hypothesis, thesis and, interpretations on how and why cultures evolved over time.

Several roles will be established in the social network that will dynamically change, according to the level of participation of the member to the network. This involvement will be stimulate through a set of serious game solutions in order to acquire points and obtain gifts and rewards of users' activities. Moreover, this social network service will be endowed with social computing techniques in order to study social network dynamics and to promote crowd-sourcing analysis that can lead to new and meaningful uses of data. Exploiting models such as pure probabilistic models [30], exponential random graph models [30, 33, 34, 38], and the latent space models [25], we aim at capturing social relationships dynamics among users in order to provide a user with suggestions based on preferences of other users according to their role in each community, their competencies, and their level of participation. In this way, in accessing the archaeological information, users will be guided by suggestions coming from other users taking into account that well-regarded members of the social network will have a higher influence in the whole process.

5.4   Analysis Support Service

By exploiting data wrapping services that contain stratigraphic information of excavation sites, this service is devised for supporting the domain experts in analyzing stratigraphies from temporal and spatial points of view, by exploiting the ArchMatrix application described in Sect. 4. The service aims at providing researchers with a visual representation of the stratigraphic units highlighting geometrical, topological, and temporal relationships. Stratigraphic units are necessary to detect the relative chronological sequence of the entire excavation site but they also produce a number of supplemental data. The idea is to combine the stratigraphic visualization provided by ArchMatrix with external services able to retrieve data about landscapes, cartography, mobile findings, and architectonic structures. This solution aims at separating the layer devoted to the visualization of the graph where it is possible to define queries and algorithms able to explore stratigraphic units from the information layer used for retrieving knowledge coming from other excavation databases. Therefore, to support the complex and interdisciplinary decision-making process at the base of the archaeological practice, this service will allow to develop new opportunities for investigation (both individual and collaborative), to increase knowledge, to improve traditional working practices and to develop new ones.

6   Conclusions and Future Developments

The aim of our work, and especially the ongoing development of the cloud of services, is to enable interdisciplinary research for supporting archaeological documentation, analysis and dissemination and able to provide an environment for supporting collaboration in this field. This would push forward the boundaries of what semantic and social technologies and Archaeology can do together in order to define original means of communication for practitioners across this field.

In the archaeological literature, the concept of context as an association of objects, which can be physical, spatial and/or temporal, is strictly related to a long archaeological tradition. However, for the renowned French school of anthropology as well as for Anglo-Saxon scholars [24], the concept of pure archaeological context has been supported by the importance of the cultural environment and social structures. Of course, it is nearly impossible to follow such procedures for every category of documentation yielded by an archaeological project without the support of technological solutions and to carry out comparisons with other situations and contexts. Such procedures could be positively supported by adequate graphical environment in which combining different services that aim at helping the archaeologist to verify the validity of their interpretations and studies through sophisticated simulations of the archaeological evidence and data at different scale. The use of a cloud of services and the idea to combine them by using an ontology-based discovery and integration mechanism could be a useful solution. For example, data coming from distributed and heterogeneous databases, 3D reconstructions of archaeological materials and data-mining service could be integrated with landscapes and stratigraphic layers models allowing to combine the aforementioned activities in a unique context of analysis. In such a context, all experts involved in the process of analysis of the results and data from an archaeological project can effectively collaborate to define innovative interpretations and hypotheses. Therefore, the final aim of our current studies and development activities is addressed to explore new strategies for studying interdisciplinary knowledge by means of innovative authoring Web platform able to put together and combine part or all described services characterizing archaeological studies according to their heterogeneous expertise – geological, historical, anthropological, chemical, human, and many others. The platform will build on cutting-edge Rich Internet Application (RIA) and semantic technologies for providing domain experts with a user-centered Web application mashup platform.

References

1. Bagnasco Gianni, G.: Rappresentazioni dello spazio "sacro" nella documentazione epigrafica etrusca di epoca orientalizzante. In: Raventós, X., Ribichini, S., Verger, S. (eds.) Atti del Convegno Saturnia Tellus, pp. 267–281. Consiglio Nazionale delle Ricerche, Rome (2008)
2. Bagnasco Gianni, G: Tarquinia: excavations by the university of Milano at the Ara della Regina sanctuary. In: Edlund-Berry, I.E.M., de Grummond, N.T. (eds.) The Archaeology of Sanctuaries and Ritual in Etruria, JRA 81, pp. 45–54 (2011)
3. Bagnasco Gianni, G.: Tarquinia, sacred areas and sanctuaries on the civita plateau and on the coast: 'monumental complex', Ara della Regina, Gravisca. In: Turfa, J. M. (ed) The Etruscan World, pp. 594–612 (2013)
4. Bagnasco Gianni, G., Gobbi, A., Scoccimarro, N.: Segni eloquenti in necropoli e abitato. In: L'ecriture et l'espace de la mort. Recontres internationales (2009)
5. Barricelli, B.R.: An architecture for end-user development supporting global communities. Ph.D. dissertation, Università degli Studi di Milano, Italy (2011)
6. Barricelli, B.R., Valtolina, S., Marzullo, M.: ArchMatrix: a visual interactive system for graph-based knowledge exploration in archaeology. In: Proceedings of AVI 2012, pp. 681–684. ACM Press (2012)
7. Bianchi, A., Bottoni P., and Mussio, P.: Issues in design and implementation of multimedia software systems. In: Proceedings of IEEE International Conference on Multimedia Computing and Systems (ICMCS 1999), pp. 91–96 (1999)
8 Bilandzic, M., Venable, J.: Towards participatory action design research: adapting action research and design science research methods for urban informatics. J. Commun. Inform. 7(3), 1–23 (2011)
9. Bonghi-Jovino, M.: The Tarquinia Project: a summary of 25 years of excavation. AJA **114**, 161–180 (2010)
10. Bruns, A.: Blogs, Wikipedia, Second Life, and Beyond: From Production to Produsage. Peter Lang Publishing, New York (2008)
11. Costabile, M.F., Fogli, D., Mussio, P., Piccinno, A.: End-user development: the software shaping workshop approach. In: Lieberman, H., Paternò, F., Wulf, V. (eds.) End User Development. Springer, New York (2006)
12. Crofts, N., Doerr, M., Gill, T., Stead, S., Stiff, M.: Definition of the CIDOC Conceptual Reference Model. http://www.cidoc-crm.org/official_release_cidoc.html
13. De Souza, C.: The Semiotic Engineering of Human-Computer Interaction. The MIT Press, Cambridge (2005)
14. Dittrich, Y.: Computer Anwendungen und sprachlicher Kontext. Zu den Wechselwirkungen zwischen normaler und formaler Sprache bei Einsatz und Entwicklung von Software. PeterLang (1997)

15. Dittrich, Y.: How to make sense of software — interpretability as an issue in design. Technical report, University of Karlskrona Ronneby (1998)
16. Fischer, G.: End-user development and meta-design: foundations for cultures of participation. J. Organ. End User Comput. **22**(1), 52–82 (2010)
17. Gianni, G.B., Marzullo, M., Valtolina, S., Barricelli, B.R., Bortolotto, S., Favino, P., Garzulino, A., Simonelli, R.: An ecosystem of tools and methods for archeological research. In: Proceedings VSMM 2012, pp. 133–140. IEEE (2012)
18. Gruber, T.R.: A translation approach to portable ontology specifications. Knowl. Acquis. **5**, 199–220 (1993)
19. Gruber, T.R.: Toward principles for the design of ontologies used for knowledge sharing? Int. J. Hum. Comput. Stud. **43**(5–6), 907–928 (1995)
20. de Grummond, N.T., Bare, C., Meilleur, A.: Etruscan sigla ("graffiti"): prolegomena and some case studies. Archaeologia Transatlantica **18**, 25–38 (2000)
21. Harris, E.C.: Principles of Archaeological Stratigraphy. Academic Press, San Diego (1979)
22. Herman, I., Melancon, G., Marshall, M.: Graph visualization and navigation in information visualization: a survey visualization and computer graphics. IEEE Trans. Visual Comput. Graph. **6**(1), 24–43 (2000)
23. Hix, D., Hartson, H.R.: Developing User Interfaces: Ensuring Usability Through Product & Process. Wiley, New York (1993)
24. Hodder, I.: Archaeological Theory Today. Polity Press, Cambridge (2000)
25. Hoff, P.D., Raftery, A.E., Handcock, M.S.: Latent space approaches to social network analysis. J. Am. Stat. Assoc. **97**, 1090–1098 (2002)
26. Lieberman, H., Paternò, F., Wulf, V.: End User Development. Springer, New York (2006)
27. Marzullo, M.: Spazi sepolti e dimensioni dipinte nelle tombe tarquiniesi. Tarchna 4, Tangram Edizioni Scientifiche, Trento (in press)
28. Muller, M.J., Rebecca, C.: Using the CARD and PICTIVE participatory design methods for collaborative analysis. In: Wixon, D., Ramey, J. (eds.) Field Methods Casebook for Software Design, pp. 17–34. Wiley, New York (1996)
29. Nardi, B., Engeström, Y.: Web on the wind: the structure of invisible work. Comput.-Support. Coop. Work **8**(1–2), 1–8 (1999)
30. Newman, M.E.J., Watts, D.J., Strogatz, S.H.: Random graph models of social networks. PNAS **99**(1), 2566–2572 (2002)
31. Orngreen, R., Pejtersen, A.M., Clemmensen, T.: Themes in Human Work Interaction Design. In: Forbrig, P., Paternò, F., Pejtersen, A.M. (eds.) HCIS 2008. IFIP, vol. 272, pp. 33–46. Springer, Heidelberg (2008)
32. Osmanovic, D., Meskovic, E.: Visualization of streaming trajectories. In: 37th International Convention on Information and Communication Technology, Electronics and Microelectronics, MIPRO 2014, Opatija, Croatia, 26–30 May 2014, pp. 1633-1637 (2014)
33. Rao, M., Gadia, D., Valtolina, S., Gianni, G.B., Marzullo, M.: Designing virtual reality reconstructions of etruscan painted tombs. In: Grana, C., Cucchiara, R. (eds.) MM4CH 2011. CCIS, vol. 247, pp. 154–165. Springer, Heidelberg (2012)
34. Robins, G., Snijders, T., Wang, P., Handcock, M., Pattison, P.: Recent developments in exponential random graph (p^*) models for social networks. Soc. Netw. **29**, 192–215 (2007)
35. Shan, J., Toth, C.K.: Topographic Laser Ranging and Scanning: Principles and Processing. CRC Press, Boca Raton (2008)
36. Schneider, M.: Spatial and spatio-temporal data models and languages. In: Encyclopedia of Database Systems, pp. 2681–2685 (2009)
37. Schön, D.: The Reflective Practitioner: How Professionals Think in Action. Maurice Temple Smith, London (1983)

38. Snijders, T.A.B.: Markov chain Monte Carlo estimation of exponential random graph models. CMU J. Soc. Struct. **3**, 1–40 (2002)
39. Snow, C.P.: The Two Cultures and the Scientific Revolution. Cambridge University Press, Cambridge (1959)
40. Valtolina, S., Barricelli, B.R., Gianni, G.B., Bortolotto, S.: ArchMatrix: knowledge management and visual analytics for archaeologists. In: Yamamoto, S. (ed.) HCI 2013, Part III. LNCS, vol. 8018, pp. 258–266. Springer, Heidelberg (2013)
41. Valtolina, S., Barricelli, B.R., Dittrich, Y.: Participatory knowledge-management design: a semiotic approach. J. Visual Lang. Comput. (JVLC) **23**(2), 103–115 (2011)
42. Valtolina, S., Mussio, P., Bagnasco, G., Mazzoleni, P., Franzoni, S., Geroli, M., Ridi, C.: Media for knowledge creation and dissemination: semantic model and narrations for a new accessibility to cultural heritage. In: Proceedings of the 6th ACM SIGCHI Conference on Creativity & Cognition (C&C 2007), pp. 107–116. ACM Press (2007)

Contextual Design of Intelligent Food Carrier in Refrigerator: An Indian Perspective

Pritam Kale[1(✉)], Ganesh Bhutkar[1], Virendra Pawar[1], and Nikhil Jathar[2]

[1] Vishwakarma Institute of Technology (VIT), Pune, India
Kalepritam91@gmail.com
[2] Avansaber Technologies Pvt. Ltd., Pune, India

Abstract. Refrigerators are used to store food items mainly in food carriers such as plastic boxes, trays or bags. This research paper is focused on Contextual Inquiry (CI) of refrigerators and related contextual design of egg tray. To understand user perspectives about refrigerators, food items, food carriers and related problems, a CI is conducted with 19 home users from 12 households. The CI has provided vital insights into several major aspects of refrigerators, their usage and user interaction. For example, the maximum weight of a food item stored in refrigerator is about 2 Kg. The selected food carrier for implementation is an egg tray. Such intelligent tray is a specially designed food carrier using a load cell for sensing a weight of eggs stored on it. Thus, a contextual design of egg tray helps in providing information about number of eggs stored on a egg tray. In future, this research work will be extended to other food carriers and related mobile App.

Keywords: Contextual design · Contextual Inquiry · Refrigerator · Intelligent food carrier · Egg tray

1 Introduction

A refrigerator is common household appliance that consists of thermally insulated compartment and a heat pump that transfers heat from inside to external environment so that the inside environment remains cool [6]. It is used to store food items as it reduces a rate of food spoilage. The refrigerators are used for domestic, commercial, industrial or biomedical purposes. The domestic refrigerators can be categorized according to their storage capacity in Liters (L) from 165 L to 310 L or more [18]. This research work is focused on domestic refrigerators, which are mainly utilized by home users such as home makers, children or other family members. Domestic refrigerators are used to store cooked food items, vegetables, beverages, and other. The food storage in such refrigerator is depicted in Fig. 1. These users face major problems such as unavailability of required food items, identification of expired food items, undesired temperature control, more power usage, insufficient storage space and continuously irritating noise [6]. Therefore, home users need solutions, which cater to deal with such problems. In this paper, Contextual Inquiry (CI) is conducted for better understanding of existing system of food storage and management in refrigerators. Then, the work models are developed and incorporated in proposed contextual design of intelligent food carrier - an egg tray.

J. Abdelnour-Nocera et al. (Eds.): HWID 2015, IFIP AICT 468, pp. 212–225, 2015.
DOI: 10.1007/978-3-319-27048-7_15

Fig. 1. Food storage in domestic refrigerator

1.1 Related Work

Initially, the research papers related with intelligent refrigerators and food carriers are studied. The first study has presented an intelligent refrigerator with monitoring capability through the Internet. It has an Infrared (IR) sensor, which detects a presence of food item in the refrigerator [21] and it does not inform about item quantity as well as reorder level. Another study has discussed about automatic Chinese food identification and quantity estimation. It identifies food item quantity through a color and texture by using two cameras for size and depth [4]. When refrigerator door is closed, it fails to detect the food items in dark, which is its major limitation. A next study has presented a child-centric food advisory enabled smart system for refrigerators. It is designed especially for children and has face recognition using a camera. It provides an access to child compartment only; hiding other compartments to promote healthy food habits [20]. These studies have helped in understanding different perspectives of smart refrigerators. All studies have used image processing for detection of food items. The use of multiple and specialized cameras increases the cost of designs and also requires presence of light for item detection. To deal with these aspects, we have proposed more economical and generic solution in the form of intelligent food carriers using much cheaper sensors such as load cells for home users to detect food item quantity and to set reorder levels.

There is an Android-based App – 'Food Buddha', which helps users efficiently in managing their food items [7]. This application tracks food item expiration and quantity in percentage. The inputs are provided through manual data entry and Quick Response (QR) code. A sample QR code for food item is depicted in Fig. 2. Many food items do not have QR codes and it is not easy to generate these codes; if required. Therefore, this application can be used only with food items with QR codes. Also, manual data entry is not preferred by many users.

Fig. 2. Quick Response (QR) code

Next study has discussed about smart egg tray named egg minder which informs only quantity of eggs i.e. in number and oldest egg put into egg tray by user which doesn't inform actual freshness of eggs. A major problem in this system, there are use of verity of food items in domestic refrigerator. These food items are measured into number, kilogram and liter but such system suitable for those food items which quantity can measure into number. User needs to alert whenever quantity of food item goes to below certain level i.e. reorder level and there should be facility to set reorder level according to user's requirement [8].

Following are the major research papers studied to understand the process of CI as well as related design. A CI of car drivers has been conducted for design of application – 'Infotainment' [10]. This CI study consists of 6 real-life travel trips with a total of 8 drivers. It suggests that even though, driving itself has remained relatively unchanged; there are now a wide variety of new in-car tasks, which drivers perform such as road tracking, weather forecasting, listening music or exploring news along with social media. The drivers have preferred gesture interaction and notification of changes in the driving context. Another study is aimed at building an understanding of Automatic Teller Machine (ATM) adoption in Mumbai, India through CI, in which 20 ATM users are involved [1]. The collected data has been analyzed to identify specific cultural traits related with power distance, collective orientation and communication boundaries. The results demonstrate the unique role of the cultural context in affecting user expectations and behavioral possibilities.

2 Methodology

The methodology of research work for the design of intelligent food carrier has three major steps, which include CI, development of work models and related effective design of intelligent food carrier [12].

- **Contextual inquiry:** It is a technique of studying users in their own natural environment to get insight, understand their requirements and identify related usability problems. It involves data collection from several households to explore domestic refrigerators, their home users, related food carriers and food items.
- **Development of work models:** The work models include categorization of users, their roles, beliefs, values, work tasks, details of work space and artifacts. Six work models are developed and they include flow, sequence, cultural, physical, artifact and sensory models [11, 13].

- **Design of intelligent food carrier:** The food carrier design is represented in terms of an architecture design, which specifies development constraints as well as software and hardware requirements. An intelligent food carrier is a specially designed carrier using a load cell, which is used to detect food item quantity in number or kilogram.

3 Contextual Inquiry

During CI, several households have been visited to study domestic refrigerators and their home users. These users have been observed interacting with refrigerators. Their behavior and responses have been investigated through interviews and discussions. CI has helped in understanding user categories, artifacts, customs, systems, problems and requirements. The data analysis in CI, has led to development of related work models [13, 14].

A field work is essential for observing user interaction and understanding real requirements of home users dealing with refrigerators. Twelve households have been visited in and around city of Pune, India including both - rural and urban areas. It includes interaction with 19 participant users. These users include 9 Homemakers, 4 children and 6 other family members. This is a convenient sampling of home users, who have been targeted during CI just like other CI studies [1, 12]. Each household has been visited about 3 times and about 10 questions related with household details, experiences with refrigerator and food storage pattern are asked to users. The details of food items stored in refrigerators used in visited households are provided in Table 1. A few interesting trends about food items are observed during field work as seen in this Table. The most important food items stored in domestic refrigerators are Tomatoes, Beans, Cabbage, Lemons, Milk and Eggs. Most of the stored food items are measured in Kilogram (Kg) and maximum weight for food item stored is 2 Kg. The food items are stored mainly in plastic boxes, trays or plastic bags. Most of the users face a problem of insufficient storage capacity of refrigerators. Many food items are hidden deeper in the storage and it is difficult to find out expired food items.

Table 1. Food item details

Food item	Item type	Average quantity	Food carriers used in storage	Number of households
Tomato	Fruit vegetable	2 Kg	Plastic box	10
Beans	Fruit vegetable	1 Kg	Plastic bag	09
Cabbage	Leafy vegetable	1 Kg	Plastic bag/On rack	05 04
Lemon	Fruit vegetable	8	Tray	08
Egg	Poultry product	8	Tray	06
Milk	Dairy product	2 L	Plastic bag/Steel vessel	06 04
Curd	Dairy product	0.5 Kg	Steel bowl	06
Buttermilk	Dairy product	1 L	Steel vessel	06
Ghee (Clarified butter)	Dairy product	0.5 Kg	Glass/Plastic jar	06

4 Work Model

There are six work models, which are developed during CI [13, 14]. Developing such models is a time consuming process as it involves intensive field work, observing user interactions, interviewing users and data analysis. These six models are discussed in this section.

4.1 Flow Model

It is focused on identifying roles and responsibilities of different types of users [5, 6]. There are three types of home users viz. homemakers, children and family members. A homemaker is a primary user, who is relatively more active and acts as a decision-maker whereas; children and other family members are secondary users [2].

- **Homemaker:** A homemaker is a person whose main job is to take care of his or her own family home and children. Traditionally, the job of homemaker is done by women. She is involved in many activities such as food storage, quantity detection, message communication and monitoring the refrigerator condition. She pays special attention to milk products and also keeps a watch on the expired food items and temperature condition.
- **Children:** They are secondary users of domestic refrigerators. They are mainly interested in food items such as chocolates, ice-creams and cakes.
- **Family members:** They are also secondary users of domestic refrigerators. They are involved in food storage, quantity detection, message communication and repairing refrigerator. The repairing activity may involve getting rid of problems related with refrigerator components such as compressor, defrosting heater or condenser coil.

In Fig. 3, three main user types - homemaker, children and family members are shown enclosed in ellipses. The activities associated with user roles and responsibilities related with refrigerator, are represented using rectangles. If user is involved in an activity, a link has been created between that activity and a related user. Each activity has many items or parameters and related users are represented with smaller squares in white, black and gray respectively. For example, both – home maker and other family members communicate a message using refrigerator wall. A home maker communicates a message related with order, warning or wish; whereas other family members mostly pass on wish messages.

4.2 Sequence Model

It represents tasks and related action sequences involved in task completion, and high-lights possible problems [5]. So, it brings out related problems which are faced by users while executing specific action sequence during user interaction with the system [15]. There are several important tasks such as storage of food item, checking out its quantity and expiry, monitoring condition, cleaning of food carriers and so on. One such important sample task is 'To check food item quantity'. It has several steps as depicted in Fig. 4. There are four problems identified during execution of related action sequence.

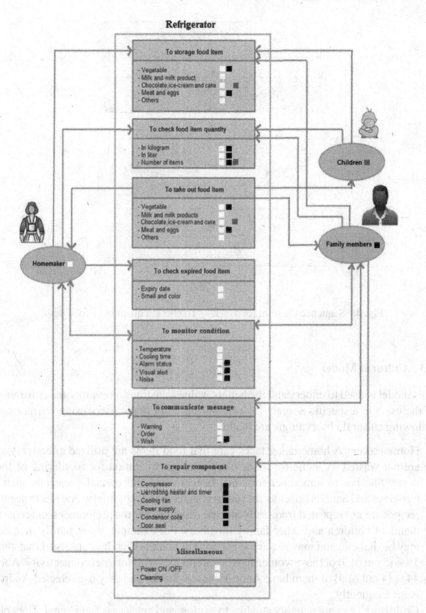

Fig. 3. Flow model for domestic refrigerator

These numbered problems are shown between successive steps and they include food item unavailable, may notice expired food item, may forget to purchase required food item, door opened or not closed properly.

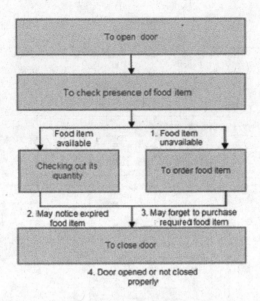

Fig. 4. Sequence diagram for a task – 'To check a quantity of food item'

4.3 Cultural Model

This model is used to understand the beliefs, values, customs, pressures and frustrations of the users in a specific domain [5, 14]. During CI of home users using refrigerators, following cultural observations are made:

- **Homemaker:** A homemaker takes care that food items are utilized effectively and are not wasted. A value for money is a vital consideration for reordering of food items. She has to remember festivals, fasts, events and special occasions such as birthdays and anniversaries as she has to plan recipes accordingly. She has to see that recipes are not repeated frequently and are served as per the preferences and require- ments of children and other family members. For example, older family members may be diabetic and may require sugar control in daily diet. It is observed that about 56 % (5 out of 9) of these women have smart phones with Internet connectivity. About 44 % (4 out of 9) of them have Android-based phones and they use selected Android Apps frequently.
- **Children:** They are naughty and like to explore and get access food items. They play with refrigerator door or even, temperature control regulator. To avoid these prob- lems, refrigerator in one of the households is found locked.
- **Family members:** They may be involved in purchasing of food items from the market. For a family member, visiting market after returning home from work, is extremely irritating experience. Young family members actively participate in exchange of messages and wishes on refrigerator door. If family member is senior citizen, he/she may forget to purchase food items on time or may miss out the refrig- erator alarm. It is observed that about 67 % (4 out of 6) of these other family members

have smart phones with Internet connectivity. About 50 % (3 out of 6) of them have Android-based phones and they use selected Android Apps frequently.

It is also found that home users prefer more economical refrigerators and food carriers in terms of both – the price and energy consumption. Most of the households prefer fresh vegetables and many branded food items. About 33 % (4 out of 12) of households visited are Indian vegetarians, who do not eat eggs, fish and meat. The food items stored in refrigerators of such vegetarian households contain larger quantity of pickles, sauces, chutneys, juices and lemons. About 83 % (10 out of 12) of households visited have five-star rated refrigerators, which have low energy consumption [20].

4.4 Physical Model

It involves the analysis of workspace dynamics. It is represented by a floor plan and arrangement [3] of related entities [5]. In CI, it is observed that the refrigerator is placed mostly in a kitchen as depicted in Fig. 5(a). If kitchen is smaller, then the refrigerator may be placed in other room (bedroom or hall) adjacent to the kitchen as seen in Fig. 5(b). If the position of refrigerator is far from the kitchen, then, users do not approach the refrigerator frequently and may store food item after a considerable delay. Many users may even forget to store the food items. This may lead to wastage or quality degradation of food items.

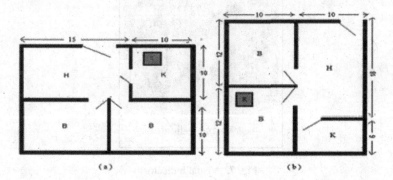

Fig. 5. Physical model depicting place of refrigerators in households

4.5 Artifact Model

It is used to understand the availability and use of artifacts. It also helps to list artifacts highlighting anything that has a potential to make a difference towards an efficient and effective working environment [5, 14]. The important artifacts observed during home user interaction with refrigerators include power stabilizers, inverters, food carriers, pasted messages or door locks along with a verity of food items. Food carriers are shown in Fig. 6.

Fig. 6. Food carrier in refrigerator

4.6 Sensory Model

It includes listing all the materialistic and non-materialistic aspects that contribute to the experience of using the system [14]. An audio alarm can be heard when refrigerator door remains opened for a long time. Sometimes, an irritating noise can be heard from a refrigerator. Also, many refrigerators generate visual indicators for power ON/OFF status and variations in cooling levels. One such indicator in the form of LED is depicted in Fig. 7.

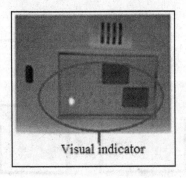

Fig. 7. Visual indicator

5 Aspects Derived from CI and Related Models for Design of Intelligent Food Carrier

Following are important aspects derived from CI and related models for preliminary design of intelligent food carrier:

- Important food items stored in refrigerators are vegetables, milk, lemons and eggs. Surprisingly, **fruits are not stored in refrigerators in majority of the households.** These items are stored mainly in food carriers such as plastic boxes, trays or plastic bags. **In vegetarian households, lemons are stored on egg trays.**

- **The maximum weight of food items stored in refrigerator is about 2 kilograms**; which may increase up to 3 Kg on special occasions. Therefore, load cell [9] for sensing system should be selected accordingly.
- **Food items have different reorder levels and home users may not remember them.** If stored food item quantity goes below reorder level, the home user requires information about it through mobile alert for reordering the food item.
- Food items stored in refrigerator vary as per the **seasons and festivals** celebrated.

6   Design of Intelligent Food Carrier

The food carriers in refrigerators include plastic trays, bags, jars, boxes, bowls or steel vessels. The design of these food carriers can be extended to that of intelligent food carriers. During the present research work, an egg tray is selected and its contextual design is proposed. A major user requirement as per the flow model depicted in Fig. 3 is to check out egg quantity stored on the egg tray. Other problems observed in the sequence model shown in Fig. 4 include unavailability of food item and user behavior of forgetting the purchase of required food item(s). The aspect of reorder level setting for eggs and generating related alert message is vital for home users. Such requirements and problems are addressed in contextual design of egg tray. Thus, an intelligent egg tray design is provided to the home users supporting remote access and effective communication for today's busy life style.

6.1   An Architecture Design of Intelligent Food Carrier

An architectural design of sample intelligent food carrier for quantity detection is depicted in Fig. 8. It has three major compartments viz. **Signal conditioning**, **Microcontroller** and **Global System for Mobile Communications (GSM) based mobile communication**. These compartments are discussed below:

- **Signal conditioning:** It has two separate blocks representing a load cell and an amplifier respectively. A load cell generates an electrical signal in mV as per the load [9, 19] i.e. a weight of food item. An amplifier is used to convert an electrical signal from mV to V since 1 Mv equal to one thousandth (10^{-3}) of a volt and Analog to Digital Converter (ADC) have one step size near about 5 mV [19]. Thus, this Signal conditioning compartment provides an amplified signal (in V) of the load cell.
- **Microcontroller:** It receives an amplified signal from Signal conditioning compartment. It has two major blocks viz. a 10-bit ADC and Data processing program respectively. It has 10-bit ADC which generates binary value with step size of 4.88 mV [16, 19]. It also has Data processing program, which is complied in C and loaded on Read Only Memory (ROM) of microcontroller. This program processes binary input into decimal output representing item quantity. Such decimal output and AT commands are provided for further mobile communication. These AT commands control the modem and are defined by European Telecommunications Standards Institute (ETSI) in GSM 07.07, and GSM 07.05.

- **GSM based mobile communication:** It communicates message about food item quantity to the home users. It has two blocks such as GSM modem and Mobile App. The GSM modem communicates Short Message Service (SMS) message containing decimal output for item quantity to and from mobile phone. The mobile App displays the quantity of food item to the home user and facilitates in setting the reorder level of the food item.

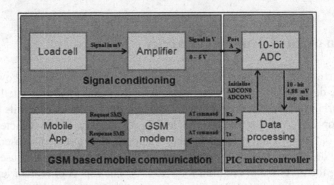

Fig. 8. Architectural diagram of intelligent food carrier for quantity detection

6.2 Load Cell and Its Parameters

A load cell is a sensor that is used to create an electrical signal whose magnitude is directly proportional to the applied load being measured. A suitable load cell is selected for detection of food item quantity based on its weight. A load cell model CZL-601 is chosen based on its maximum load capacity of 3 Kg and its temperature range of −20°C to +65°C. The capacity of this load cell is selected as per the requirement for food storage, which is 2 kg (Sect. 5) as observed in contextual inquiry. It has a dimension of 30 mm × 130 mm and an excitation voltage range of 5–12 V [17].

6.3 Implementation of Intelligent Egg Tray

An egg tray is selected for implementation of intelligent food carrier as it stores 6–12 eggs only and the food item quantity often needs to be expressed in one or two-digit integer. This tray is also used for storage of lemons in vegetarian households. Therefore, the tray design may also be extended to lemon storage in future.

An experimental setup of intelligent egg tray is depicted in Fig. 9. It consists of egg tray placed on the top of a load cell, which is connected to microcontroller kit through an amplifier circuit mounted on a breadboard as discussed in an architectural design in Fig. 8 [17]. The load cell (CZL-601) and microcontroller kit are provided with +5 V DC power supply. An Amplifier has +5 V and −5 V DC power supply with gain of 1000. An output pin of an amplifier is connected to port A (RA0) of a microcontroller - PIC18f4520. A 10-bit ADC in microcontroller kit is at fosc/64 clock i.e. 2 μs (microseconds) with a 4.88 mV step size. The part of GSM-based mobile communication have GSM modem which communicates the message about quantity of eggs and reorder level alert with mobile App through a SMS message.

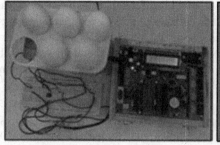

Fig. 9. Experimental setup of intelligent egg tray

6.4 Testing and Result

An intelligent egg tray is tested using its experimental setup as shown in Fig. 2(b). The eggs are placed on egg tray and the result - egg quantity in numbers is observed on Liquid Crystal Display (LCD) display of microcontroller kit. It has been observed during experimentation that as average weight of eggs is 53 gm. It means a decimal value of 5–7 represents item quantity of 1 egg. Similarly, a value of 12–14 represents 2 eggs; a value of 19–21 represents 3 eggs and so on. The observation table for this testing is provided in Table 2, which shows that the design of intelligent egg tray is able count the number of eggs accurately.

Table 2. Observation table for egg tray

Eggs on tray in numbers	Egg weight in gm	ADC step sizes in V	Decimal value	Egg quantity in numbers
01	48	0.024	6	01
03	160	0.080	19	03
07	368	0.168	40	07
10	530	0.280	50	10
12	650	0.320	58	12

7 Conclusion and Future Work

The CI and related six work models have highlighted many important aspects and requirements for refrigerator usage in Indian households. These aspects include selection of key food items, maximum quantity estimates, reorder levels and related home culture. The preliminary setup of an intelligent egg tray for refrigerators is designed and is able to detect the number eggs placed on an egg tray accurately.

In future, mobile communication will be implemented as per the architectural design of intelligent food carrier. The food carrier should differentiate between eggs and lemons. There is a plan of developing an Android-based App as a complete integrated solution for dealing with several user requirements identified in CI. Such contextual design can also be extended to the other food carriers used in refrigerators. It will help home users to reduce their frustrations with refrigerators and manage stored food items effectively.

Acknowledgements. We would like to thank and appreciate help from **Mr. Suresh Nagargoje**, Mr. Rohit Kewalramani, Mr. Vinay Thamke and Mr. Pranay Nandanwar in assembling of electronic components and valuable suggestions. I also thank to **Prof. Dhiraj Jadhav, Mr. Uday Sagale,** Mr. Mahadev Karad, and Mr. Shrikant Savale in design of diagrams. I am very grateful to all the home users who participated in Contextual Inquiry.

References

1. Angeli, A., Athavankar, U., Joshi, A., Coventry, L., Johnson, G.: Introducing ATMs in India: a contextual inquiry. Interact. Comput. **16**(1), 29–44 (2004)
2. Bhutkar, G., Katre, D., Rajhans, N., Deshmukh, S.: Scope of ergonomics and usability issues with intensive care unit (ICU): an Indian perspective. HFESA J. Ergon. Aust. **22**(1), 26–32 (2008)
3. Bhutkar, G., Katre, D., Ray, G.G., Deshmukh, S.: Usability model for medical user interface of ventilator system in intensive care unit. In: Campos, P., Clemmensen, T., Nocera, J.A., Katre, D., Lopes, A., Ørngreen, R. (eds.) Human Work Interaction Design: Work Analysis and HCI. IFIP AICT, vol. 407, pp. 46–64. Springer, Heidelberg (2013)
4. Chen, M., Yang, H., Ho, C, Wang, S., Liu, S., et al.: Automatic Chinese food identification and quantity estimation. In: SIGGRAPH Asia 2012, Singapore, November 2012
5. Chinnapattan, P.: A guide to conducting contextual inquiry user research (2013). http://www.webcredible.com/blog-reports/web-usability/contextual-inquiry.shtml. Accessed 7 March 2014
6. Devotta, S., Sicars, S., et al.: Safeguarding the ozone layer and the global climate system. Special Report of the Intergovernmental Panel on Climate change, October 2005
7. Food Budhha: Contextual inquiry. https://sites.google.com/site/foodbuddhacorp/milestones/contextual-inquiry. Accessed 8 April 2014
8. Garun, N.: Egg Minder smart tray lets you remotely check the freshness of your eggs. http://www.digitaltrends.com/home/egg-minder-smart-tray-lets-you-remotely-check-the-freshness-of-your-eggs/ Accessed 8 July 2015
9. Gross, C., Germanton, D.: Load cell with bossed sensor plate for an electrical weighing scale. U.S. Patent 6,417,466, July 2002
10. Heikkinen, J., Mäkinen, E., Lylykangas, J., Pakkanen, T., Väänänen-Vainio-Mattila, K., Raisamo, R.: Mobile devices as infotainment user interfaces in the car: contextual study and design implications. In: Proceeding of MobileHCI 2013, Munich, Germany, pp. 137–146, August 2013

11. Holtzblatt, K.: Contextual design. Human-Computer Interaction: Development Process (2009)
12. Holtzblatt, K., Hugh, B.: Making customer-centered design work for teams. Commun. ACM **36**(10), 92–103 (1993)
13. Hugh, B., Holtzblatt, K.: Contextual Design: Defining Customer-Centered Systems. Morgan Caufmann Publications, San Francisco (1998)
14. Hung, Y., Winchester, W.: Using contextual design techniques to identify work task problems in dynamic work environments – A field study of isolating safety challenges for small builders. In: Proceeding of the Human Factors and Ergonomics Society 52nd Annual Meeting, New York, USA, pp. 1718–1722, September 2008
15. Jadhav, D., Bhutkar, G., Mehta, V.: Usability evaluation of messenger applications for Android phones using cognitive walkthrough. In: Proceedings of the 11th Asia Pacific Conference on Computer Human Interaction, pp. 9–18. ACM (2013)
16. Jawarkar, N., Vasif, A., Siddharth, A., et al.: Micro-controller based remote monitoring using mobile through spoken commands. J. Netw. **3**(2), 58–63 (2008)
17. Kale, P., Pawar, V., Bhutkar G.: Design of intelligent food carrier for android–based application – 'Refrigerometer', ICCIG3, IIM Ahmedabad (2015)
18. McNeil, M.: Progress towards managing residential electricity demand: impacts of standards and labeling for refrigerators and air conditioners in India. Lawrence Berkeley National Laboratory (2010). https://escholarship.org/uc/item/6cd588t4.pdf. Accessed 15 June 2014
19. Muhamma, M., Mazidi, J., McKinlay, R., Ingendorf, P.: Pic microcontroller and embedded systems. Prentice-Hall Inc., New York (2005)
20. Mulay, P., Kumar, M., Patil, S.: Child centric food advisory enabled smart system for refrigerators. IJCSMC **3**(12), 507–513 (2014)
21. Nayak, S., Gangadhar, G., and Puttamadappa, C.: Intelligent refrigerator with monitoring capability through Internet. Special Issue on Wireless Information Networks & Business Information System (WINBIS), Int. J. Comput. Appl. **2**, 65-68 (2011)

Author Index